STEAL AWAY HOME

STEAL AWAY HOME

CHARLES SPURGEON & THOMAS JOHNSON

UNLIKELY FRIENDS ON THE PASSAGE TO FREEDOM

MATT CARTER AND AARON IVEY

B&H
PUBLISHING GROUP
NASHVILLE, TENNESSEE

978-1-4336-9065-5

Published by B&H Publishing Group
Nashville, Tennessee

Cover design and illustration by Abe Goolsby,
Officina Abrahae.

Dewey Decimal Classification: 233.7
Subject Heading: SPURGEON, CHARLES \ JOHNSON,
THOMAS \ FREEDOM

All Scripture is taken from the King James Version.
Public domain.

1 2 3 4 5 6 7 • 21 20 19 18 17

DEDICATION

FROM MATT

For my son, Samuel Haddon Carter—

I love you more than you'll know until you have children of your own. And I pray that your faithfulness exceeds that of the three men after whom you were named.

FROM AARON

For Jamie—my best friend on this blessed pilgrimage

Contents

Introduction 1

Section 1

Chapter 1: Waking Up 7

Chapter 2: From a Tobacco Plantation 19

Chapter 3: The Bottomless Pit 29

Chapter 4: The Eye of Faith 42

Chapter 5: A Little More of That Sun 54

Section 2

Chapter 6: Susannah 65

Chapter 7: Back to Stambourne 79

Chapter 8: Steal Away to Jesus 91

Chapter 9: Sermon Writing 101

Chapter 10: More Dead Than Alive .109

Section 3

Chapter 11: An Oak Tree in Clapham Common 119

Chapter 12: Thanksgiving 133

Chapter 13: The Foulest Blot 142

Chapter 14: Emancipation 153

Chapter 15: Great Mercies 167

Chapter 16: What Freedom Feels Like 181

Chapter 17: Let the Man Come 194

SECTION 4

Chapter 18: Whisperings 205

Chapter 19: The New Forest 220

Chapter 20: Africa for Christ 239

Chapter 21: In Cursive Letters 250

Chapter 22: The Fog of 1880 253

Chapter 23: Jubilee 271

Chapter 24: Falling Asleep 281

Acknowledgments 291

About the Authors 293

INTRODUCTION

The idea for this book came years ago when I was reading a novel by author Michael Shaara called *The Killer Angels*. The Pulitzer Prize-winning book was written in a unique way. It's a novel about the Battle of Gettysburg in the American Civil War, but it was written from the perspective of the historical characters themselves. The beautiful thing about the novel was that it made these men, who through the fog and time of history had become larger than life, seem real and accessible in a way that I had never experienced.

I often wondered through the reading of *The Killer Angels* what it would be like to write in a similar way, bringing to life some men who had a profound impact on church history as a whole and my life in particular. I thought of Charles H. Spurgeon, the man who pastored the Metropolitan Tabernacle of London, England, in the late 1800s.

Untold volumes of Spurgeon's writings and sermons have been published throughout the decades. Scores of biographies and books lauding the praises of the great "Prince of Preachers" have been written, uncovering every rock and nuance of the man who accomplished so much in the name of Christ. As a result of the sheer volume of academic attention Mr. Spurgeon has received, I fear, for many, that he has become larger than life. His oratory ability and obvious passion and skill in the pulpit tend to overshadow the stark reality that he was a mortal man and a sinner, just like the rest of us. Charles struggled with doubt, pride, fear of failure, and poor health in the same way that every man does. For many of his admirers, the sheer magnitude of this man's gifting has unfortunately hidden that, above all else, he was a flawed man, trying to make it, day by day with the help of God's grace.

How This Book Came to Life

My coauthor, Aaron Ivey, and I spent nearly two years reading everything we could get our hands on with the attempt to better know the main characters of this story. While recognizing that you can never truly know someone who lived two hundred years ago, we nonetheless spent untold hours poring over journals, sermons, and autobiographies of the men in this book, not only learning the facts about their lives, but attempting to understand how they thought, spoke, and felt.

During the course of our research, we spent a few days at Midwestern Seminary, giddy as school boys, looking through Charles Spurgeon's personal library, hoping for direction as to what part of his life we might focus on. During our time at Midwestern, in an interview with Dr. Christian George (one of America's top Spurgeon scholars), we first heard the name Thomas Johnson. Dr. George mentioned a former slave that had been trained at Spurgeon's college in England and commissioned by Spurgeon as a missionary to Africa. After further investigation, we found the out-of-print autobiography of Thomas Johnson titled *Twenty-Eight Years a Slave*. The real-life story of the friendship between the former slave and Charles Spurgeon is the subject of this book.

TELLING A DIFFERENT KIND OF STORY

It's important to understand that what you hold in your hands is not a biography, and it's not a history book, but a story, based on real events that occurred in history. Many passages in the book are word-for-word quotations from Spurgeon's or Johnson's own writing. While my coauthor and I, in several instances for the sake of flow and continuity, were forced to "fill in the blanks," take literary license, and deviate slightly from the historical record, the overwhelming majority of the persons, places, dates, and even the dialogue of this book are based on real events. While the line between fiction and history is blurred, our hope is that you walk away from the reading of this story with a better glimpse of the heart and life of Charles Spurgeon than you have ever had before. It is also our hope that you enjoy meeting Thomas Johnson. His is a story the world needs to hear. It's important to note that Aaron and I are very aware of our limitations in giving life to the voice of an African-American from the 1800s. We approached this task with reverence and an understanding that Thomas Johnson experienced a reality that, even through the most ardent research, we could never fully understand. Through counsel and much discussion with trusted friends from the African-American community, we have attempted to present him in a way that is both historically accurate and honoring to the legacy of this brilliant man of God.

After years of research and writing, setting down the pen and walking away from these two men that Aaron and I have lived with for so long was harder than we expected. We felt like we came to know them in such intimate ways that the last sentence was like a farewell note to two dear friends. I'm looking forward to seeing them one day in Heaven and asking them both what parts of the story we got wrong. Until then, it is our pleasure to introduce you to these two wonderful men of God and it is our hope you enjoy getting to know them as much as we did.

Dr. Matt Carter, Austin, Texas

SECTION 1

CHAPTER 1

WAKING UP

Essex, England 1841

T here was not a village in the world more pleasant than
Stambourne, and although London was only forty
miles southward, there was rarely a need to leave.
Quilted patchworks of lush gardens and orchards surrounded
the entire village, neatly tucking the good people of Stambourne
inside fences of leafy hedges and fruit trees. Here, the rural
beauty of Essex was at its finest. Only a few homes sat alongside
Church Road, the tiny dirt road that meandered through the
town, but from his grandfather's front porch, Charles could see
every single one.

The covered porch sat a few feet above the ground and
wrapped along the front of the "Gentleman's Mansion," as
his grandfather cleverly referred to it. Although it had many
charms, it was quite simple. Eight large windows lined the front
of the white brick home, but almost all of these were covered
with cement, painted black, then marked with white squares to

mimic glass window panes. Since the ridiculous "window tax" swept through Essex a few years ago, homeowners were forced to brick up their windows. The tax was meant to help estimate the size of a house based on how many windows it contained, but sadly, it left unwealthy homeowners with darkened houses, completely shut off from the sunlight that they were not fortunate enough to afford.

No tax could keep seven-year-old Charles from enjoying the light his grandfather couldn't buy, so the porch became a morning haven, an outpost of tranquility and deep pondering. It wasn't normal for a boy to wake before anyone else in Stambourne, much less before the nightingales and roosters in the farm across the road, but Charles was no ordinary boy. There was a hardly a day in Stambourne that didn't begin with Charles on his grandfather's porch waiting for the drowsy village to stretch and yawn, and wipe the sleep from its eyes.

While the mellow sun began to peel back the night, exposing giant oak trees and illuminating redbrick chimneys up and down the street, he felt relief that morning had returned. Slivers of brilliant light traced the wood-thatched roofs, and within a matter of minutes, white-stained brick houses were covered in a brilliant glow of orange. Like tiny embers stoked by the hand of God, morning began to blaze. As it did, blackness gave way to color, color nudged the light, light beckoned the wind, and the cool breeze of morning chased through the roads of Stambourne, climbing into every fruit tree and shaking it ever so gently, as if to say, "Wake up. Darkness is gone!"

As the village awakened, so did Charles.

Something unpleasant stirred deep within Charles as he sat completely still, observing the darkness creep and crawl away. Since he could remember, darkness had always been his real, and only, enemy. From within the echoing chambers of its dungeon, darkness constantly wooed, whispered, and lulled him to sleep, while it prepared to pierce Charles's heart with ten thousand darts of terrible fear and sorrow. Like the best captain of war, it watched his every move, plotted and planned, stalked and stared, then crouched in the trenches of his thoughts, waiting for another perfect strike. It was a familiar stranger to Charles, one that he noticed in his nightmares, on the gravel road to the garden, in the grassy fields, under the pews of the church, along the halls of the schoolhouse, in every conversation, and thought, and step, and breath, and blink of the eye. Darkness always seemed to be pressing down on his fragile body like a water-logged wool blanket.

Charles hated darkness, but while he watched the town of Stambourne radiate and brighten with new morning light, a rush of wonderful memories overwhelmed his unpleasant thoughts.

Nests of young nightingales and songbirds began to chirp as the horses in Mr. Tagley's horsing block shuffled around and snorted. They stood next to a patch of vibrant lime trees, already beginning to show signs that they were ready to shed their summer leaves. The time would come when the old caretaker would sweep the leaves and shove them under the horsing block, but not today, or tomorrow, for that matter. The little creek bed that ran from Bailey Hill down to the front of Hogs Norton was full as could be, bustling with creeping critters and fish hardly worth a catch. The stream ran along wooden fences, iron gates, and century-old trees, all the way to the Meeting House, where Charles's grandfather was the preacher. This solid rectangular building with porch and pent roof wouldn't be used today—there's no need for a chapel on the day before Sabbath—but, tomorrow it would be bouncing with eager Essex men and women, ready to hear the words of the fiery Congregationalist preacher.

A few years ago, there was a rather intense thunderstorm, the kind that shakes walls and rattles rib cages. For hours, hard rain hammered the parsonage roof, and it felt as though all of hell's fury was ramming against every wall of his grandfather's humble abode. The deathly black night camouflaged the intensity of the clouds, and without the occasional blast of lightning flashing through the windows and all the cracks in the walls, Charles couldn't see his hand when he pulled it to his nose. He lay alone in his bed, terrified of the kind of darkness he dreaded most. All at once, a torrent of pure evil and fear piled upon his chest like an iron mountain. It weighed so hard, he could barely breathe. The familiar, terrible darkness whispered in his ear, just loud enough to be heard over the booming thunder,

"Charles. Charles. You're mine."

Charles clenched his eyelids together and dug his fingers into the soft sheets. He waited for the storm to blow down the house, and for the darkness to swallow him whole.

Then suddenly, from somewhere within the house, he heard his grandfather shouting, "Charles, come here! Quickly, grandson!" The urgency in his voice startled Charles, and without delay he jumped from his bed and ran into the main hallway of the house. Lightning flashed thin lines of bright silver through the joints connecting the walls to the ceiling and doorframe. Placing his hands under Charles's chin, his grandfather lifted the boy's terrified eyes to his own, and reassured him, "It's alright, Charles. The storm is powerful, but I want you to see something extraordinary."

He turned his grandson's head towards the open door of the washroom, just adjacent to the kitchen and study. There, Charles instantly noticed the washtub, full to the brim with rainwater that had poured off the roof, and was now running along the top of the doorframe and spilling down the walls like a waterfall. In confusion and panic, Charles thought surely his grandfather must be angry about the condition of the leaky parsonage, as it was an old house that leaked often.

"Charles, quickly. Cup your hands like this," he said while gathering his hands and forming a goblet of skin. Charles mimicked the shape of his grandfather's hands, prompting a warm and confused smile on his face. Walking towards the ceramic washtub, he beckoned Charles to follow, and then they both knelt in front of the washtub. Lightning flashed like fireworks as thunder cocked its gun and prepared to pull the trigger again. The wooden floors rumbled beneath their knees as his grandfather gently pushed his cupped hands into the water. His hands filled with water and he slowly carried it to his mouth, closed his eyes, and drank every drop. He licked his lips and wiped water from his grey beard before turning to Charles, who was still quite perplexed by the scene.

"My boy!" his grandfather shouted, having to yell over the terrible volume of the storm. "There is no sweeter tasting water than that which falls straight from Heaven!" He thrust his hands in again and again, each time savoring and smiling. Timidly, Charles followed. He tightened his fingers, plunged his hands into the water, and slowly brought it to his lips. It was the sweetest and brightest water he had ever tasted, crisp and airy like sunshine, earthy like freshly clipped field grass. With each swallow, he imagined tiny rain droplets making their way from Heaven's river and falling through feathered clouds before they gathered into his boyish hands. They drank happily, as Charles's heart slowly melted into childlike glee.

"What bliss to taste the sweetness of God, even as it pours through the fiercest of thunderstorms!" said his grandfather confidently, over another crackle of thunder. Charles drank from the overflow of Heaven until his belly was round and full. While the lightning continued to scream and his bones rattled and clanked from the thunder, the taste of Heaven's sweet rainwater overshadowed and muted the thunderstorm. He would never again taste or smell the sweetness of rain without thinking of his grandfather, and of Heaven.

James Spurgeon, his grandfather, was a venerable man—sturdy as an ox, gentle as a breeze, yet unrivaled in his conviction and love for the Holy Scriptures. For more than fifty years, he fathered numerous children, literally and spiritually, and the good people of Stambourne gloried in the goodness of God they saw in their pastor and friend. In his early days, he was a dissenting teacher, removed from the Church of England because of his nonconformist views. Now he was simply the "Pastor of the Flock" and the proud grandfather of Charles Haddon Spurgeon. He had never been happier.

Charles wasn't born in Stambourne, but it was all he knew. His mother and father, unable to bear the financial weight of their many children, decided it would be best for Charles to grow up in the countryside with his grandparents, and as he grew, Charles agreed. His grandfather taught him many meaningful things: how to count the stars, how to read the Scriptures at meal times, and the importance of good Puritan books. His reading parlor was littered with books too heavy for little Charles to carry, but the stories in these volumes were a relief to the soul, a healing balm that he would treasure for years to come.

"Come, read this," his grandfather would say. "This, is a treasure . . . Oh, what about this! Yes, this!" He'd tower over the shelf of leatherback books, running his bony finger over each spine until he found the right one. "Bunyan and his pilgrim," he said with a softened voice. "This one, Charles." This happened regularly, and like a beggar ready to eat, Charles would take one of the books, sit alone, and ingest stories of martyrs, old theologians, and characters in the Scriptures.

There was another spot in the old parsonage, a place of solace, that always enchanted Charles. Extending from one of the bedrooms, there was a cramped chamber with a large window, just large enough for a chair, a boy with a book, and a candle. The original owner of the house built this little chamber for the sole purpose of reading and praying, but after the window tax, it became a darkened and unused den. This didn't stop Charles. With a candlestick in one hand and a book in the other, he'd sit and read for hours. Heaven's light was enough to beam through the darkened chamber and warm nearly every part of his heart, mind, and soul. It was brighter than a candle, stronger than the darkness, and demanded no tax payment.

Charles finished recalling other memories of his grandfather from the front porch as he silently watched morning continue to waken. Finally, when the village streets were full of light and the citizens of Stambourne began to hustle and bustle around, his grandmother opened the front door and greeted him with a glorious smile.

"Good morning, Charles!" his grandmother said, interrupting his thoughts. "Can I disturb you for a morning hug?" Charles jumped to his feet and stretched his arms around her waist. Feeling the knot of her apron, and noticing the aroma of pastry and sugar, he knew breakfast pastries and cool milk were on their way.

"I watched the sunrise again, this morning," said Charles. "It never gets old, Grandmother."

"I've seen it a thousand times, and each time this old woman turns into a soupy mess just pondering how good the Lord is to give us another day. Come inside and eat your breakfast, Charles." Inside the kitchen, she placed a plate of pastries and glass of cold milk in front of him and rubbed her strong hand through his boyish hair. "Are you tending the garden with Grandfather today? It's Saturday, and the apple trees are just starting to bud," she said.

"Yes, Grandmother. Just as soon as he wakes up," said Charles, smiling with affection.

"As soon as he wakes up?" she said through a chuckle. "Your grandfather has been up for hours, praying and reading. He was up before the songbirds, silly child!" She was right. Not even morning's first light could beat his grandfather out of bed. He didn't go a single day without kneeling to the floor of his reading parlor and begging the good Lord for a spoil of manna from Heaven. Every single day, Heaven relinquished, and he ate from the bounty of that Bible he so dearly loved.

When Charles was nearly finished with his pastry and milk, the door of the parlor next to the kitchen opened. "Another good morning with the Lord," said his grandfather. "And now, another good day unto Him." His words were inspiring to Charles. When he spoke, Charles listened, paying careful attention to how he spoke, and how often he spoke of the Lord. It was as if "the Lord" were a true friend, a soulmate, a lover, and Charles hoped very much to meet and enjoy the Lord one day, as well.

"I made fresh pastries for you and Charles. Come eat," said Charles's grandmother. "The apple trees are beginning to bud, my dears. Mrs. Thompson saw nearly thirty fresh buds in her garden, and from the looks of ours, I'm sure I'll be making apple biscuits in no time."

They finished their breakfast as the sacred walls of the kitchen watched along. From floor to ceiling hung portraits of grandparents, uncles, and nieces, and portraits of men that grandfather had baptized in the river. There were also the portraits of Charles's father and mother, clasping the newly born and pale-faced Charles. Next to these, one of the only real windows of the house was carved within the brick. Roses generally peeked through the open window, and whenever they could, they'd climb into the window frame and drop a few of their ripened petals.

"Let's hurry on, Charles," said his grandfather. "Bring along some fresh water, an empty wine bottle, and a little spool of string. I believe there is a treasure in store for us today." He smiled and pushed himself from the table. He wasn't a man of delay. When he was ready, he was ready. When he was finished with something, he was already halfway to the next thing. "Come along, boy!"

Charles scurried off to fetch the bottle and string that his grandfather requested. Charles was only three feet tall and weighed less than fifty-five pounds, much smaller than all the other boys his age. It never bothered him and, honestly, you'd never know it because he bounced and sprung around so quickly you couldn't compare him to anyone else. His coal-black hair pulled neatly across the top of his head, parted down the middle, and laid flat against his scalp, revealing his attractive face. The only things more mature than his heart and mind were his eyes. They were steady and resolved—much more than other kids'—and always taking note of things, cataloguing and thinking deeply upon them. His face was soft with a timid joy, and no part of his bright countenance suggested he was being ravaged with inner turmoil.

"What are you thinking about, Charles?" his grandfather asked, as he opened the iron gate next to the parsonage, revealing the pathway to the garden. "What's got your mind going this morning?"

It was a wide, grassy walk from the house to the garden, one that Charles had run along since he could barely stand. He thought about his grandfather's question, then slowly answered, "I don't know, Grandfather. The other day, Mr. Tagley showed me a baby fox he had captured."

"Mr. Tagley captured a fox?" asked his grandfather, suspiciously.

"Yes. It was wonderful, really. Its fur was perfectly red, like a rusty iron fence. It was beautiful, Grandfather. I've never seen one up close. And it didn't bark. Or snap. It didn't curl away. It just stood like a warrior, even though I'm sure it was frightened. And, he was stuck in this metal cage." Charles made a motion with both of his hands, creating an imaginary cage. "And it seemed very wrong. A baby fox—it shouldn't be in a cage, should it?"

The walk was green and quiet as Charles's question hung in the morning mist. They passed along an old hedge of yew trees that extended all the way around the garden. They had been freshly trimmed, and stood as a perfectly lush boundary around the outer edges. Beyond the hedge, bright green and open fields extended for what seemed like miles. The grass inside the hedge, in the garden, was perfectly mown, but the open fields outside the garden were rustic and natural.

"It just felt odd to see something so beautiful become a prisoner in a cage. Especially, when—didn't God make foxes to be out there, instead? Why would God let it be put in a cage?" Charles pointed to the open fields and looked up at his grandfather, trying desperately to unravel what his heart was feeling about Mr. Tagley and the beautiful little fox. His grandfather remained quiet as they walked, unsure of the questioning, but sure of an answer.

They finally stopped underneath a deliciously plump apple tree in the center of the garden, just between the Meeting House and the parsonage. His grandfather cleared his throat and said, "Charles, we don't always know the ways of the Lord." He gathered his thoughts and chose his words.

"Sometimes, the Lord gives us the opportunity to see things—things that seem wrong—so that we can do something about them. So we can change them. But other times, the Lord lets us see things—things that seem wrong—so those things can change *us*."

Charles listened and catalogued every word.

"Son, the most important thing to understand about God," continued his grandfather, "is that He is God, and we are not. He is in charge of baby foxes, not Mr. Tagley. God made the rising of the Essex hills, the twinkling of the stars, and He whispers the wind to climb all through the treetops. He turns the fall leaves to hues of brown and grey. He crafted the bottomless pit of hell, and He decorated the hallways of the Heavenly City. Nothing happens without His knowing, His acting, His doing."

Charles nodded his head, partly intrigued, but mostly confused. "But what about the pretty fox?" he asked.

His grandfather chuckled as he fished around his pocket for the spool of string that Charles gathered from the parlor desk. "I'm sure the pretty little fox was put into that cage for a reason, Charles. I bet my afternoon tea that Mr. Tagley will eventually let him go. That man loves animals. And if not, by God, we'll go break that furry little dog out of jail!"

A forced grin crept across Charles's face, content with his grandfather's vigilance, discontent with an answer he couldn't understand. "Hand me that bottle, Charles. You hold the string." Charles handed him a golden empty wine bottle, and together they tied a string around the center of it as his grandfather quietly continued, "Remember what I said. The most important thing to understand about our mysterious God is that He is God, and we are not. When we are least expecting it, He will put something so deep inside the caverns of our heart. We won't see it at first, we won't even know it's there. But one day we'll look back and see He was in control of everything, all along the way."

He reached his arm high above his head and carefully pulled one of the branches of the apple tree towards them. The leaves were gorgeous green, and the entire branch was filled with several buds that would soon bloom into baby apples. "Reach your hand up here, son. Hold the branch near to the bottle. That's right, hold it right there." Charles clenched the bottle and the

branch, and held them tightly, but kept his eyes fixed on the face
of his grandfather.

"God," he said as he peered into his grandson's eyes, "being
the best gardener I know, takes His own branches and bends
them all the way down towards us. Then, He takes a budding
little seed from His branch, and places that seed in us." He took
one of the apple buds and gently pushed it into the bottle, still
keeping it connected to the branch. With his other hand, he
gently tied the bottle to the branch, fastening it tight enough
that it wouldn't fall, and close enough that the bud stayed in the
bottle. Charles stared and waited for his grandfather's illustration to make sense. *But, what about the fox?* he thought. *And why
does God need to be mysterious?* he wondered.

After his grandfather finished tying the glass bottle around
the branch, he released it from the grip of their hands. It sprung
back above their heads, and Charles looked up to see the rather
strange sight: a shiny golden bottle hanging from an apple tree
branch, with a tiny budding seed stuffed inside.

"Then," his grandfather whispered to Charles, "God does
what we cannot do. So, we wait. We watch. It is He who places
the seed exactly where it should go. It is He who waters the budding seed, He who grows it, and it is only He who makes any
sense of it. And when He's ready, that seed will grow into a delicious piece of fruit, shiny and fattened, more glorious than we
could ever imagine. So we wait and watch, my grandson."

They turned their backs to the apple tree and the golden
bottle hanging from its branches, and quietly walked through
the wide green grass, along the hedge of yew towards the parsonage. The fox remained in his cage, the seedling rested in the
bottle, and Charles wrestled with silent disbelief. But God was
up to something. Something that would one day crash through
the fences of Stambourne, trample the borders of Essex, and
eventually change the entire world.

CHAPTER 2

FROM A TOBACCO PLANTATION

Virginia, USA 1846

Thomas Johnson was ten years old when he first saw the Devil. Its eyes were black, small, piercing—just like the ones Thomas had seen in his dreams. It was more than the form of the beast, but rather his eyes that brought real fear to Thomas. This first encounter with the Devil brought to him the kind of fear that instantly pulses waves of sickening nausea through your stomach and beads of cold sweat to your brow. In that one fateful moment, Thomas felt the kind of terror that a man can recall in an instant, years later, when more peaceful days prevail.

The morning began like every other morning of his life at his master's plantation on the outskirts of Fairfax, Virginia. Every slave woke up with the sunrise, stumbling slowly from their quarters, empty looks in their eyes, stiffness being stretched from their backs. The smell of fresh bread, fryback, and eggs cooked in grease wafted from the main house and made Thomas's stomach hurt. Hunger was the little boy's constant companion, his worst friend. He often lay in bed at night and wondered what it would be like to eat such meals, every day, just like his master and his master's family. The only time Thomas ever got to taste the salty, sweet flesh of pigs was on Christmas Day, and only then if his master was in a good mood and not drinking too much. But this wasn't Christmas Day. It was Tuesday. And Tuesday only offered the enticing scent of a white man's breakfast from the big house on the other side of the yard.

"Get over here now, boy!" screamed the plantation's foreman, startling Thomas from his thoughts.

He ran, without hesitation, to the foreman's wagon where the man who controlled his life stood every morning in the shade, assigning the day's work to each slave. The man's name was Quentin Ellis. Quentin was of Irish descent, and carried a bitter anger and a head full of red hair that was passed down from his father's father. His lean and muscular build made him taller than most men. He was probably handsome at some point in his youth, before the disappointment of life clouded his eyes and tobacco stained his beard.

At the age of thirty-two, Quentin was given the position of plantation foreman. The master, Mr. Bennett, liked that Quentin was a hard man who felt no remorse when it became necessary to give lashes to a slave. Quentin Ellis had learned hate at an early age. He was possessed by a natural cruelty—the worst of its kind. His father made a sport out of beating him and his mother, and she was the only human being Quentin had ever loved. Many years ago, on a sultry summer afternoon, Quentin walked into his father's house and found his mother laying on the floor in a pool of blood. His father stood over her, emotionless, breathing heavy, reeking of whiskey.

Most people experience a profound metamorphosis in moments after they become victims of unfathomable violence. Surprisingly, many become peacemakers. They grow in gentleness, and become the opposite of the very cruelty they once incurred. This unlikely transformation brings some semblance of peace, and serves as a salve to the festering wounds of their souls. Others though, in an instant, are reborn by the bloodletting they fell prey to. They succumb to cruelty they once sustained, now capable of even worse. This was the man that Quentin Ellis had become.

"Grab a pail," said Quentin to Thomas. "Go down to Turkey Creek. Look by that big oak, and fetch some blackberries for the master." He rested the palm of his hand on the handle of the leather whip that hung from his side. "And, when you get back, that pail better be full. And you best not take more than an hour."

Thomas nodded obediently, and without a word, he turned and ran towards the shed where the pails were kept. Grabbing a pail, he quickly opened the back door of the shed and began his journey down the well-worn path that led to Turkey Creek. He knew the way by heart, because every slave was allowed to bathe in the cool waters on Sunday afternoons. This privilege had been instituted by the master's wife, Mrs. Bennett, who finally convinced her husband that cleanliness was a virtue—next only to godliness—and one day she would stand before the Lord in judgment if she kept a plantation full of dirty slaves.

Once Thomas was out of the sight of the foreman, he slowed his run to a leisurely walk to allow himself time to enjoy the peace and quiet that came with this small taste of freedom. The air hung thick and moist in the creek bottom, too moist for his taste. Sweat beaded lightly on his forehead. Ancient oaks, thick with green moss hanging from their branches, lined the path to the creek and kept the moisture of the morning from being evaporated by the hot Virginia sun.

As Thomas reached the last sharp bend in the trail, he entered a large opening in the trees. There, an oak tree, ancient and majestic, stood in the middle of the opening. Old, rotting leaves coated the floor beside the oak tree, and a crooked fence lined its furthest boundary. Thomas heard the sounds of Turkey Creek, clean and bubbling just beyond the fence line, and immediately felt a sense of peace.

Thomas inhaled the sweet, sticky smell of summer and, as often happened in his rare times of solitude, he thought of his mother. He missed her dearly. She was the most wonderful person he had ever known. He often tried to push thoughts of her away—the fond memories were sometimes too much to bear— but he could no more keep them away than the mosquitoes that tortured him at night. They were always there.

Thomas had never known his father; he lived in Alexandria, and died as a free man when Thomas was only nine. News of his death reached the plantation, and Thomas's mother explained that his father spent seven years trying to earn enough money to purchase their freedom. Mr. Bennett had received the money from Thomas's father, more than enough to purchase their freedom, but he refused.

The evils of slavery, perhaps, were most greatly displayed when slave owners separated husbands from their wives, and mothers from their children. To masters, slave children were a valuable commodity, and they were publicly sold at auction, torn from their mother's arms, never again to be reunited. Such had been the case with Thomas, and now at ten years of age, he felt completely alone in the world. Thomas desperately loved his mother, and missed her in a way that made his chest ache and hot tears roll down his face. She had been the only person in his life to show him kindness, and her gentle embrace provided the only refuge he had ever known.

All the thoughts of his mother vanished from his mind as Thomas laid his eyes on a thick blackberry bush that circled and entwined the rungs of the wooden fence. "Woohoo!" Thomas shouted to nobody in particular, as he drew closer to the thick berries he had come to harvest. He loved the sweet taste of the fruit, and it always made him giggle when he bit into a blackberry and its juice exploded in his mouth. It offered a brief moment of childlike excitement to Thomas; blackberries were as close to candy as a young slave boy could get.

Thomas's excitement vanished as he heard a rustling in the leaves near the oak tree behind him. He held a blackberry in his mouth and grew quiet, daring not to turn around, but waiting to see if he had imagined the noise. *Is someone watching me?* he thought, wondering if the foreman had sent a spy to see if he was eating too many blackberries.

His legs were thick and heavy with fear. He could feel his pulse growing stronger and hotter in his neck. The rustling began again, and his tiny hands tensed tightly around the handle of the pail, knowing it could serve as a weapon, if necessary. Mustering enough courage, Thomas finally turned towards the noise. He lifted his eyes, and there within the shadows of the oak tree, just a few feet from the purple blackberry bush, he saw it. The Devil.

Time seemed to stall, as Thomas's head rushed with a thousand thoughts. He remembered the last conversation he had with his mother. "Be a good boy," she said with tears. "Always be nice to the master. And never forget to stay clear of the Devil." In those last moments with the woman who occupied the greatest affections of his heart, Thomas was overcome with too much grief to ask her what she meant about avoiding the Devil.

And yet, now he stood, still stunned, white-knuckling the empty pail, facing his greatest fear.

A few days after the painful separation from his mother, Thomas was working in the tobacco fields and asked a fellow slave what he thought Thomas's mother could have been talking about. "Who's the Devil? And, what does he look like?" Thomas asked his friend Ezekiel. There were few people in the world who felt comfortable to Thomas, and although no one could ever take the place of a parent, Thomas found a steadiness in Ezekiel, one he could lean heavily upon. He was an older man, weathered with wisdom, and tall with confidence.

"Why you ask that, child?" Ezekiel said, raising his eyebrow and setting his full basket to the ground.

"Before she left, my momma said I was supposed to stay clear of him," said Thomas with a sadness in his voice. "But I don't even know who he is. And I don't know what he looks like."

"Well, from what I been told," said Ezekiel, "the Devil—he came into the Garden—where God put the first people. Adam and Eve was their names. And, the Devil, he lied to 'em. Made 'em eat an apple. And they died. That's 'bout all I know." Ezekiel picked up his basket to continue gathering tobacco leaves.

"And he's still around? What's he look like, Ezekiel?" asked Thomas, intrigued.

"He's a snake! If he gets you to eat some fruit, you gonna die too. But don't you bother yourself with that boy," Ezekiel said, turning and leaving Thomas with his thoughts.

❋ ❋ ❋

Those distant words rang loudly in Thomas's mind as he stood near the blackberry bush, facing the Devil himself. The stage was set exactly as Ezekiel had described. He was in a garden, surrounded by fruit, with a snake slithering towards his quivering legs. The serpent's tongue rolled quietly in and out of its mouth. Its shiny skin sparkled, and Thomas was sure the Devil would start talking any minute. Paralyzed with fear,

Thomas faced the greatest dilemma of his young life: if he were to stay, the Devil would force him to eat some fruit like Adam and Eve, which would surely result in his death, but if he ran back to the plantation without berries, he would face the wrath of Quentin Ellis.

Thomas decided between the lesser of two evils; he was certain he'd rather face the wrath of Quentin Ellis than take his chances with the Devil—after all, it didn't work out very well for Adam and Eve. Quickly, Thomas dropped the pail, spun on his heels, and ran towards the path with a speed only achieved by someone being chased by evil, himself.

Thomas arrived at the plantation, empty-handed, dusty, and glistening with sweat. He forced himself to walk, hoping not to draw unwanted attention, then snuck past the slave quarters towards the tobacco fields, where he knew Ezekiel would be stationed for the day.

Ezekiel looked up from his work and saw the boy approaching from a distance. The little boy's eyes were wide with terror. As their eyes met, Thomas burst into tears and ran the last few yards into the tobacco field. Ezekiel looked cautiously to his left and right to see if the foreman was near, then quickly dropped his bag of tobacco leaves just in time to catch the crying little boy in his arms.

"I saw the Devil! I saw it!" Thomas yelled, spilling tears onto his friend's shirt. Ezekiel held the boy tight in his muscular arms and patted his head.

"What in the world do you mean, child? What'd you see?" asked Ezekiel.

"Down by the creek. The foreman told me to get blackberries for the master." Thomas tried to catch his breath as he explained. "Right next to that old oak by the creek, I saw him, Ezekiel! It was the Devil. He almost got me. Just like he got them people you told me about. But I ran. I dropped my pail and ran. Just like

I'd stole a loaf of bread from the big house," said Thomas, as he clenched Ezekiel's arms.

Ezekiel smiled sympathetically and took the boy by the shoulders, pulling him gently away from his chest.

"You didn't see no Devil, boy. All you saw was a snake. The Devil got better things to do than mess around with a ten-year-old slave boy on a rundown plantation in Virginia," Ezekiel said, laughing.

Thomas hung his head in embarrassment, as he realized his error in judgment.

"One thing's for sure, honey," said Ezekiel, his tone changing darkly. "We have to figure out what to say to the foreman. He ain't gonna be happy when he sees you came home without them berries."

A fresh and hot wave of despair came over Thomas as he remembered the blackberries and the job Quentin Ellis had given him. Thomas had been beaten only once by the foreman, but it was enough to remember.

❊ ❊ ❊

Last year, Thomas worked in the big house as a servant to the master's son. At night, he was responsible for bringing slippers to the young white boy before he went to bed. Thomas didn't know right from left, so each night he simply guessed as to which shoe was to be put on which of his master's feet. On the nights he guessed wrong, the master's son hit him on the head and called him names. On the nights Thomas guessed correctly, the master's son accused him of knowing all along and deliberately trying to sabotage the evening ritual. The master's son complained to the foreman, who promptly found Thomas and tied his hands to the whipping post in the middle of the grassy lawn outside the big house. He only received five lashes with a leather belt—a lesser punishment than a whipping with the normal three-pronged whip. But even so, Thomas had never experienced anything that compared to the shame and hopelessness he felt as that belt lashed across his shoulders, lower back, and buttocks.

The first lash sent a searing pain up and down his tiny back. It shot like a bolt of lightning through his arms and legs, all the way to his fingers and toes. As he held onto the wooden post, he prayed for God to rescue him from the torture. The second lash hit Thomas on the left part of his back, in between his backbone and ribs, and he swore all of hell's fury had been unleashed to his tiny body. As he continued to grip the post, he made eye contact with Mrs. Bennett, who had walked into the shade of the front porch to see the commotion.

Thomas's eyes welled with a sadness too heavy for a child's eyes to bear, and by the time the third and fourth lashes slammed across his shoulders, his knees gave way and he let out a heavy moan. He looked again at Mrs. Bennett and thought, *She's a mother. She has sons! Maybe she will stop this!* But Mrs. Bennett only watched, silently unmoved. As the final blow landed on Thomas's shaking legs, Mrs. Bennett simply shook her head and turned towards the front door of the big house.

❈ ❈ ❈

"What do I do, Ezekiel? I ran off without the berries and the foreman's gonna beat me like he done before. Except, I'm ten now. And ten means I get the whip, not the belt!" Thomas shouted from within the tobacco field.

"Don't you worry, honey. I ain't gonna let no man beat you. Not today," said Ezekiel sternly.

Thomas and Ezekiel gathered tobacco leaves until the falling sun rested behind the plantation. That evening, Thomas lay alone in his bed and wept bitterly. He recalled his encounter with the Devil, the terrible beating last year, the turning away of Mrs. Bennett, and he thought of his mother. He thought of her sweet embrace and strong arms. He longed to be caught in those strong arms, but he knew his mother was gone, and he could never return. Deep loneliness slithered within his sheets and crawled throughout his thoughts, as Thomas clenched his eyes and closed his fists.

In a distant wooden building, just past the grassy lawn and the whipping post, Ezekiel, too, lay alone in his bed. Blood drenched his shirt, and pain sped along every bruised bone and fiber of his body. Ezekiel had told the foreman about all that happened with the Devil by the blackberry bush and Thomas's empty pail, and he begged for Thomas's punishment to be given to him instead. Ezekiel was whipped with twenty lashes too many for a child, too many for a man. Long cuts and bruises covered Ezekiel's back and body, but not a single tear was shed.

Ezekiel would have gladly taken twenty more.

Thomas desperately tried to fall asleep as he listened to the familiar nighttime sounds of Mr. Bennett's tobacco plantation through his open window—the clanking of pans as slaves cleaned the kitchen, the flapping of clean linens strung on the lines, and the laughter of white men drunk on whiskey and power. Then surprisingly, from just beyond his shack, Thomas heard a sound like none he had ever heard. It was the faint sound of singing— low as a whisper, quiet as the moon. The hushed voices, defiant in their quietness, sang of a place called Heaven—a land where slaves were free forever. The melody was haunting and slow, but the whispered voices were hopeful and steady.

For just a moment, Thomas savored the sounds of Heaven, and he longed for such a place. He longed for the place where boys could run and roam without fear, without struggle, without whip- pings. But as he lay within a hardened bed frame in the corner of a clapboard shack on a tobacco plantation in Virginia, he swore Heaven was a place to sing about, but never reach. For Thomas Johnson lived in the real world, one ruled by men like Quentin Ellis, who made sure freedom was enjoyed only by white men.

CHAPTER 3

THE BOTTOMLESS PIT

Essex, England 1844

Since the winter of 1841, remnants of Stambourne cluttered every space of Charles's heart and soul. It was hard to be away from his grandfather and grandmother, but going back to Colchester to stay with his parents from time to time made absolute sense, even to his stubborn, little brain. The twenty-three-mile horse ride from Colchester to Stambourne took many bends and dips through Earls Colne, Halstead, and Toppesfield, and it always brought a delirious excitement to Charles. Throughout the years, he'd make the trek countless times, and each time the journey itself became a heaven for him. And it wasn't merely the idyllic scenery, the thrills of nature, or the sound of hoof-beats on the gravel road; instead, it was the quiet that invigorated him. It gave Charles time to think, and as much as he loved the mingling of conversation and laughter, he always preferred a journey through the countryside with a strong horse and his own thoughts.

By the time his feet hit the floor that morning, ten-year-old Charles Spurgeon was already halfway out the door. Breakfast was on the table, and his father, John, was nearly finished readying the horse. Charles swooped through the kitchen to fetch two warm biscuits, then scarfed them down as he flew to the front yard of the tiny thatched cottage. On this much-awaited day, the liberal smile painted across Charles's cheeks betrayed his excitement.

"Oh Father, how I've missed Grandfather! How long will I stay this time?" asked Charles as he jumped into his father's arms. Reeling from the surprise attack, John chuckled mightily, squeezed his boy tight enough to burst a melon, then sat him to the ground and brushed off the leftover biscuit crumbs that trimmed Charles's rosy lips.

"Good morning, Charlie. Delightful morning it is! And, did any of that biscuit make it into your mouth?" he said, as he knelt eye-level to Charles. His eyes were deep as caverns, and when he spoke, it was as if he could peer into every recess of your soul. Not a cold stare, nor the kind that spills shivers down your backbone, but rather, it was the warmest, proudest, and most earnest stare in all of Essex, one that always comforted Charles and made him feel visible.

❈ ❈ ❈

Children need to be seen by their fathers. When the heart of a son or daughter goes unattended by a father, it becomes a golden lamp without the flame with which it was intended to sparkle. They rust and wither away, while hoping to find something—someone—that will strike a match and set fire to their wick.

A few years ago, John traveled to Cambridge, where he preached night after night the gospel of Jesus and God's love for the sinner. As he spoke of the beautiful "All-Seeing Eyes of God," hundreds of golden souls suddenly lit up as they realized the eye of God had sought them out and found them. But despite the thrill of watching souls come to faith in Christ, John feared he was neglecting his own children at the cost of caring for the souls of complete strangers.

He departed right away, traveled through the evening, burst through the front door of his sleeping household, and wept as he quietly prayed, "Oh God, may my children have an earthly father who sees them and a heavenly Father who saves them!" As Charles slept, unaware, in the adjacent room, he was seen by the jealous eyes of a good, earthly father, and a very good heavenly Father as well.

❈ ❈ ❈

"Father, come on! We must hurry. I've got to get on my way to Stambourne! Help me finish packing? What's the weather there? Has Grandfather got any new books? And how long can I stay this time, Father?" rattled Charles as he busied about like a bumblebee counting luggage bags, carefully peering inside each one to make sure he packed everything. Sometimes Charles asked so many questions all at once, barely giving time for any answers, that when he finished asking all of them, he'd forgotten what he asked. This always made his mother and father laugh heartily, as they thoroughly enjoyed this part of his quirky personality.

"Father, tell me! How long can I stay this time?" sweetly demanded Charles again.

"I'm not sure," answered his father. "How about you just stay until Grandfather gets tired of you?"

"Well, how long will that be?" Charles asked, perplexed that anyone could tire of him.

"It depends how many questions you ask of him every morning." His father carved a sarcastic grin across his face and continued, "You might want to let him get his morning tea and pastry before you go buzzing around asking a bucket of questions, Charlie. He's an old man, and old men require . . . a bit more quiet." He winked at Charles and began securing several leather bags to both sides of the favorite family horse. Stuck was a short horse, but a strong one, and was aptly named, as she was the only creature more stubborn than Charles himself. The old girl decided when she would move and when she would not, and no amount of prodding, pleading, or pushing could change her mind. Maybe that's why Charles loved her so much. He appreciated that attribute in people, and he certainly respected it in a creature that weighed a ton.

"Ah, Charles! Charles!" his mama yelled as she flung open the front door and ran towards Stuck, who was ironically loaded with so much luggage it would tempt a much larger horse to defiantly sit and shake its head in refusal.

"Packed you a few boiled potatoes, my boy. And a loaf of raisin bread for your grandmother. And your books. Charlie—you forgot your books." She handed him another bag, loaded to the edge with all his favorite books. He instantly thought of the little reading chamber extending from the parsonage bedroom and could smell the melting of his grandfather's candles, handmade from rushes and tallow. "And don't forget your dear mother while you're gone. I will continue to pray for you every night, my sweet boy. Every single night."

Charles's mother was a true woman of virtue—bright as ten thousand rubies and lovely as a diamond—and she loved Charles with every beating of her heart. Her plump, soft hand caressed his smiling face, as love seeped from her warm hands. She was the mother of seventeen children, and even the nine that would eventually die in infancy always danced in her dreams at night and haunted her thoughts by day.

Charles remembered the time he woke to the sweetest sound from his mother's lips, pursed and proper, whispering a plea to God to save him. "Oh, that my son might live before Thee!" She must have said that a hundred times that night, and each time, she whispered it with more fervency and command. Her peaceful countenance camouflaged her strong will, but Charles could easily imagine her standing before God demanding that He save her boy. "Oh, that my son *might* live before Thee! Oh that my son *will* live before Thee! My son *must* live before Thee! I beg it of you!" she prayed.

It was her nightly custom to gather the children around the family table to read from the Holy Scriptures. Even as her immature congregation struggled to pay attention, she brought the biblical stories to life with her patient heart and loving words. "And what do you say Elijah *should* have done Charles?" she gently asked, stirring up blank stares and thinking faces. "I suppose," answered Charles reluctantly, "I'd say he should have eaten that goat before it burned to a crisp char!" She never tired of teaching, never became impatient with silly answers, and closed every table meeting with the sweetest of motherly prayers.

"Now Lord," she prayed often, clasping her hands and lifting one eyelid to dart her policing eye around the table. "If my children go on in their sins, it will not be from ignorance that they perish. My soul must bear a swift witness at the day of judgment if they lay not hold of Christ." She felt the weight of wanting her children to know the Christ she knew, and never missed an opportunity to plead on their behalf. Each time she prayed, it nudged Charles's conscience and stirred his fragile heart.

Some children are blessed to grow up with a maternal care-taker, one who nurtures and protects and tends. But Charles was given an unimaginable gift that superseded even the most prized mother: a tender woman who knew God. Charles was unknow-ingly bathed in a sea of invisible tears and prayers offered to Heaven from his godly mother, and it's perhaps one of the greatest reasons that darkness could never fully defeat Charles Spurgeon. When he wept in bed at night, as he often wrestled with thoughts of depression and loneliness, she stood by his door reading aloud the Word of God, her sword unsheathed. When Charles closed his eyes and had visions of demons bind-ing his hands, she cried aloud to her mighty God, "Release my boy from the grip of anyone but You, God! Secure my boy!" And, when the heart of young Charles Spurgeon was fallow and covered with weeds, she kept her blistered hand to the plow, never questioning the seed of the gospel that would eventually bloom and trample over the barrenness of his troubled heart.

"Charles, you must be on your way! From the looks of it, you'll have a fierce thunder shower chasing you towards Stambourne," his father said, as he helped him climb onto Stuck, who held her ground and swatted flies with her black tail.

"Stay on the path, stay on Stuck, and God be with you, my boy," he said firmly. "Get on now."

Charles gave Stuck a gentle nudge in her underbelly, and to his surprise, she nodded her head and stepped into a gentle trot down the dusty road.

"Good-bye! I love you both!" he turned and yelled as they shrunk in the distance. "Don't worry about me, Mama!" She would—and he knew it—but, it's always comforting to know a mother has just a twinge of worry in her. *It'll keep her praying,* he thought to himself, and smiled as he nudged Stuck to pick up the pace. It was a long ride to Stambourne, but he was ready to take a deep plunge into his thoughts, savoring the beauty all around him.

It was an eight-hour journey from Colchester to Stambourne, though Charles could make it in six if Stuck ever felt the urge to run, and the first five hours were an absolute delight to Charles. The gears of his imagination seemed to churn as fast as the new Royal Train he'd heard about in London. He often wondered what it would be like to ride a locomotive across Essex, but quickly dismissed the idea, fearing it would be impossible to truly enjoy nature from a boxcar traveling 120 kilometers per hour.

Charles had the rare ability to see beauty in everything. From the tiniest of crawling creatures to the vast blanket of pinhole stars at night, Charles couldn't help but see the finger-prints of God in all things. To him, the world seemed to echo constantly like a drum the heartbeat of God. He often imagined the Creator as a brilliant architect, delighted to sketch every detail of His Creation. Perhaps the Creator pulled a chair to His wooden desk, sharpened His pencil and gathered His paper, then outlined every leaf that would hang from every tree in the world. With scissors and a careful eye, He trimmed each one, then dyed them in beautiful colors from His divine palette.

"These shall be gold," Charles imagined God whispering as He proudly stacked and catalogued them. *"And these, amber-green with streaks of caramel-blue. And these, the purest of heavenly green, just like the ones in my Garden!"* The trees stretched their arms wide with anticipation as the Creator sewed each leaf with needle and thread to the wooden branches He had carved. Then when the Creator had finished, He brushed his hands with delight, and sat down to work on His next project.

Charles imagined God smiling on the day He drew up the plans for his parents and grandparents. His strong hands must have pressed and kneaded with special diligence, ecstatic to craft them from the finest of clays. And there in the clay, He placed bits of compassion and empathy, truth and wisdom, then painted them in silvers and whites, bright as linen. What an act of brilliance when He lit their hearts with a holy spark, then roamed His finger along a map of the world to find the perfect place to set them in motion.

Sadly though, when Charles dared to imagine the Creator designing Charles Haddon Spurgeon, born in Essex to a lineage of fine Congregationalist pastors, son of a godly mother, grandson of a God-fearing grandmother, smart, witty, and destined to lead, he could never seem to find a smile on the face of God. When he imagined God at the same desk, he saw nothing but frustration and contempt upon His face. Wrinkled and frowned, the mouth of God drooped with disappointment. His face shook in bitter disgust as He crumpled up the half-sketched design and threw it into His empty trash bin. God had never needed to throw anything away until that day; even the devils had some place in the storybook of God. But surely, Charles thought, it was a sad day when God closed His eyes, drew a deep and frustrated breath, then pushed Himself away from the desk.

Charles wondered why God had even tried in the first place.

With the sun hidden behind stacks of thunderclouds, Charles hadn't realized it was an hour past noon. His stomach rumbled as he fished around one of the sacks looking for a potato. It tasted plain, and as it filled his empty belly, he noticed a peculiar sense of plainness filling his heart as well. Because there was no sunlight to spill shadows onto the road, everything suddenly appeared flat and muted. Endless rows of trees marched towards him, passed his left and right, then cowered and blurred into the distant horizon.

Each of Stuck's pressing hooves sank into the gravel, lifted and spun a little dust backwards, then reached forward and pressed into the never-ending path again. Birds whistled and chirped the only song they knew. As soon as Charles passed one, the next picked up right where the other had left off. Like a terribly long and boring symphony, the song never changed keys, it had no ebb or flow, and quickly became an endless monotone horn blasting his ears. Usually he loved being engulfed by the sights and thrills of nature, but today, delight was all too dim as he felt the claws of darkness once again reaching for him.

Rain began to trickle from the darkening clouds above. One drop turned into two, two to ten, ten to millions. A cold wind blew through his hair and swirled around his back, then hugged him and placed its hands in all of his pockets. Lightning and thunder, brilliant and terrible, rattled all throughout the trees that surrounded him. They bent in submission, kneeling almost to the ground from the weight of the wind and rain. All at once, Charles was completely swallowed by the storm that had been chasing him since Colchester. His spine shivered as he wiped the cold water from his face, squinting through the sheets of rain to find shelter for him and Stuck. A torrent of black clouds rushed in, changing midday to what seemed like midnight, and all of a sudden Charles could only see Stuck's mane and the outline of a cattle barn in the far distance.

"C'mon, Stuck! Faster!"

His heart raced, fast as fire, and while the thunder cracked and crawled through the sky, fear began to pierce his bones. He thought of Grandfather, trying to recall his gracious eyes and warm affection, reaching to remember the smell of sweet heavenly rainwater, the taste of fresh honey from the backyard beehive, and warm pastries in the kitchen. But as the fear and the storm increased, the face of his grandfather blurred, and the memories were unable to bring any comfort.

The wind howled around him. To his left, a sword of lightning streaked from the heavens, igniting a giant tree into flashes of roaring fire. Within seconds the entire tree was ablaze, shooting branches in every direction like cannonballs. As it erupted, a fiery branch, thick as an English foxhound, cracked off the highest point and crashed onto the pathway right in front of him.

Charles gasped, ripping Stuck's reins to the right, barely dodging the falling branch. Haunted by the fiery tree and drenched in rain and fear, Charles burst into tears and held onto Stuck for dear life. He felt the thunder rumble through the ground, up Stuck's legs, all the way to his saddle. It seemed as though the floor of the earth was buckling from the storm, and all of hell's fury was waiting to pull him in.

"C'mon, Stuck! We must make it to that barn ahead! C'mon, girl!" She ran towards the shadowy outline, but even at her fastest speed, it still seemed so far away.

"Help! Help! Help!" he cried out in despair. But, there was no one to hear him—no one close enough to save him. As he and Stuck fumbled through the blackness of the storm, Charles's mind began to spiral down toward a thousand fears and worries until it came to a halt at the ever-darkened pit of hell.

❖ ❖ ❖

"There is a deep pit, Charles," said his grandfather while sitting around the wooden dining table one day. "The soul without Christ is always falling down that deep pit." His grandfather held his clenched fist as far above the table as his arm could reach, then let it spiral towards the table. Inch by inch, it moved downward, slow as a snail. Charles watched in wonder and intrigue. "And oh, how slowly it is falling! Look! The last ray of light at the top has disappeared, and now the soul falls on—on—on. And so it goes on falling—on—on—on—for a thousand years."

"But is it getting near the bottom yet?" Charles asked, as his grandfather's fist came closer to the wooden table. "Won't it stop when it hits the bottom, Grandfather?"

"No, son. As the soul is falling down, it cries out in terror, 'Help! Help! Help!' but all it can do is keep falling." As soon as his fist came near the surface of the table, he pulled his hand as high as he could reach, and let it slowly spiral again. As Charles watched it fall towards the table, he was overcome with sadness. A knot of anxiety swelled in his throat as he listened and watched. Charles knew his grandfather believed with all of his heart in the reality of that bottomless pit. He heard the conviction in his voice. He saw it in his eyes.

"What if—what if that soul falls for a million years? Does it not go near the bottom?" Charles asked, as pools of water began to fill his eyes.

"No, Charles. You are never near the bottom. It is a *bottomless* pit. It goes on—on—on, and the soul goes on falling into deeper depths. Forever—and ever—and ever. On—on—on into the pit that has no bottom. And there's no hope of ever hitting the bottom or climbing out the top. It's the worst thing imaginable, Charles."

❊ ❊ ❊

Suddenly, another crack of lightning filled the storm-cluttered sky, jolting Charles from the memory of his grandfather around the kitchen table. It had haunted him for so many years, but today it echoed in his heart as loudly as the thunder above. Charles's eyes swelled with tears as he gripped the reins and stared at the outline of the cattle barn, still so far away.

On—on—on Charles went.

On—on—on Stuck ran.

"C'mon, girl. Don't stop," he pleaded. Her hooves became heavier, nearly buckling under the weight of rain-soaked

Charles, bulky luggage, and the terrible storm. She struggled to keep the pace, but her strong and stubborn legs kept marching forward.

In a sudden moment, Charles was hurled forward over the horse's head and into the sticky mud. Stuck's hoof had landed in a small hole in the path and tripped her, sending her knees straight to the ground and Charles into the sticky mire. The leather straps that held the luggage ripped from the saddle, and luggage scattered all across the muddy road. Stuck neighed and screamed in the darkness as she gathered the strength to stand back up. Charles, squinting through the rain and darkness, ran towards her and fondled the ground, desperately trying to collect all the wet books and clothing.

"Help! Anyone! Please, help! Help!" he cried.

The floodgates of hell had opened. His mind was pandemonium as ten thousand evil spirits seemed to hold a carnival within his brain. He clenched his teeth and pressed his lips as hard as he could, trying to hold back the volumes of blasphemous words that rang through his ears and heart. Fear and outrage stirred together, violent as a hurricane, and Charles was sure he was spiraling in the bottomless pit. It seemed the Devil himself was throwing and tearing Charles, whipping and tossing him without remorse. As the torturous storm continued to beat his body, he cried out the most horrific insults to the God he assumed was just watching it all happen.

"Where are You, God?!" he yelled and beat his hands into the thick mud. "What kind of god are You that You'd throw a child into the pit?!" His face was completely drenched in mud, cold rain, and bitter tears. When he opened his mouth, he inhaled the rain and exhaled cursing.

On—on—on he seemed to fall.

On—on—on he cried.

His words, fierier than the burning tree, finally gave vent to his bursting heart.

"You're no god. . . . You're a tyrant! Are You deaf and dumb? Why won't You help me?!" As he screamed at God with vile curses and insults, the weight of darkness, the sting of his fall, and memories of the terrible bottomless pit seemed to break Charles into a million pieces. There he lay, shattered and alone, six kilometers from the comforts of Stambourne. And as he gasped for air and cupped his muddy hands around his face, he swore he saw God shake His head in disgust and slowly walk away.

CHAPTER 4

THE EYE OF FAITH

Essex, England 1844

Sunlight always sends shadows away, as even the most arrogant darkness cannot tolerate the invading presence of light. As the sun began to cast yellow beams onto Charles and Stuck in the abandoned cattle barn, fear and darkness crawled away in silence. Like a wounded soldier reeling from defeat on the battlefield, Charles mounted Stuck and somberly made his way towards Stambourne. Though the storm had subsided, it was his darkest night—the one where God walked away and looked for someone else to save, someone else to forgive. He felt alone, more alone than he ever had.

Weekly prayer meetings in the Stambourne Meeting House were always kept, although during certain seasons of the year, only a few farmers and old women gathered to sing hymns and recite prayers. Sundays were reserved for sober celebration, and Charles's grandfather never neglected the opportunity to teach the glorious beauty of the gospel. His pulpit was a sturdy box crafted from an oak tree and finished in a dark mustard stain. From the back row of the six-hundred-seat chapel, it loomed over the flock like a tower. On the pulpit's surface, there was plenty of space for a Bible and two hands, which James frequently thundered and pounded with conviction. Behind the pulpit was a shelf for water and a wooden peg to hold his hat, as it would be inappropriate for a Puritan preacher to wear a hat in the presence of Almighty God.

Just in front of the pulpit stood the table-pew, adorned with fresh bread and ruby-red wine for the Lord's Supper. Here, the elders of the congregation gathered every Sunday morning to pray and prepare for the sacred assembly. They were "men of light and leading," as Charles's grandfather referred to them, and they accepted the gravity of their role. Their knees bore callouses from kneeling often in prayer. Their eyesight was damaged from years of meticulously reading the Scriptures by candlelight, and their hearts groaned for the Spirit of God to save souls.

The pews were crafted from dense wood, and stretched all across the room, taking up nearly every inch of the floor. They were square and roomy, waiting to embrace members of the flock every Sunday morning, afternoon, and evening. Lined with faded blue and golden fabrics, they offered enough comfort to silence any complaints, but not enough comfort to fall asleep during long sermons. James's flock was made of simple people, real Essex folk, and they were drawn to his commonsense sort of preaching. There were a few rough fellows in Stambourne who never dared to darken the doors or sit in the pews of the Meeting House, but nearly every member of the village found it to be a place of delight and refuge.

While the rest of the town streamed towards the Meeting House with eager anticipation, Charles felt distant, reluctant to join. As he tied Stuck to the wooden post outside the church doors, he heard the congregation begin to sing upbeat songs of freedom and glory, but his heart hummed slow songs in minor keys. From within the walls of the Meeting House, they sang songs of hope and the coming Promised Land, but Charles imagined spiraling down the pit, convinced it was the only promised place he would land. They sang of the cross of Christ and the forgiveness of every sin, but Charles couldn't forget shaking his fist and cursing God on the side of that little road from Colchester to Stambourne.

Charles desperately wished someone could see him as he truly was. He knew he wasn't invisible—people saw him all the time. His grandparents saw a good Puritan child, buoyant and excited, without any extraordinary sin. Charles's parents saw him as a bright child full of intellect and humor, not like the other boys who were disobedient, prone to swearing, Sabbath-breaking, and so on. The good people of Stambourne would frequently say, "That Charles Spurgeon! What a fine young man he is!" But to Charles, there was something incomprehensibly worse than being invisible—being *seen* but remaining *unknown*. He was a fake, an imposter, and he was the only one that knew it. A prisoner to his private thoughts, fears, and anguish.

If Charles held up a looking glass, he saw a much different and more grotesque reflection of himself. His handsome face was smeared with darkness like thick paint; it polluted every part of his face—around his eyes, along his forehead, over his cheeks, and pudgy chin. Every vile sin he could imagine, and all his blasphemous thoughts about God, were neatly written on his face in bright red ink. If he looked close enough, every single one of his youthful lusts and imaginations were spelled out in vivid detail, in cursive letters and fine print. *If God does not send me to hell, He ought to,* he thought. He wondered why the skies didn't fall on him, why the stars didn't explode from the sky and crush his guilty soul. Wishing he had never been born, he thought of the commission of suicide, not by means of blade or blood, but through grief and sorrow.

When he slept at night, he dreamt of the pit, and when he awoke, he felt the misery of his all-too-real nightmare. No matter how hard he tried put away that looking glass, morning and night, he was shackled to it—a prisoner to his own internal anguish. And, no one knew but him.

⌧ ⌧ ⌧

As the singing ended, Charles slipped quietly through the entrance, and crawled into the pew that nudged against the back wall.

"Friends, today we turn to Hebrews chapter two for our Scripture reading," an out-of-town preacher spoke to the packed Meeting House. "Today we will see the glory of God in the face of Christ, and I pray you find great comfort in seeing Him today."

This particular Sunday, Charles's grandfather relinquished the pulpit to Richard Knill, an English missionary who was traveling through Stambourne to preach. Charles's grandfather loved Mr. Knill very much, and experienced a profound delight in hearing the old man recount stories of mission work, salvation, and dead people coming to life. Mr. Knill's heart blazed with the true spirit of a missionary, for he constantly craved the souls of young and old to confess the name of Jesus. He was nearly sixty years old, but the strength in his voice and the boldness of his countenance fooled one into thinking him no older than thirty. After spending years as a missionary in India before returning to England because of bad health in 1833, he spent most of his days traveling up and down the United Kingdom preaching and distributing gospel tracts wherever he went. It was rumored that five million of his tracts were in circulation throughout England and America, so on this special Sunday, every pew in the Meeting House was filled.

"This is the Word of God," said Mr. Knill, pausing to take a deep breath. Charles gripped the pew and listened as the old preacher continued. "The Word of God pierces and convicts, but like a rushing river of life, it always offers peace."

Mr. Knill bowed his greying head and placed his hands on the pulpit. His demeanor was incredibly captivating. Not a sound was heard in or around the Meeting House as they waited for the preacher—the prophet—to speak.

"But we see Jesus." He read slowly, deliberately, and then repeated the verse again, even slower, "But. We. See. Jesus." He paused again, letting the words sink deeply into the soil of any troubled soul that listened.

Charles had heard the book of Hebrews explained many times—his grandfather had preached on it, his father had delivered countless sermons from it—but, every time Charles heard the words "We see Jesus," he took another peek at the looking glass, and struggled to see Jesus anywhere.

When Charles read the Bible, all the threatening words of God were printed in capitals, while the promises were in such a small type that he could barely make them out, even through a squint. The threatening words of God made sense to him, but the promises surely must have been for someone else. In the Stambourne Meeting House, as Mr. Knill preached of the promises of God, Charles's grandfather nodded his head in agreement, and Puritan men and women sat in wild wonder.

Charles squinted, desperate to believe the words, desperate to *see* Jesus.

Mr. Knill looked across the crowded room, making eye contact with every single member of the congregation. Clasping his hands and leaning into the crowd, he continued, "Perhaps one of the greatest things written in the Scriptures, my dear friends! We have the profound ability to *see* Jesus! Do you see Jesus, my friends? Can you see Him today?"

Charles's heart began to race as a thick lump grew in his throat. He sat up in the pew, adjusted the blue cushion under him, and leaned forward with curiosity. There was a subtle stirring in his heart, much different than he usually felt. It wasn't like the anguish he felt when the darkness rumbled within—or the sour feeling in his gut when he looked into the looking glass. This was a gentle caressing within the inner most part of his soul, something he had never had the pleasure of experiencing.

"The apostle," continued Mr. Knill with compassion, "is not boasting in seeing Jesus with the *natural* eye. To see Jesus with the natural eye, my dear friends, would be an incredible thing! Surely, He would radiate with beauty and power. He would startle us with majestic glory. But, until we enter the Heavenly City and set our natural eyes to His, we must *see* Him with a *different* eye. You cannot believe your own natural eye, anyway. We all know that even our eyesight must not be trusted, since the most extraordinary illusions have been imagined with them. Sometimes you see a great many things, or think you do, which aren't really there—perhaps they are illusions or delusions— either way we are deceived by our natural eye. You know the phrase, 'To see is to believe?'" he asked the crowd rhetorically. "My friends, it is but a worldly proverb, and since some of you have seen and heard the story of Jesus but *know* Him not—there must be a different set of eyes that the apostle is speaking of."

Charles inched towards the edge of his seat. *This describes me to a letter!* he thought.

"The Word of God is speaking of a better eye—the eye of faith—and when we see Jesus with the eye of faith, we find salva- tion. We *see* Jesus. My brothers, my sisters, come to Jesus and *see* Him! See the precious blood of the Lamb of God slain for you. See the nail-pierced hands and the crown of thorns. See where love and justice flowed to release you from being a slave to sin. See Him with the eye of faith, then fly to the fountain of living water and wash in His cool waters."

His words traveled throughout the Meeting House, and with every repetition of the name of Jesus, something detonated in Charles's heart like cannon fire.

"My brother," began Mr. Knill as he stepped to the side of the pulpit and pointed to Mr. Tagley, "is your soul downcast?" Mr. Tagley listened without nodding or looking away. "Do you *see* Jesus? He empathizes with your downcast soul, brother. And He longs to embrace you with His comforting arms."

Mr. Knill walked across the small stage to the other side of the room and pointed to an old woman listening from the fourth row. "You, my dear sister. Are you grieving because you've been betrayed? Look and see Jesus being kissed by Judas. See Jesus as He embraces Peter. See Him as He understands your betrayal, and compels you to forgive . . . as He did." The woman nodded and then hung her head in humility as Mr. Knill returned to the pulpit, continuing to address the now-captivated congregation.

"You there, in the back of the room—you will never be alone if you see Jesus. Brother, on the edge of the pew—you will not feel weak if you see His strength. Sister, near the center aisle— you will not feel helpless if you simply look upon Jesus and see your Great Helper. My friends—oh, that you would *see* Jesus! You have heard of Him as a Savior, now *see* Him with the eye of faith. See Him as your friend, upon whom you can rest your weary head, and into whose ear you can whisper your tale of sorrow. Even though you walk through a valley of shadows, you can lean on your beloved Jesus and experience the sweetest of joys. Even in your desert, you can truly see Jesus with the eye of faith, and the barrenness of your soul will bloom like a garden of pink roses. Oh, how sweet it is to see Jesus, to truly see Him and know Him."

Mr. Knill continued to preach and read from the book of Hebrews, while Charles listened and nodded. The Word of God had pierced like a dagger, and he quietly received the gentle wounds that would eventually turn to rivers of peace.

I do not see Him, but I want to, thought Charles.

At the close of the service, the congregation stood to sing a hymn. Then, one by one, they received Communion and exited the church building. Charles was nearly the last person to leave the Meeting House. He sat glued to the dense wood, heavy in heart, deep in thought, holding nothing but his little imaginary looking glass, wondering if Jesus could actually forgive him.

"Hello there, son," Mr. Knill said, causing Charles to jitter with surprise. "Looks like we're the last ones to leave tonight. You're the grandson of James Spurgeon, aren't you?"

"Yes sir, I am," he said looking up at the old man, towering above him. He was surprised by the number of wrinkles on his face, seeing him up close for the first time. Like splintered valleys, they carved in and around his forehead and spilled out around his eyes. His hair was now neatly tucked under a tan hat, and his appearance was graceful and kingly. "I'm one of his many grandsons," said Charles, "but I have always been Grandfather's favorite, of course."

Mr. Knill chuckled, put a warm hand on the boy's shoulder, and said through a grin, "Ah! You must be Charles! Charles Haddon Spurgeon. Your grandfather thinks very highly of you, boy."

"Well, sir, I think highly of him as well. Are you staying with us in the parsonage tonight?" asked Charles.

"I am, indeed. And I hear your grandmother has been roasting a shoulder of pig all day. I can almost smell it from here! Can't you?" Mr. Knill closed his eyes, and drew his head back while taking in a deep breath through his nose. "Ah, and I hope she's made her apple biscuits for dessert. Come along, Charles. Let's not keep them waiting."

Charles, now feeling a rumble of hunger in his belly, stood and walked with Mr. Knill out of the Meeting House. They talked as they walked along the dirt path through the garden, beside the old hedges of yew, through the front porch of the parsonage, and into the kitchen where the potent aromas of fresh bread and roasted pig danced in the air.

Dinner was brief and delightful as Mr. Knill told grand stories of traveling through India and preaching the Good News. At the end of dinner, Mr. Knill—exhausted from the busy day of preaching—thanked Charles's grandparents, and then turned to Charles. "Son, when will you wake in the morning?" he asked. "Your grandfather says you have quite the intellect, and before I get on my way tomorrow, maybe you can teach this old man something new!" He cracked a gentle smile, and waited for an answer.

"Alright, Mr. Knill!" replied a wide-eyed Charles. "But it would be best for you to bring paper and a pencil, or you might forget all the treasures of wisdom I have to teach you!" Charles giggled cheekily; his infectious laugh caused everyone else at the table to join in.

"Well, then. I shall wake you at six o'clock, with blank paper and a sharp pencil!" He nodded, agreeing to the terms of their negotiation. Mr. Knill gracefully pushed his chair from the table, folded his napkin, and said good night to Charles and his grandparents.

The next morning at exactly six o'clock, Mr. Knill woke Charles and they walked to a spot beneath the yew trees in his grandfather's garden, where they ate breakfast and watched the rising sun magnificently light up all the trees and flowers and hedges.

"Charles," said Mr. Knill, breaking the silence, "I couldn't help spy you last night during the sermon. And it seemed you were at war with your thoughts. What was troubling you, son?"

"I—I'm not sure, Mr. Knill," Charles stammered, stumbling over his words, trying to articulate the darkness that always seemed to stalk him.

"It's just—I see a lot of things very clearly, but I've never seen Jesus—not like you talked about. When I close my eyes, I

see darkness. But, when I open them, darkness is still there."
Mr. Knill continued to listen to Charles, without interrupting.
"And no matter how hard I pray—no matter how hard I try—I
can never seem to *see* Jesus."

"Ah, child," replied Mr. Knill with excitement, "it's not
strange that when people are coming to Jesus, they are so much
in the dark they can't see their own hands. They are even so
blind, they can't see themselves. But, I do believe that the Holy
Ghost is beckoning you to come close—to call out to Jesus."

"But what if He rejects me?"

"Charles, what do you imagine when you look at the face of
Jesus?" Mr. Knill asked politely.

"Anger. Outrage. I see Him pushing me away. I see all the
grossest things I've ever imagined—and I—I know He sees them
plainly too, and so I imagine Him casting me away . . . into a pit."

"Oh, my boy," Mr. Knill said as he slumped down to peer
closer into Charles's eyes, now damp with tears. "I have never
heard a man say that he sought Christ, but Christ said 'no.'
Child, you do not imagine the Jesus that I have come to know as
Friend and Lord." His voice melted with compassion and empathy. "I see the shame and fear in your eyes, Charles. I *know* the
anguish in your head, and I *know* the sorrow in your heart. And
I also know that my Friend, Jesus, sees it too. And His heart—
well, it erupts with love for you, Charles. You must believe."

For the first time Charles could remember, he felt as though
someone else could see into the looking glass into which he all
too often stared. "But, how could Jesus do that? Why would
He?" Charles asked Mr. Knill, barely able to get the words out.

"Let me ask you this: In your memory, what's the worst thing
you have done to make Jesus cast you aside—into the pit?" Mr.
Knill asked.

Charles told him about the storm on the road from
Colchester to Stambourne, and all the blasphemous words
he uttered to God, both in his thoughts and from his mouth.

Mr. Knill listened, completely focused, for there was a spark of something great igniting in Charles, and he was cautious not to disturb it.

"Do you hate these thoughts, son?" he asked.

"I do," Charles answered truly, wiping away the flowing tears.

"Then they are not yours. Treat them like the old parish officers do with guilty vagrants who steal and murder. They whip them, and they send them off to prison! Do that with your evil thoughts. Groan over them, Charles. Repent of them." Mr. Knill took a deep breath and nodded his head. Then, he gently placed both hands on either of Charles's arms. "Send all those dark thoughts onto the Devil, the father of them, to whom they belong—for they are not yours, Charles."

At once, all the corners of his heart began to light up, as the bricked-up windows crumbled and fell away. Mr. Knill continued to tell Charles of the love of Jesus and the blessedness of trusting in Him and loving Him in childhood. They talked for hours about the patient love of Christ, the glorious beauty of Him crucified and risen, and work of salvation that He intends to do, even in the vilest of men. Charles listened intently, and every part of his heart began to soften as he drew near to the God he had never truly seen.

"Call out to Jesus, Charles. He will hear you. I promise it," said Mr. Knill.

Charles turned his gaze to the morning sky, closed his eyelids, and groaned with conviction, "God, be merciful to me, a sinner." Full of honesty and pleading, Charles continued, "God, be merciful to me. Please. Help. Help. Help." His troubled soul was suddenly overpowered, and he cried out, "God, I have heard of You with my ear. But now, my God, I want to see You with the eye of faith."

Mr. Knill sat next to Charles on a bench in the garden and placed his arms around Charles's neck as he began to pray for the boy.

"Almighty God," prayed Mr. Knill, "may this boy one day preach the gospel of Jesus Christ. And may he preach it to the masses with power and might. Use him powerfully, God. Go beyond his wildest imagination."

For as long as Charles lived, he would never forget the dear prayer from the old man on the bench. And, there in the cool of his grandfather's garden, under the branches of a mature apple tree, Charles looked up through the bright rays of sunshine and noticed the golden wine bottle still tied with string to the branch of that old tree. It glittered and swayed in the morning breeze, and although the original apple budding his grandfather had placed inside had long blossomed into fruit and perished, the seed of the gospel in the heart of Charles Spurgeon was buried inside fertile soil, where it would bloom and flourish for years to come.

CHAPTER 5

A Little More of That Sun

Virginia, USA 1851

Thomas felt deeply out of place as he stood formally, just inside of the wood-paneled entrance to the great dining hall of the big house. Arrangements of freshly cut flowers and Mrs. Bennett's best china lined each side of the massive table in the center of the room, giving the large, open space an air of rigid formality and elegance. Thick cigar smoke, combined with the smell of boiling potatoes, thyme, and carrots, filled the dining hall and stifled the air. The light from candles around the room flickered through the smoke and cast a warm glow onto the portraits of long-dead ancestors that lined the surrounding walls. They frowned and scowled, as they stoically watched the mingling of strangers and friends. Thomas wondered why white people were always sad. Actually, the only time Thomas saw happy white people is when they had their hand to a glass of whiskey or to the end of a whip.

Thomas nodded and smiled nervously at a hundred strangers who filled the house that night. A chorus of sounds—polite-talk, laughter, and violin music—added to the anxiety already felt by a young man who was more comfortable with the quiet sound of crickets and wind whistling through oak trees. That morning, the foreman had given Thomas the rare privilege of leaving the tobacco fields to serve inside the big house for the master's fifty-first birthday celebration. On the plantation, only Christmas Eve could rival the festive atmosphere the master demanded to celebrate the day he came screaming into the world. And by eight o'clock, the big house was filled with Richmond's finest—doctors, lawyers, military generals, and congressmen from Washington.

When Thomas received the day's assignment, he was excited to be given the task of carrying trays of food and washing dinner dishes. It was a much better way to spend the day compared to the back-breaking labor of working in the tobacco fields. Yet, Thomas's excitement was tempered. He knew all too well that the smallest mistake, on this momentous night, would certainly mean a trip to the whipping post the following morning.

Thomas wore a black, woolen suit—it was the first he'd ever worn—and carried a delicate white towel that hung from his left arm. With his other hand, he held an ornate silver platter stacked high with food, delicious with scents of garlic, butter, and basil. The aroma woke his stomach to a waltz as it rumbled with hunger.

The suffocating tightness of his necktie, along with the heat of the crowded room, caused sweat to trickle down the muscles of his back, disappearing into the fabric of his shirt that clung tightly to his waist. He briefly entertained the idea of setting down the platter to reach his hands around his back, as the irritating combination of wool and moisture caused an insatiable itching. But he knew it would be a costly mistake if Mrs. Bennett witnessed such a horrible breach of protocol.

"Boy, what sort of food is this?" asked a beautifully dressed white woman. Thomas's muscles tensed. Her voice was smooth and elegant, heavy with the drawl of North Virginia's wealthiest folk.

"Honestly, ma'am, I don't know," said Thomas, smiling, hoping his kindness would diffuse his lack of knowledge of the evening's food. "But people seem to like it. So go on and try one for yourself." He leaned the platter towards the woman and smiled. It was rare to see a young slave with such a radiant smile. Thomas seemed to grin with his entire face. It was captivating and contagious.

The woman placed the dainty bite of food between her red, painted lips, and bit into the pastry filled with blackberries and cream. Her eyes widened, as Thomas nodded his head in agreement.

"This is outstanding! What's your name, boy?" she asked while wiping pastry crumbs from the corner of her mouth with her kerchief.

The question took Thomas by surprise, for it had been asked with warmth and kindness, as if the beautiful woman was genuinely interested in his response. Thomas was rarely surprised by even the most erratic behavior from white people, but the strangeness of this woman—to engage him in a conversation in front of so many important people—filled him with a startling fear and caused the muscles in his back to stiffen like steel.

There were two unpardonable sins a slave could commit on the tobacco plantations of Northern Virginia. The first was to escape. If a slave dared to run, all of the resources of the sovereign state of Virginia were pledged to the apprehension of the black man who had the audacity to pursue freedom. Second, and equally as egregious, was the inappropriate interaction of a black man with a white woman. If a slave boy had the audacity to flirt with, much less speak to, a white woman, the consequences were often worse than death.

"My name is Thomas. Thomas Johnson, ma'am," he replied, glancing nervously to his left and right, looking for anyone who might have perceived the casual nature of their conversation.

The woman continued talking nonchalantly. How long she talked, Thomas didn't know, but for him, it felt like an eternity. She asked what life was like for Thomas on the plantation, what kind of food he ate, and if he was treated well by Quentin Ellis, an old friend of the woman.

As she spoke, Thomas couldn't help but think of his friend Moses who worked in the blacksmith shop of the plantation. Not long ago, the foreman accused Moses of being "too familiar" in his conversation with Mr. Bennett's daughter. And for punishment, Quentin Ellis gathered all of the slaves to the whipping post in the middle of the grassy lawn, tied Moses to the post, stripped him of his clothes, and beat him senselessly for almost an hour. Everyone shook their heads and gritted their teeth as they saw Moses's body, limp and unconscious, torn and red with blood, collapse against the whipping post. Strips of flesh hung in tattered pieces from his shoulders and buttocks. The crimson puddle beneath the whipping post shocked Thomas, and he wondered if his friend would live through the night.

In time, Moses regained consciousness, but he was unable to walk for a week. The scars on his back would remain for the rest of his life, and worse, the scars on his pride would as well. All of this because Moses entertained an innocent conversation with a white woman.

"Pardon me, ma'am," said Thomas, turning abruptly and moving swiftly from the entryway of the dining hall and down the long hallway toward the kitchen. Thomas looked back anxiously to see if the woman had been offended by his sudden exit, but was reassured to see her move on to the next house slave, carrying the next silver platter of the next tiny bite of fanciful food.

Thomas was light-headed and dizzy, and feared the entire mansion was spinning. Pushing his way through the crowded kitchen and towards the back door of the big house, Thomas flew through the opened the door and stumbled down the steps into the cool night air. Thomas, now alone, breathed fiercely and loosened his black tie. Within the sweet, fresh aroma of the evening wind, his pulse and his spinning brain began to slow.

He laughed to himself, wondering what he must have looked like stumbling uncontrollably down the steps of the kitchen. Mr. Bennett was a notorious drunk, and Thomas had seen the master stumble down those steps more than a few times. Every day around six o'clock, after he had finished the day's affairs, Mr. Bennett sunk into one of the wooden chairs on the porch and poured caramel-brown whiskey from a beautiful crystal decanter into a deep glass. He rarely showed interest in the comings and goings of the plantation he owned, but much interest was shown to the imbibing of warm whiskey and a cool sunset. After drinking three—sometimes four—glasses, Mr. Bennett would rise slowly, keeping his hands on the chair for support, shuffle unsteadily, then make his way back into the house, not to be seen again until the next morning. Thomas had never been drunk or had even tasted alcohol for that matter, but in the quiet and refreshing cool night air, he wondered if his encounter with the white woman was similar to whiskey's intoxicating effects.

Thomas, feeling the tension dissolve from his shoulders and neck, walked quietly toward the thick trees that lined the backyard of the big house. The busy sounds of the master's celebration faded softly as the steady rhythm of cricket calls bounced through the trees, slowly and methodically, like waves lapping peacefully against the white sands of a foreign shore. Night birds sang along, gently and without words. But Thomas recognized their song. They sang the song of freedom. They belted out a chorus so beautiful, so cheerful, that it could only come from an unconfined creature. Thomas longed to sing a song of freedom with them, uncaged.

Thomas held loosely to hope, for nothing was truer than this: Thomas was a slave. He was in bondage, caged, the property of another man. The master and foreman held absolute power over him. He had no rights, no voice, no recourse, no future. The depth of this reality consumed him, and it was slowly suffocating what little hope he held.

"What in the world are you doing, boy?" whispered Ezekiel loudly through clenched teeth. "I saw you from the yard, and followed you out here. You know what kinda trouble you gonna be in?"

"I don't belong in there, Ezekiel," said Thomas quietly, relieved the shadowy figure was his friend and not the foreman. "That house is all filled up with white people. They're all dressed like the president himself came for supper."

"What you mean, you don't belong in there? The foreman told you this morning that's where you'd be working tonight. So I say you better get your backside in there before somebody sees you," said Ezekiel, nearly shouting.

"I can't, Ezekiel," Thomas replied, his eyes stern with frustration. "I was in the dining room. Wearing a white man's suit. When, next thing I know, this white lady starts talking to me. I'm tellin' you, Ezekiel, this woman would not stop talkin'. There she was. Her mouth movin' and me not hearing a word she was saying 'cause all I could think about was *Moses*! You remember what happened to him? Moses got the life beat outta him for talkin' too long to the master's daughter. I didn't want that to happen to me, Ezekiel—so, I just turned around and ran out the back door of the kitchen. I figured, if I gotta get beat, I'd rather get beat for leavin' a party than talkin' too long to a white woman."

Ezekiel sighed deeply. "Son, you best get back inside—now." Ezekiel placed his hand on the boy's shoulder and turned him toward the big house.

Ezekiel loved Thomas, and since the day he was ripped from his mother's side, Ezekiel made it a point to take him under his wing. Ezekiel had always known that Thomas was a restless soul, and his restlessness had only increased as he became a young man. Some slaves, throughout the course of their lives, come to terms with their lot in life. They surrender and quietly submit to an undeserved life on a terrible plantation that cages them, tortures them, and eventually numbs their soul. But this could never be true of Thomas. With each passing year, Ezekiel watched a restlessness and longing grow within the depths of Thomas Johnson.

"Let me ask you a question," said Ezekiel, stopping before the two approached the back door of the big house. "You ain't thinkin' about tryin' to escape, are you?"

Thomas stopped to look up at the stars, so distant from tree line and fences that blanketed the plantation from horizon to horizon. "I'd be lyin' if I told you it ain't never crossed my mind. What these people do to us ain't right, Ezekiel. There ain't a day goes by, that there ain't some poor soul g'tting' the life whipped from him by the foreman. They keep us dressed in rags, feedin' us the same thing they feed pigs. They tell us where we go, when to go, and how we gonna get there. There is one thing—one thing I want more than anythin' in the world, Ezekiel—I want freedom. The sun shines on a black man, same as a white man, and I'm ready for a little more of that sun to shine on me."

Ezekiel listened, absorbing the words of the young slave, paused, then moved slowly toward Thomas. When Ezekiel began to speak, their faces were less than an inch apart.

"That's the dumbest thing I ever heard in all my life, boy."

Ezekiel never let his gaze waver from Thomas. "You get back in that house. And you do your job. You got a lot to learn about freedom, boy. 'Cause I'm tellin' you, you lookin' for it in the wrong place."

With that, Ezekiel gripped the boy's shoulder firmly, pushed him towards the back door to the big house, then turned into the night.

SECTION 2

CHAPTER 6

SUSANNAH

London, England 1854

F ar removed from the stunning beauty of Essex, the city of London was a towering landscape of incredible need and terrible sorrow. The first few years of the 1850s had ushered in a decade of impeccable progress—telegraph cables were laid beneath the English Channel, the window tax was abolished, the Crystal Palace was opened by Queen Victoria, railroads were expanded, technology and art flourished. But by the middle of the decade, London's streets were filthy, the Thames River was contaminated with refuse and debris, and London fell prey to the worst epidemic of cholera in its history. This terrible disease invaded the borders of the city and stole tens of thousands of lives. There was no part of the city untouched, as residential and urban families felt the repeated effects of death.

"Ten thousand seven hundred thirty-eight dead," whispered Susannah as she placed the *London Daily News* on the table next to her afternoon tea. "It seems death is in our backyard." She pursed her lips and slowly shook her head as she thought of neighbors, friends, her family. No one was exempt from the fiery dart of cholera. It showed no bias.

"English ladies shouldn't read the newspaper anyhow, Susannah," said Mrs. Onley as she entered the room and picked up the paper from the wooden table in the center of the kitchen. Susannah frequented Mr. and Mrs. Onley's house for Sunday afternoon tea. She loved the tastefully decorated house in Southwark, where many wonderful meals and tasty conversations of politics and city life ensued. Mr. and Mrs. Onley had become quite good friends of and mentors to Susannah, and she treasured them.

"I suppose not," smiled Susannah reluctantly. Her sweet face was always calming, and her skin smooth as silk. Although there was hardly anything proper about Susannah Thompson, she was a woman of daring radiance. Sensitive and strong, her countenance neither demanded attention nor allowed for dismissal. Susannah was simply captivating, and everyone knew it. Raised in a modest South London neighborhood, Susannah grew up in a Christian family with earnest friends and good parents. In her childhood, she never met another child who spoke of Jesus, since English churches tended to disregard their youth, rarely telling them of the gospel story. This left a staleness and coldness in her heart towards the things of God. As a twenty-one-year-old woman, though she hadn't learned to treasure the Lord or give Him solemn surrender of everything she had, she still frequented the New Park Street Chapel with Mr. and Mrs. Onley on Sundays.

"Are you ready to go to the chapel?" asked Mrs. Onley. "The new preacher is a fine young man." Mrs. Onley, a woman in her middle years, had a perfectly engaging face and smile, and it always seemed to shine with happiness, especially when she spoke to Susannah about young men.

"Ah, Mrs. Onley. A proper English lady would never give eye to a preacher," Susannah said through a grin. Her face blushed with a lovely stroke of pale pink and softened red. "Surely, I'd never notice if he was fine or not."

"You're blushing, Susannah," laughed Mrs. Onley as she got up from the table and cleared the empty cups of tea. "Spurgeon," she continued, speaking over her shoulder, washing a few fine ceramic cups. "Charles Spurgeon. That's his name. Would you believe he's only nineteen years old? He's a country boy. From Essex, I believe. Just a rural village lad, but this morning at the chapel service, when he opened his mouth and spoke of the Lord, I'm telling you—every last ear turned to hear. There was something very peculiar—special, really—about him. All of the congregation is overjoyed. And, tonight every seat in the chapel will be filled. And did I mention how handsome Mr. Spurgeon is, Susannah?"

"Alright, Mrs. Onley. Let us suppose this new preacher is handsome . . . and stunning . . . a true gentleman . . . and a brilliant scholar," she stated sarcastically, leaving the sentence hanging in the air.

"Yes," replied Mrs. Onley, turning from the kitchen sink to listen. "Let us suppose." She folded her hands and held them in front of her purple cotton apron, anxiously awaiting Susannah's reply.

"Then, suppose he sets his eye on me," she blinked her eyes rapidly and continued, "and I set mine to his?"

"Yes," said Mrs. Onley with more excitement in her voice.

"Well. What preacher should be *rewarded* for setting his eye to a beautiful English lady on the very first Sunday he sees her at the chapel?" Susannah brushed her curled brown hair behind her ear, revealing her pretty, delicate face. "Mrs. Onley, I am Susannah Thompson," she said slowly, deliberately. "And, I will be no reward to a preacher's wandering eye."

"Oh, Susannah," winked Mrs. Onley. "You are such a treasure of a woman. And, what mercy it is that your life is not yours to plan. Thank heavens that our Father chooses it all for you. Or else—you might just turn away from your greatest blessings."

"Sure, Mrs. Onley. Now, stop torturing me, and let's get to the chapel," replied Susannah, rolling her eyes.

The walk from Mr. and Mrs. Onley's house to New Park Street Chapel was a cold one, especially on December evenings. The wet winter winds, however, didn't keep a crowd from flooding into every pew of the chapel. News of the young preacher had quickly traveled through London, so the congregation—normally around two hundred people—had doubled in size from the morning service. Mr. Spurgeon was said to be much different than the other preachers of his day. While others were stoic in delivery and used tired, antiquated illustrations, Charles was full of charisma, charm, and wisdom beyond his age.

Susannah and Mrs. Onley squeezed into the chapel and made their way to a pew near the front, next to the center aisle. Susannah always preferred to sit near an aisle, as large and rowdy crowds had a way of making her feel anxious. Nearly every seat in the chapel was occupied by both young and old, while at least fifty men stood along the side and back walls, unable to find a seat.

Since she was a child, Susannah always thought the New Park Street Chapel pulpit looked so curious. It had no stairs surrounding the stage, and she swore it looked like an unsightly bird's nest. She frequently snickered at the sneaky manner in which the minister made his appearance. Entering from behind a hidden door along the back wall, it seemed he appeared out of nowhere. One moment the bird's nest was empty, but if she glanced at her hymnal for just one second, she'd look back up to see the old preacher nestled in the bird's nest. She was charmed and humored every single time she saw it.

The chapel was modest in design, with no extra frills or fancies, but tonight's buzzing crowd gave it the mystique of a packed music hall in central London. At exactly six o'clock, a hush fell on the crowd as the hidden door in the wall opened and the young preacher made his way to the pulpit in the middle of the stage.

"He's not what I was expecting," whispered Susannah to Mrs. Onley, cupping her hand over her mouth as to not disrupt the hushed crowd. "He's quite contrary to what a preacher should be, isn't he?" she asked, turning her head back towards the stage.

It was undeniable that young Charles Spurgeon was from the country. His clothes were simple and unpretentious, but there was a peculiarity about them that gave nod to his youthfulness. He wore a long village-tailored coat made of black silk and cotton, and underneath it, a fanciful white shirt and collar hugged his stocky, round neck. A dark satin scarf dangled from his shoulders towards his waist, and in his hand he held a bright blue handkerchief with large white circles.

What business does a boy have in the pulpit? thought Susannah to herself. The question was probably not just her own, as it was odd to see such a young person stand behind the famed pulpit of New Park Street Chapel, the very one that countless giants of the faith had preached from. Charles, however, never felt he was too young to preach the gospel.

❖ ❖ ❖

The eyes of Charles's faith were first opened as a child, when he *saw* Jesus for the first time, but it wasn't until he was sixteen, sitting in a tiny Primitive Methodist Church, that he finally realized, *I am forgiven! I am a sinner saved by the blood of Jesus!* He had found Christ, and Christ quickly became the most satisfying well from which he had ever drank. The love of Jesus—strong as death, fierce as hell, and lasting as eternity—completely changed Charles. And, like a slave newly emancipated, drunk with joy that he was free, Charles could not be silent about the One who released him from darkness and marked him with a life of freedom and fruitfulness.

When a man or woman is truly rescued by God, they cannot stop themselves from shouting from every rooftop. They cannot be silenced. Even if they have no human listeners, they tell it to waterfalls and babbling brooks, they travel to the wilderness to speak to rocks and dust, they fly to the mountains and yell it over canyons and riverbeds, because once a person has heard the call of Heaven, they become unstoppable. They carry lanterns through rainstorms to burst through front doors exclaiming, "I've got a story to tell you!" They darken the den of pubs and whiskey houses, saying, "Look at Him! He's magnificent!" They sit in farmers' kitchens to mourn with those mourning. They gather in old men's gardens to rejoice with the happy. They comfort the broken, lift the downcast, and just like the fire within their bones, their influence blazes and lights up the darkest towns and the dimmest souls.

Everywhere Charles went, every place he walked, and every person that he spoke to was affected by the love of Christ. He became a friend to the friendless, for he took careful notice of people that were typically overlooked and forgotten. He had the ability to stitch stories and illustrations together, finer than Dickens, and preached to common people in their own language. Typical ministers, priests, and evangelists of the day spoke with fanciful phrasing and meaningless monotony, but Charles offered something of rare value—he captivated the interest of common people.

A man once told Mr. Spurgeon, "You are such a natural. You preach effortlessly!"

To which Charles brashly responded, "Ah, but sir, you do not see the thousands of hours I have studied and labored, prayed and pleaded, scoured books and commentaries, begging the Lord to equip me to preach His Word with power and simple words. You only see the pulpit, and hear the sermon, yet you miss the candlelit nights of God wrestling my heart to the ground to say, 'Son, I must preach this through you tomorrow.'"

Charles studied the Word of God diligently. He was an avid student of the Bible, as well as many other theologians and authors of commentaries. Breaking with typical tradition and convention, Charles refused to preach boring or lifeless sermons. Preaching was no trite task to him; he never approached it lightly. He insisted that the preparation of the sermon required much labor, and his whole heart was absorbed in every part of it. Although most assumed he was simply a naturally gifted communicator, Charles knew preaching required much of the Holy Spirit, and very little of Charles Spurgeon.

❈ ❈ ❈

As Charles stood behind the New Park Street Chapel pulpit, he looked up and down each row of pews, taking time to look into nearly every single eye. Rarely did a preacher take the time to look into the eyes of his congregation. Charles never missed an opportunity. As he slowly scanned the room and prayed for the Holy Spirit's power, a resolute calm came over his spirit.

"My brothers and sisters in Christ," said Charles in a noticeably countrified accent. "We may not yet be acquainted, since I do not know each of you by name. We are, however, living stones perfectly joined together by the cement of Christ's blood." He raised his hands and brought his palms together, slowly folding his fingers around his hands, illustrating the firm bond of cement. The crowd watched and listened, as he held his hands together and continued, "And tonight, I wish to tell of the devotion and service He deserves from us, His joined-together, living stones."

The crowd leaned in, their hearts roused, ready to hear more.

As the sermon continued, Susannah thought of her own heart. While she had attended the chapel nearly every Sunday since she was a young child, her spiritual life was marked with indifference and a lack of service. As her heart was stirred by the words of the gospel on this night, she realized that her life was far from what it should be. Susannah listened, not simply to an eloquent sermon from a handsome country preacher from Essex, but to the Holy Spirit of God that was speaking something louder than words to the entire congregation on that very cold December evening.

Oh, could I ever be a living stone for you, God? Susannah pondered, as Charles continued to preach.

Susannah didn't hear the rest of the sermon, her heart too focused on this newfound question. As the sermon concluded, the crowd stood to sing a good Puritan hymn—one filled with eloquent and robust words of worship and admiration—then they exited the chapel with warm, full hearts.

It was customary for a preacher to stand outside the door of the church after a service, and Charles enjoyed the opportunity to shake each person's hand and speak words of gratitude for attending.

"It was a pleasure to have you in the chapel today, Mr. Spurgeon," said Susannah as she nervously extended her hand towards his.

"Thank you, madam. The honor was mine," he said sincerely as his hand met hers. The warmth of his hand surprised Susannah. He had been standing outside for nearly forty-five minutes, but his hands were comfortable and warm. "My dear, your hands are freezing," said Charles, as a gentle smile filled his face. "What is your name?" asked Charles.

"Miss Thompson," she replied gracefully.

"Ah, wonderful to meet you, Miss Thompson," he said. "I am Charles, and I am very glad you came to the chapel tonight. I do hope to see you again." It seemed their hands lingered together for minutes, as Susannah looked into Charles's young face and smiled. His face, plump and pale, was the most welcoming she had ever seen.

Mrs. Onley, standing behind Susannah, unashamedly took the opportunity to disrupt the moment and join the conversation. "Excuse me, Mr. Spurgeon," she exclaimed. "Do you have plans for dinner? My husband and I, and Miss Thompson here, would be happy to host you this evening for dinner. I have a pot of warm potato and beef stew, large enough to feed the whole Southwark neighborhood. We would love to dine with you, and further enjoy the fellowship of your company, wouldn't we Miss Thompson?" Mrs. Onley asked, awkwardly knocking Susannah's elbow, then looking to Charles for his answer.

"It would be a delight. And, what is your name, madam?" asked Charles, releasing Susannah's hands and turning to Mrs. Onley.

"Mrs. Onley. And my husband, Mr. Onley, is right over there." Charles shook her hand, and cast a casual wave to Mr. Onley, who was standing underneath the gas street lamp at the corner of the chapel and the cobblestone road. "Do come quickly, Mr. Spurgeon. It is getting colder by the minute."

Charles buttoned his long coat, tightened his silk scarf, and placed a large top hat over his long and badly trimmed black hair.

"After you, Miss Thompson," said Charles, tipping the corner of his hat. Mr. and Mrs. Onley, Charles, and Susannah briskly walked along the darkened south London street, eager for warm conversation and good food.

⊞ ⊞ ⊞

Words were scarce on the journey, as the cold had numbed all the travelers' lips, but as soon as they sat at the Onleys' wooden table, poured bowls of steaming stew, and asked the Lord to bless the meal, a fountain of conversation and laughter flowed forth. Charles, unmatched in his ability to tell a good story, was never short for words. He told stories of Essex, reminiscing the quiet country days where he and his adolescent friends would sit by the creek in Colchester and fish until dark. He told of his time at St. Augustine's College, where he learned strong theology, not from a professor but from a woman who served as a humble cook in the college cafeteria. From her, Charles learned the paramount importance of the Word of God, as well as the proper sugar and flour to use for baking the best pastries in Maidstone. He told of his baptism at Isleham Village, in Cambridgeshire, and how astonished he was to become the youngest pastor of Waterbeach Baptist Chapel. With every single story he told, Charles both bragged on God and downplayed his own accomplishment and ability. His humility was not forced—not fake—but strangely strong. It was, in a sense, the rarest form of humble confidence that Susannah had ever witnessed.

"Mr. Spurgeon," started Susannah after plunging a wide spoon into her piping hot stew.

"Please, you must call me Charles," he said plainly.

"Alright, Charles." She felt awkward calling a preacher by his first name, but she quickly reminded herself he was just a boy, hardly old enough to be a real minister. "I have heard that you enjoy reading books."

"I do, indeed, Miss Thompson. I dream of owning a house in time—one with its own library." His voice lowered almost to a whisper. He squinted his eyes nearly shut, and with his hands, formed an imaginary box onto the wooden kitchen table. "See it with me—floor to ceiling, wall-to-wall, nothing but books, shelves, and more shelves, loaded to the edge with books on all subjects, books filling the entire room. I swear, Miss Thompson, I would spend all that I could afford to purchase enough books to fill a thousand shelves."

Susannah closed her eyes, trying to imagine a house big enough to justify having an entire room devoted to books, much less one with a thousand shelves. She had only seen a library in a house one time, and it was a royal mansion next to the river in central London.

"Can you see it, Miss Thompson?" he asked, keeping his eyes closed and continuing to move his hands up and down the table as he described what he saw. "Along the side nearest the windows, the whole bay is filled with books on history and science. On either side of the bay, the entire wall is filled to the top with books of travel, and adventure, biographies of explorers, and storytellers. There is an entire shelf for Dickens's works—like David Copperfield, Nicholas Nickleby, and Oliver Twist. Another shelf for American and Latin authors. Ah! Then, the opposite wall . . . the one without windows, since it will require the whole space . . . books allotted to the subjects of the Bible and theology, and hymnals. Oh, how I love hymnals!"

"This is a very big room, Mr. Spurgeon," said Susannah squinting, trying to imagine a room with such grandeur.

Charles kept his eyes closed, undeterred by Susannah's interruption. "Oh, and here, in this corner, behind my desk—this corner shelf is reserved for the Puritans."

"Will there be rare books, Mr. Spurgeon?" asked Mrs. Onley, startling Charles, who had seemingly forgotten that he and Susannah were not alone at the table.

"I do not particularly concern myself with a book simply because it is rare, as there are many rare books without any value. But, a rare *Puritan* book . . . maybe a very old and used copy of Bunyan's *The Pilgrim's Progress* . . . that will absolutely find a special place in my library."

Charles opened his eyes and fiddled around the inner pocket of his coat as the rest of the table curiously looked on.

"Are you searching for one of your gaudy handkerchiefs, Mr. Spurgeon?" Susannah grinned mischievously, and slumped back in her seat.

"My name is Charles. And no, Miss Thompson. After all, one should only own a *single* outrageous handkerchief." From his pocket, Charles pulled a small and very used book, and placed it on the table. The hard cover was tattered but not torn, and had contoured to the shape of Charles's chest, since it had hardly left his interior pocket in a decade. The cover was green as moss, and possessed a beautiful golden inlay of embossed images and letters.

"Other than the Holy Scriptures, *this* is my favorite book. My grandfather gave it to me when I was just seven years old, and I've read it fifty times at least. Each time, I'm charmed all over again." Charles ran his fingers along the gold-embossed letters that read *The Pilgrim's Progress*. He thought of his grandfather, and a familiar peace rushed through his body.

"You carry this with you always? Why?" asked Susannah as she leaned towards the table. Charles handed her the worn-out book, and she gently put her fingers on the embossed title. Without thinking, she, too, caressed the bright embossing that carved long, skinny letters within the stiff fiber cover.

"If you read any book by Bunyan, you will see it is almost like reading the Bible itself." Charles's eyes were wide, focused on Susannah's. He found himself enjoying her eyes as much as the conversation.

"Go on," she said, as she brought the book to her nose, smelling its brown, paper pages. The delightful aroma of ink and dusty paper swirled around her nostrils, instantly filling her thoughts with nostalgic memories of girlhood.

"You see, Bunyan had read the Bible enough . . . till his very soul was saturated with Scripture. And though all of his writings are charming and full of poetry, the sweetest of all those poems is *The Pilgrim's Progress.*" He paused to see if she was still interested. "And you ask 'Why?' Miss Thompson?"

"Why, Mr. Spurgeon?" said Susannah, now smiling and incredibly interested.

"Because, when you read this book, it makes you feel like the author is a *living* Bible. You can prick him anywhere, and he bleeds the Bible. He cannot speak without quoting a verse or a section of Scripture. It's as if his very soul is full of the Word of God." Charles placed both elbows on the table in front of him, and extended his hands towards the green and gold book in Susannah's hands. "So this story—which I never seem to tire of—is the best description of the Christian life. And the secret of its freshness is that it's essentially biblical teaching in the form of a beautiful and striking allegory."

No matter how hard she tried, Susannah could not quit smiling. While other boys bored her with childish and dull conversation, she found herself completely captivated by her new acquaintance. Her affection towards Charles was not one of infatuation, but rather, profound intrigue and genuine interest.

"I see. I suppose I must read Bunyan very soon. After all, every pilgrim is in need of progress. Right, Mr. Spurgeon?" asked Susannah.

"Charles. Call me Charles, won't you?" he pleaded.

"Susannah. Call the young man Charles!" exclaimed Mr. Onley through a wheezy laugh.

"Mr. Onley!" responded Charles with liveliness. "That's the first thing I've heard you speak all evening. And I agree, completely!"

Susannah and Mr. and Mrs. Onley chuckled along, as Charles slipped the treasured book back into his coat pocket as the dinner guests finished their last—now cold—sips of potato and beef stew. The tiny kitchen was filled with the sweet aroma of homemade food and good conversation, and while the furnace barely kept the drafty kitchen at a comfortable temperature in the winter, no one shivered or complained on this night. It was one of the warmest and most enjoyable dinners that Susannah had ever experienced. Somehow, she knew this would not be the last time she would laugh, dream, and eat around the comforts of a dining table with Charles Spurgeon. A shared table is a shared life, and the friendship that was kindled between Charles and Susannah would very soon ignite into a shared life, unimaginable.

Susannah savored the moment, then leaned into Charles's ear and softly spoke, "Charles, isn't it rare and beautiful to begin a meal as strangers, but end as friends?"

"Yes, it is."

CHAPTER 7

BACK TO STAMBOURNE

England 1856

As soon as the final passenger whistle sounded, the six wheels of the steam engine slowly crawled from the Bishopsgate Station platform. While the helmsmen continued shoveling mounds of coal into the firebox, the boiler erupted with steam, moving the strong pistons forward and backward, faster and faster. It was a modern work of mechanical genius, and although it could only pull a few second-class passenger carriages and two smoking carriages, it was all the rage in Great Britain for commuters and tourists. During weekday rush hours, the station jumbled with men and women hurrying in and out of the heart of London, but on this quiet Sunday afternoon, the train heading northward to Colchester was as peaceful as its destination.

Exhausted from the long weekend and early morning, Charles and Susannah slumped into the plush seating that stretched all around the edges of the long smoking carriage. Lined with bright red fabric, fine and puffy, the bench was comfortable and proper. Square windowpanes wrapped the entire carriage, filling the space with natural light. The older carriage models were dark and dingy with few windows, but after patrons complained of barely being able to read their newspapers and gasping from all the cigar and cigarette smoke, the Eastern Counties Railway got wise and introduced a new and improved line of airy, delightful smoking carriages.

On busier mornings, the long table in the center of the carriage was cluttered with bags and newspapers and elbows, the coat hooks were loaded with long coats and scarfs, the stunning patterns of the carpet covered by passengers' legs and luggage, and the roar of the steam engine could be hardly heard over the buzz of happy conversation. However, on this Sunday morning, the carriage only carried three passengers, and Charles and Susannah embraced the quiet relief. Sighing with contentment, Charles nodded at the other passenger, a proper English gentleman huddled in the corner reading the *London Daily News.* Charles removed his top hat and ran both of his hands over his face and through his long black hair, then fumbled through his leather satchel, pushing aside sermon notes and his Bible to find his half-smoked cigar from earlier in the morning.

Since a few years ago, when his grandfather gave him his first cigar on his birthday, Charles was a fan of the "blessed leaf," as he liked to call it. Susannah disapproved, but he loved the taste of burning tobacco leaves; more important, he loved that a cigar made him stop and enjoy something. Too many times, people missed the lovely things in life because they were too busy to stop and notice. But Charles made it a point to stop—pause, really—and enjoy blessed things every day.

"Now, grandson," he remembered his grandfather say, "this isn't very *'Puritan'* of me . . . and I'll deny it if you ever say I said this, but an inexpensive cigar is one of God's finest measures of common grace!" Charles smiled, remembering his first cigar with his grandfather in the garden. "Don't inhale it though, Charles. It'll turn your stomach green."

Throughout the years of living in London, Charles often thought of his grandfather's friendship and the attentiveness with which he cared for Charles's soul. His grandfather was a constant source of hope and encouragement, and a warrior of prayer, not on the battleground with Charles, but nestled within the Essex hills, hunkered on his knees, begging God to endure his grandson.

And Charles needed it.

In many ways, Charles had taken London by storm. After he became the pastor of New Park Street Chapel, his notoriety and influence increased daily, it seemed. Sunday crowds outgrew the small chapel, so the congregation moved just north of the river, making Exeter Hall their new Sunday gathering place. The main hall's auditorium, which held nearly four thousand people, was typically used for religious and philanthropic rallies, but on Sundays, its walls were packed with vast crowds of people eager to hear sermons from Charles Spurgeon. He attracted young people of every background, from nearly every part of the city of London. There was something special—sacred—about God's work through Charles, and yet, outside the walls of Exeter Hall, the polarizing message of Jesus caused many to dislike the messenger.

"Mr. Spurgeon is a stupid, irrational bigot. An ignorant, conceited fanatic," said a reporter with the *Saturday Review*. "This ranting fellow is like an overgrown cucumber, a buffoon in the pulpit, just a spoiled boy with ignorant theology!" Such was the general consensus for many of the newspapers in London, but the news of this strange new preacher-boy also invaded the headlines of Belfast's *North Whig* newspaper, the *Illustrated Times*, the *Ipswich Express*, the *Christian News of Scotland*, and the *Essex Standard*. It seemed everyone was talking about Charles Spurgeon. Most newspapers devoted more than half of their words to the country preacher from Stambourne, and the more criticism he received, the more people filled his pews.

On his best day, Charles would skim a negative news article, smile, and shake his head. But on his worst day, the barb would cut deeply and inflict a pain that pierced all the way to his bones. Few knew of his internal torment. From outward appearance, one would never know Charles Spurgeon suffered from depression. But the same darkness that stalked him as a young child in Stambourne continued to haunt him as a famous twenty-year-old in the big city of London. And no matter how hard he tried to manage it, shake it off, or hide, that old evil voice of darkness continued to whisper in his thoughts the lie, *Charles, you're still mine!*

In the drawer of his office desk, Charles kept every letter his grandfather wrote him. They were treasures of wisdom, love, and a constant motivation to endure.

Grandson,

A company of mean-spirited, wicked men, who are no bigger than bees, can get together and sting a man in a thousand places, 'till he is maddened by their scorn. But, it is their very littleness that gives them the power to wound with immunity. Do not be grieved, Grandson. For their stings will leave no scars. The Lord is on your side. Whom shall you fear?

Charles lit the end of his cigar with a match, then puffed and exhaled a patch of smoke that hung in the air of the carriage. The taste was sweet, hinted with flavors of currant and cocoa, and as he sat still, gratitude for his grandfather filled Charles's heart. He tilted his head towards the back of his plush seat and closed his eyes, grateful for his grandfather and for countless others who had prayed and yearned for his salvation for so many years.

As Charles unfolded his newspaper, he noticed a headline in the center of the front page: "The West End Wedding That Captured London." He gently tapped Susannah's hand, nestled next to his, and whispered, "Good news, today, my dear."

"Read it to me, Charles." Susannah pulled the cigar from his mouth, placed it in the ashtray—nearly extinguishing it—then nestled into Charles's shoulder as she listened.

"Friday morning," Charles read aloud, dramatically, "a curious scene was witnessed in the neighborhood of New Park Street Chapel, Southwark, at the rear of the Borough Market. Yesterday morning, the popular young preacher, Rev. Charles Haddon Spurgeon, was married; and although the persons who took an interest in the proceedings were not of the aristocratic character of those who usually attend West End weddings, they far outstripped any display which the West End is in the habit of witnessing. The bride was Miss Susannah Thompson, only daughter of Mr. Thompson, of Falcon Square, London," continued Charles, grinning with absolute delight.

"Oh, Charles. What a day!" said Susannah as she fell further into Charles's chest and closed her eyes.

"What a day, my dear." He spun his fingers through the soft brown curls of her hair and brushed her cheek with the backside of his hand. Then, smiling, he picked up the smoldering cigar and brought it back to life.

All over London, news of Charles and Susannah's marriage had spread like fire, and nearly two thousand people attended the marriage ceremony. Charles shook his head with disbelief as he recounted all that the Lord had done uniting their hearts.

Together, they shared an inseparable sort of bond. The clever mind of God knew that Charles would need a woman such as Susannah, and she, him. Through their courtship, they spent countless hours under the cool shade of the beech trees which lined the gardens of the Crystal Palace. It was their favorite place to rest, and they found that just a few hours of conversation in the lovely gardens, with the pure air and golden winds, brought both of them a sweet sense of delight. Often, Charles would scatter piles of sermon notes along the grass, while Susannah sat quietly, listening to the songbirds and occasionally offering suggestions on how to phrase certain sentences in his sermon. Several nights of the week, Charles and Susannah would meet under the gas lamp in the center of the gardens, reading Puritan writers and discussing the gems of wisdom found within.

※ ※ ※

One of Susannah's fondest memories of courtship was the night that Charles professed his unwavering desire to marry. It was an unusually busy evening in the Crystal Palace, as hundreds of families and couples played in the gardens, enjoying the sweetness of blooming flowers and the rustling of fresh water fountains. As they sat closely on the edge of a stone fountain, talking and laughing for what seemed like hours, Charles clasped his hand to hers and said, "Susie, do you ever pray for the one who is to be your husband?"

Her heart began to leap, and a telltale brushstroke of red flushed along her cheeks. The quiet and subdued Susannah Thompson sat by the pastor's side, waiting to hear his next words.

"I would very much like to be yours, Susie," he said. Reaching into the inner pocket of his coat, Charles revealed an unused copy of *The Pilgrim's Progress*. Its untattered, unblemished, and embossed cover sparkled like the setting sun reflecting from the fountain. "I would not like to be on this pilgrimage alone, Susie. Shall we do it together?"

A crowd of newly awakened emotions fluttered within her heart as she whispered in reply, "I would like that very much, Charles." He handed her the book, and as she opened the front cover, she saw the handwritten words that would always be a treasure to her. Inscribed in purple ink and cursive letters, it simply read: "Miss Thompson, with desires for her progress in the blessed pilgrimage, from C. H. Spurgeon."

Throughout their courtship, the couple's love for the Lord and each other grew strong as trees. She was his source of constant encouragement, often reminding him of the great calling God had placed on his life to pastor the city of London. She gave her whole heart to Charles, and was closer to him than any other human being. Charles never once took for granted the blessing of the woman who embraced him with a language of love straight from Heaven.

❇ ❇ ❇

The steam engine lurched forward, startling Susannah from her nap as the complete stranger in the corner politely asked, "Where are you lovely people heading today?" He spoke with a proper English accent as he kept his eyes on his newspaper.

"Well, sir, we are off to Paris for our wedding trip. But first, this train will take us to Colchester, where we will get off to head to Stambourne," said Charles. "Have you ever been?" Charles slid forward in his seat and handed the *London Daily News* to Susannah.

"To Stambourne? Oh, yes of course. Delightful this time of year. Truthfully, I'm usually the only person to ride this train on a Sunday afternoon. What has you chasing Stambourne today?" he asked, curiously.

"Ah, my family. They were unable to make the trip to London for our wedding ceremony." Charles smiled with pride. "We were married on Friday. This is my wife, Susannah." It felt strangely comfortable for Charles to refer to Susannah as his wife.

"Madam, a pleasure," said the man as he nodded and placed his paper into his carrying bag. "Looks like we have arrived in Colchester. You two will be on your way soon."

"Indeed," said Charles. He took his time to replace his top hat to his head and finish his nearly defeated cigar. After snuffing the end into the ashtray, he stood to look through the windows at Colchester quickly approaching. "She has not changed much, has she?" Charles asked the man.

"Nay. But changing soon she will be. Word is getting out about her ravishing charm. You do know that Colchester is the oldest town in all of Britain?" asked the man.

"Old as can be!" Charles slid his arms through his coat, then fumbled through all the pockets trying to find his train tickets. He unbuttoned and opened every flap of fabric in his coat and shirt, patted up and down his trousers, then shook his head with bewilderment.

The man sat up in his seat and sincerely inquired, "I hope you have not lost anything?"

"Thank you, my friend," Charles said. "But I've gone and lost our train tickets, and by a remarkable coincidence I have no money with me—not even a wristwatch to haggle with the platform collector!" Charles seldom wore a watch, and usually gave all of his spare coins to beggars as he walked the streets of London, so it was no surprise he had neither. "But, I am not at all troubled, sir. I am quite sure all will be well."

"I'm sure it will be well, sir," nodded the man as they waited for the train to come to a stop at the station in Colchester. As the train stalled into the platform, the door of the carriage opened, revealing a young official waiting to receive their tickets.

"Good afternoon to you," said the platform collector to Charles and Susannah. "Your train tickets, please."

"Ah, that won't be necessary today, Mr. Crawley," shouted the man to the platform collector. He stood to shake the official's hand, interrupting Charles from the need to explain the missing ticket or haggle his boots or topcoat as payment.

"Yes. Absolutely, sir. A good day to you all," the platform collector said, touching his hat and stepping back onto the platform. Charles and Susannah reeled with surprise.

"How strange," said Charles to the man. "He did not demand our tickets, nor any payment. Have you ever seen such a thing?"

"Ah, Reverend Spurgeon," the man replied earnestly. "How delightful to know that God is watching over us in the littlest of things. I am the General Manager of this train line, and no doubt I was divinely appointed to be your traveling companion just so I could be of service to you." A look of shock filled Charles and Susannah's faces as they continued to listen. "I know of the many ways you have blessed the people of London, and it was a great pleasure to meet under such happy circumstances." He tipped his hat at Charles, and walked through the door onto the platform. Then, turning with a smile, he said to Susannah, "And many congratulations on your extraordinary wedding, Mrs. Spurgeon. It was stunning."

Once again, gratitude and glee rushed into the heart of Charles Spurgeon like a tidal wave. He never took for granted when complete strangers recognized him in train stations, or along the London Bridge at night, or in his horse carriage driving down New Kent Road. Popularity was never something he expected. Ironically, it hadn't puffed him up or made him arrogant; instead, it humbled him profoundly to be a pastor that was well-loved in his city. By divine providence, many in the city of London had fully embraced him as a revolutionary leader and preacher. All throughout the city—sacred and secular, harlots and queens, drunkards and professors, rich and poor—found Charles Spurgeon to be a man of great character and intrigue.

❋ ❋ ❋

As Charles and Susannah stepped onto the station platform in Colchester, they were immediately greeted by Charles's
mother, father, and brother James. It had been some time since
he had visited home, and they were pleasantly surprised by the
roundness of his face and belly.

"My boy, London has treated you well!" said his mother, as
she embraced him and kissed his rosy cheeks. There was nothing like the comfort of family to Charles, and he had been looking forward to this trip for quite some time.

"My, you look fantastic, Mother. Not a day over twenty-three,"
Charles said, causing her to swat his hand playfully.

"As do you, Charlie," she said. "And Susannah, my goodness! You look spectacular, as always."

"Charles," said his little brother James, "what is this silly hat
you're wearing!? And why is it so large?" He pointed to Charles's
top hat, a symbol of London fashion at the time, and snarled
again. "You, my brother, look like a leprechaun. Where's your
pot of gold?" James was a feisty little fellow who borrowed his
wit and quick-thinking from his older brother.

"It's a *top hat*, James. I know it's excruciating for your adolescent mind to comprehend something of such high fashion,"
Charles said through a smirk.

"Charles, what have you prepared for a sermon today?" his
father asked him, inquisitively. "The townspeople of Stambourne
have been talking about this day for quite some time, and word
has spread that you'll be preaching a sermon tonight. Some say
a thousand will show up. Everyone is very proud, Charles!"

"I am proud as well, Father. It's a great honor to preach in
my grandfather's pulpit," he said.

"Enough about sermons!" interrupted his mother. "Tell me of your wedding. Tell me this instant! You know London is so far for us, or we surely would have come."

"I still have trouble believing that God would be so kind as to grant me union to a woman of such love, grace, and beauty. Our wedding was bright as the morning light. As delicious as the Essex winds." His eyes melted with childlike happiness.

"I still have trouble believing that a duff like you has a lady like that," said James sarcastically. "You tricked her real good, Charlie."

"A prophet is not without honor except in his hometown. Right, little brother? It seems you have not changed a bit," said Charles while reaching across the platform to punch his arm. "Alright, we must get to it; we have a long ride."

❋ ❋ ❋

The ride from Colchester seemed to pass unusually fast, and as the carriage turned onto Church Road, the town of Stambourne glowed bright as an orange from the setting summer sun. They passed the creek bed underneath Bailey Hill, and Charles immediately noticed the sweet aroma of the countryside. As they passed the parsonage and Grandfather's garden, the sound of singing filled his ears. He could hear the congregation from afar, a small army of voices singing.

When the carriage finally stopped at old Mr. Tagley's horse block, Charles couldn't believe his eyes. Nearly three thousand people stood in the horse barn and spilled into the grassy field next to the Meeting House. Tents and canvas tarpaulins strung from every post and tree, and as far as Charles could see, men and women and children stood facing the little temporary platform in the corner of the barn. The volume of their singing was the loudest he had ever heard, and it reverberated all throughout the countryside of Stambourne, in every direction.

Without wasting a second, Charles burst from the carriage and made his way to the front row of people. There, in front of the table-pew and pulpit, his grandfather stood with eyes closed and mouth wide, singing louder than the entire crowd. Charles gently nudged his grandfather, startling him from his singing, and without skipping a single lyric, his grandfather squeezed and held him tight as they both finished the hymn, "Jesus, Lover of My Soul, Let Me to Thy Bosom Fall."

Charles closed his eyes and thought of Heaven, for in that final hallelujah, the mighty waves of singing seemed to roll towards the sky, in grand majesty, like ocean billows bursting to the shore.

Charles stepped behind the pulpit and motioned for the mass of people to have a seat. Some sat in chairs, but most sat on blankets in the grassy field surrounding the horse barn. He scanned the crowd of family and strangers, then locked eyes with his bride, who sat perfectly poised next to the center aisle of the second row. Charles said no words; he couldn't. The crowd eagerly awaited what he would say, but Charles silently wrestled with an unshakable darkness in the depth of his gut. It was unexplainable.

Somehow in that moment, Charles knew that a season of terrible suffering and sorrow was coming. And, when it came, he and Susannah would have to rely on the mingling of flesh and soul to endure not just marriage and ministry—but life, itself.

CHAPTER 8

STEAL AWAY TO JESUS

Virginia, USA 1857

Most slave owners in the South firmly believed that any hint of freedom in a slave's daily schedule would lead to a slippery slope of disobedience, and that disobedience most certainly would lead to all-out rebellion. In the heart of every slave owner, especially Mr. Bennett, there lived a gnawing fear of rebellion. This fear lurked under the surface of their humanity, crouching like a lion—sweaty and muscled— ready to pounce from the shadows to shred the life and security they worked so hard to achieve. It haunted their dreams at night; it frolicked in their thoughts by day. *If our slaves ever got a mind to do it,* the owners worried, *they have the numbers, the power, and a reason to burn this house, raze our crops, kill our families, and walk out the gates none the worse.* It was a well-founded fear.

Mr. Bennett, ever the student of history, was well aware of incidents like the slave rebellion of the Danish West Indies of 1733. In the early morning of November 23 of that year, one hundred and fifty African slaves organized an insurrection that ended with the island beaches soaked red with the blood of its landowners. It took an army of Swiss and French militia months to quell the massive uprising. Mr. Bennett spent many a sleepless night, stomach churning with anxiety, planning contingencies in case the same scenario occurred on his plantation. And more important, he schemed on how to prevent it from happening in the first place.

As a result, the life of Thomas Johnson was ruled by rhythms, schedules, and order. From sunrise to sunset, time did not belong to him, but solely to the master and his foreman. He was told when to wake up, when to eat, when to work, and when to sleep. Any deviance from the master's design was met with sharp and brutal punishment. This sort of daily oppression robbed Thomas of what little humanity onto which he still clung. His childhood had been steeped in loneliness and anger, and now a slave for over two decades, Thomas felt barely human.

This sense of hopelessness festered, choking Thomas from the inside. His only reprieve was the soothing balm of a few short hours each night of blessed sleep. Then, as Thomas rose from his slumber, just like the day before and a thousand days before that, hopelessness waited for him at the side of his bed, hovering like a houseguest that has long overstayed their welcome.

It was close to midnight, and with his daily duties finally completed, Thomas stirred in bed. Slow waves of pain pulsed through his knees and feet, up his aching back, and down towards his calloused hands. The pain pierced his skin and bones, but a much deeper pain kept him awake on this sticky summer night.

"I'm going to escape," Thomas said, almost aloud, as he lay motionless in the dark. For twenty-one years, freedom had been the subject he thought about more than any other, and yet, he had never mustered the resolve to fight for it. With ever-increasing courage, Thomas slowly lifted his head from the pillow and sat upright in his bed. Lazy candlelight flickered in the corner of his small clapboard shack and cast just enough light to reveal holes at the base of the wall. The holes were much too small for a man to crawl through, but field mice often used them as an entrance and exit. Thomas chuckled as he thought of the time a large rat wiggled her way through, ran underneath his bed, and scared the living breath out of him. As quickly as the chuckle began, it fell away, overcome by the sobering reality that freedom belonged to mice and rats, but not all men.

Escaping to the North was an idea that had consumed his thoughts since boyhood. A large map of the United States of America hung in the dining room hallway of the big house, and Thomas, on more than one occasion, neglected his duties long enough to steal a passing glance at what lay north of Virginia. One Sunday morning when the master's family had gone into town to attend services at the Episcopal Church, Thomas studied the map. There were very few words he could read, but when he finally recognized "Richmond," he traced his finger upward, slightly to the right, then crossed the Potomac River into Washington, D.C., then all the way up through several states to Boston, Massachusetts. His finger often roamed along the spider web of roads that connected so many American cities, and Thomas wondered if he would ever be able to freely roam the land where he was born. He imagined waving good-bye to Virginia before he crossed rivers and valleys, scaled to the tops of mountain peaks, and dipped his toes into the cool waters of the Atlantic Ocean.

Two things, and two things alone, kept Thomas tethered to Mr. Bennett's godforsaken plantation in Richmond, Virginia. The first was fear. What would happen if he were caught escaping? Would he receive a beating that would scar him for the rest of his life? Or would he receive death, and be buried under the grassy lawn between the big house and the whipping post?

The second was the unknown. What would he do if he actually succeeded in his escape? Where would he live? How would he make a living? Thomas could barely read and write, and his best skills were harvesting tobacco and passing out food to white people. Fear and the unknown, like fetter and chain, held a firm grip on Thomas, and he wondered if he'd ever leave Mr. Bennett's tobacco plantation in the southern state of Virginia, in the United States of America, where all men were not equal.

As Thomas waged a silent war in his bed, the hopelessness, anger, and frustration of his position began to drown out the voices of reason that held him in bondage for so long. It suddenly seemed reasonable that the pain of the whip—even the pain of death—*had* to be more tolerable than the pain of a meaningless life. Just the chance of tasting freedom, as miniscule as the chance may be, seemed like a risk worth taking.

Thomas desperately wanted to bolt to his feet, blow out the flickering candle, push open the door, point his feet to the North, and walk daringly into the dark of the woods, never turning back. But every time he thought of escape, the haunting words of Ezekiel rattled around his head.

I'm telling you boy, you are looking for freedom in all the wrong places.

Those words held Thomas to the plantation for so many years. His friend claimed that freedom was found somewhere other than the North, and although Ezekiel was the most trustworthy person Thomas knew, he had to find out whether Ezekiel was right.

Thomas placed his feet on the hard, wooden floor and slid his tattered cotton shirt over his head. He blew out the candle in the corner of his room, hoping that any passerby would assume that he had fallen asleep. Slowly, Thomas pushed his head out the entrance of his quarters and scanned to the left and to the right. Like a shifting shadow, he inched slowly toward Ezekiel's shack.

Midnight on the southern plantation was both beautiful and haunting. The sound of many men working and a few men shouting orders had long silenced, leaving only the sound of soft winds blowing through apathetic trees. Long-neglected windmills creaked and whined, providing the steady rhythm to which the crickets and night birds added their lulling harmonies. The moon and stars seemed to shine brighter outside the town of Fairfax, a long way from the street lamps and bonfires of the city, a light ample enough to illuminate the silhouettes of slaves crawling around the plantation past curfew.

Quentin Ellis rarely issued nighttime passes, and only for extreme reasons. If a slave woman was having a child, or a direct member of a slave's family lay on his deathbed, the foreman would begrudgingly issue a pass. Apart from these, and without exception, a slave was to remain in their quarters until morning. Thomas knew that if he was caught outside his quarters without a pass, it would mean lashes. Five, ten, maybe more.

Ezekiel's quarters were a short hundred yards away, and once Thomas gained confidence, he burst into a sprint, dashing between the trees and old rusty wagons that cluttered the darkness. As Thomas reached the quarters, breathing heavily, he knelt below the open window of Ezekiel's room. Ezekiel's shack was completely darkened, and his boyish heart sank at the realization that his friend was asleep. Thomas glanced up at the cloud-thick night sky, and noticed how quickly the clouds sped through the air. They billowed and danced, rolled and crawled, freely. A cool blast of wind blew through Thomas's hair and down his face. The wind, caged by nothing, seemed to hug and caress Thomas with a calming comfort.

Thomas's senses were fully alive. He almost felt free. He wanted to keep running into the night, past the fences and into the spiderweb of roads that splintered across state lines. He took a long breath to slow the throbbing of his heart, then heard a faint sound emanating from the window above his head. The sound was small and steady, almost a whisper.

Then, in an instant, it stopped.

Thomas wondered if he had imagined the noise, when suddenly, it began again. Ever so slowly, he raised his head, just enough to see beyond the base of the window frame. Thomas peeked into the pitch-black of Ezekiel's shack and waited for his eyes to slowly adjust from the relative light of the moon-washed plantation. As the pitch-black gave way to clarity, the source of the melodic whispers was revealed. There, crammed within the walls of Ezekiel's quarters, sat a sacred circle of men and women with heads bowed to the floor. Some sat, others knelt, one lay completely prostrate with his face to the dirt. Thomas had never seen a grown man lay face down on the floor without someone forcing him to do so. The scene bewildered Thomas.

In the middle of the circle of men and women stood Ezekiel, with both arms rhythmically and slowly moving, pausing briefly at the top and bottom of his motion, leading the circle in whisper-singing. For fear of being heard by the master and the foreman, they sang not with melody or harmony, but whispers. Strangely, the volume of their hearts far outweighed the volume of their whispers. Thomas leaned further towards the window, and heard clearly for the first time:

> *Steal away, Steal away.*
> *Steal away to Jesus;*
> *Steal away, Steal away home;*
> *I ain't got long to stay here.*
> *So steal away, Steal away to Jesus.*

Thomas found himself peering through the window frame, completely mesmerized by the depth of emotion in their whisperings. He looked around the room and saw that some had expressions of joy, others of pain. There are rare moments when one can see, from the outside, what the inside of a person looks like. It was as if Thomas could see the inside of his fellow slaves, clearly. Pain became visible. Sorrow was seen. Hope couldn't be contained, so it spilled out onto their faces, from their eyes, down their cheeks, to their chins. Joy burst from their hearts, and caused their hands to sway and dance. In that rare and vulnerable moment, Thomas saw what he had never seen: faith that Jesus was enough. It was a faith of which Thomas knew nothing.

As they whispered the final line, "Steal away to Jesus," Ezekiel noticed Thomas peering through the window frame. Ezekiel solemnly motioned his head toward the room, signaling for Thomas to come in, and without saying a word, Thomas opened the door and entered the sacred space. Several of the slaves lifted their heads as they noticed his entrance, but none said a word. They quietly shuffled their bodies to the left and right, allowing room for the young man to sit on the floor. Thomas sat peacefully, and crossed his legs as Ezekiel began to speak.

"I got one question for each one of you tonight," whispered Ezekiel as he looked directly at Thomas. Even in the darkness of the room, Thomas could see his friend's eyes—bright and piercing—speaking to everyone, but looking only at him.

"Have you stolen away to Jesus?" Ezekiel paused, letting the question soak.

"Have you stolen away from this place—your work, your troubles—have you gotten alone with the Lord? 'Cause that might be the most important question you answer all day long. 'Cause you see, the master . . . he owns our body. The master, he owns our time. The master, he owns everything about us," Ezekiel continued to whisper, looking only to Thomas.

"But. There is something you can't ever forget. There is one thing that man don't own. There is one thing that man can't ever own."

"He don't own your soul."

Several of the slaves moaned quietly in agreement, gently rocking back and forth to the slow, rhythmic cadence of the whispering preacher. "There is another Master. And this Master—He the Master of this whole world. He's the One that your soul *really* belongs to. His name is Jesus."

Ezekiel lifted his gaze from the boy and moved his eyes back and forth across the rest of his captivated audience.

"Some of you picked tobacco today. Some of you washed dishes and clothes today. Couple of you even took a whippin' from the foreman today. And you might be thinkin' to yourself, *I ain't never gonna get out of this place. I ain't never gonna know what it's like to be a free man. A free woman.* Some of you been thinking, *I ain't never gonna know what it's like to do what I wanna do. To be who I wanna be. To go where I wanna go.*"

Ezekiel paused, and Thomas could hear the word "yes" gently leave the tear-stained lips of a young mother staring at the face of her infant, sleeping in her arms. A large man who sat next to Thomas nodded his head in sad agreement, and deeply whispered, "That's right."

"And the truth be told . . . the bad news is that may never change. You and me, we may very well live our whole entire lives in these chains." Ezekiel paused, filled his lungs, and straightened his back. "But here's the Good News—you can be free. Really free. Right here. Right now. No matter where you are. No matter what you do. No matter what kinda chains you carryin' with you."

Thomas sat, barely breathing, hanging on every word of his friend. He listened as if he were hearing a great and powerful secret for the first time, one that had been kept from him until now, and was then suddenly revealed in all of its beauty and glory.

Ezekiel once again looked at Thomas, wide-eyed and passionate, like no one else was in the room, and spoke the words
that would forever change the life of Thomas Johnson.

"Jesus sets slaves like us free. He may not take away the
chains from your hands and your feet. He may never let you off
this plantation. But, Jesus will do something even better than
that. He will take off the chains from your heart."

Ezekiel looked at each face in the room. Then, offering an
assuring smile, he stated, "That . . . He will do."

When his short sermon concluded, Ezekiel closed his eyes,
thought of Heaven, and began to whisper-sing, "Steal away to
Jesus. Steal away home."

Thomas pressed the palm of his hand towards his heart and
joined their song. Although a mere whisper, there were something about the singing of those words that Thomas couldn't
explain. His heart beat fast and his breath was shallow, but for
the first time in his life, it wasn't because of fear. The lifelong
companion of Thomas Johnson—dreadful fear—seemed to run
away into the distant shadows of the quiet tobacco plantation.

As he continued to sing, joining the other whispers in the
shack, a flood of relief gently pushed years of anguish and grief
from his young heart. His eyes released a flood of joyful tears,
as Thomas felt like he was sitting right next to this man—Jesus—
the One who could finally set him free from the bondage that
held his heart. There in Ezekiel's shack, in the middle of the
darkened slave quarters, surrounded by the gentle whisper-
songs, beneath a clouded night sky—Thomas believed.

Thomas wouldn't remember the conversations he had with
his fellow slaves after the whisper-singing was finished. As
hard as he tried to recount the sacred evening, he would never

remember what it felt like to dance across the moonlit field between Ezekiel's quarters and his own. He wouldn't recall washing the dirt from his feet before he crawled into his crooked bed. But one thing Thomas would never forget until his dying breath—he would never forget how it felt to sleep that night.

Because for the first time in his entire life, Thomas Johnson slept in peace.

CHAPTER 9

SERMON WRITING

London, England 1856

When Charles sat at his desk on Saturday, he had no idea that Sunday would bring a sadness that would shackle him all the way to the grave.

The tiny amber flame fluttered and flickered as the cool London breeze whispered through the window of Charles's study on 217 New Kent Road. It was half past seven, and even though Susannah had been asleep for an hour, Charles kept to his candlelit desk, barely making progress on tomorrow's sermon. He was overly familiar with the painstaking process of crafting a Sunday sermon, but since Susannah gave birth to two lovely twin boys just a month ago, ample time for sermon writing was inconceivable.

Susannah's pregnancy had been difficult. Her body buckled under the stress of carrying two children. Doctors couldn't explain exactly what happened, but after delivery, Susannah knew something wasn't right. When babies Charles and Thomas entered the world, they were blessed with a mother and father whose relationship was founded on pure love and devotion. There was not a better family in all of the United Kingdom to be born into; and yet, pregnancy and childbirth brought devastating effects on Susannah Spurgeon.

As the boys slept at the foot of Susannah's bed just down the hall, Charles thought of the many souls that would attend church tomorrow. It would certainly be the largest Protestant gathering in the history of London, and Charles could barely sit still or stick to one thought in his head.

⁂

"We are out of room, Mr. Spurgeon," Charles recalled one of his deacons saying to him emphatically. "Unless we turn five thousand people away and tell them they cannot hear of Jesus and His Good News, we must find a building in London large enough to house them all!"

"Indeed, brother," Charles replied with wonder and excitement. "We are getting on too fast. Souls are being converted and are flying like doves to their windows! Our harvest is too rich for the barn; we must find a bigger one."

For months, the elders of New Park Street Chapel turned thousands of people away each Sunday, as they could not fit another human being inside Exeter Hall. During the dreadful summer months, the temperature reached ninety degrees, and was nearly impossible to bear. Still, thirty minutes before the sermon began, every aisle was stacked with a solid block of people wedged shoulder to shoulder. Every seat, nook, cranny, and corner was invaded by a beating heart, a longing soul, and an inclined ear. Children sat in windowsills and fanned their sweaty faces, women shook crying babies as they sat on wooden benches, men stood along the edge of the Victorian-decorated walls, while others leaned against the golden banisters that lined the front of the balconies. Behind the podium, people stood for hours in the orchestra section to listen to Charles. They could only see his slick black hair and the occasional side of his plump face when he turned to the side, but as his billowing voice reverberated around the massive room and echoed back towards their ears, it was impossible for them to lose interest. If crowds could have hung from all eighteen ornate chandeliers that majestically hung from the white plastered ceiling, they surely would have, but as there was no more room inside—their only option was to peer through an open windowpane and hang their chins on the black iron that fenced them from the holy spectacle inside. It was like trying to cram the whole ocean into a teapot, and beautifully, it was nothing short of revival.

It seemed ridiculous, really. Ridiculous that most churches were dying, shrinking, while New Park Street Chapel couldn't possibly find a building with walls far enough apart. Burdened by the magnitude of the need and the limitation of space, Charles and the elders pleaded and begged God for a larger meeting space.

"Have you considered the Gardens?" asked Susannah during a quiet breakfast.

"What do you mean, Susie?"

"The new music hall. In the Gardens. It's become a favorite haunt of my dreams at night. Have you considered it?"

"Well, no . . . I don't think I have," said Charles, as he wondered why he had never thought about leasing the largest and most commodious building in all of London. "I . . . I have never even considered it, Susie," he said with pause. "But, I will this instant."

The Surrey Music Hall had recently been built in the Royal Surrey Gardens, just south of the Thames River. In addition to the beautiful gardens that Charles and Susannah had enjoyed during courtship, the Surrey Gardens now housed one of the largest music venues in all of England. The newly built hall was home to symphonies and orchestras, city events and operas, and on most occasions, attracted ten to twelve thousand people. It was the center of London's art culture. So, when Susannah cast the idea to use it as a place of worship and preaching, it set off the alarms of Charles's emotions and stirred him with a curious excitement.

※ ※ ※

Charles gathered the elders and deacons of New Park Street Chapel, and announced that the church would begin meeting in the Surrey Gardens Music Hall on October 19. News of the move flew quickly throughout the United Kingdom. "Preposterous," said some people. "The church is moving into a devil's house!" said others. Charles had already broken with tradition by moving the congregation into Exeter Hall, so when Londoners heard that he was overtaking the twelve-thousand-seat palace every Sunday, the concept seemed nearly impossible to comprehend. But Charles did not choose the Surrey Music Hall because it was fanciful in appearance. He did not choose it because it was as the epicenter of English culture and amusement. He did not choose it because it puffed his ego, or inflated his sense of approval. Charles simply had no other choice; he wanted every person in London, England, to hear the Good News of Jesus. And, in less than twenty-four hours, Charles would stand in front of the largest Protestant audience that had ever gathered in the city of London.

"God, what must Your people hear tomorrow? There are so many coming. There are so many needs. What must they hear?" he whispered in the dark. An appropriate blend of anticipation and fear whisked around his heart—excited by the responsibility of preaching to so many people, and plagued by a strange premonition that the Enemy would do whatever necessary to derail the sacred gathering.

Charles stared at a blank sheet of paper on his desk, and twirled a wide-nib, black resin fountain pen in his right hand. The silken curtains around the opened window danced in the cool wind, while the tiny flame of the waxen candle continued to sway, bending orange light along the leather surface of the desk.

He tapped his pen on his front two teeth three times, rhythmically, as the words *Prove Yourself, God* filled his imagination.

He tapped his teeth again—another three times—then, whispered, "Prove Yourself faithful, God."

He continued to pray as he held his pen, "God, I want you to prove Yourself tomorrow. Perhaps I may be called to stand where the thunderclouds brew, where the lightning plays, and the tempestuous winds are howling on the mountaintop. But amidst all dangers, I am born to prove the power and majesty of our God. Inspire me with courage. Make me strong!"

He lowered his fountain pen to the top corner of the blank piece of paper and wrote in purple ink, *October 19, 1856. Our first Sabbath at the Surrey Gardens Music Hall.* The ink continued to spill out as Charles kept writing, his hand hardly lifting from the page as he covered each square inch. Heaven spoke; Charles listened.

We are gathered together, tonight, where an unprecedented mass of people have assembled, perhaps from idle curiosity to hear the Word of God.

Why should we be unbelieving?

Have we one thing to make us not believe?

Are we not strongest in our God when we are weakest in ourselves?

We are weak, but God hath chosen the weak things of the world to prove Him now!

Lift up that life-giving cross, and let it again be exhibited.

Charles pressed his entire self into the sacred moment of sermon writing—the intersection of the Spirit's leading and man's listening. As his pen continued to spill ink on the now-cluttered paper, Charles knew that he was simply an instrument, simply a pen in the hand of Almighty God.

It is a rare thing for a human being to press all of their physical energy, all of their intellectual capital, all of their spiritual force into a task, then humbly cast it at the feet of Jesus for Him to use according to His purpose and plan. And, in this rare endeavor, Charles discovered a deep dependency on the Spirit of God to accomplish what his talents never could—the setting on fire of human hearts and the igniting of souls. Because when the light of Christ shines brightly through a humble and surrendered servant, God proves Himself very good.

As the hour hand of the clock slowly spun in circles, the hand of Charles continued to pen his sermon for tomorrow's gathering. And when the last period was placed at the end of the sheet of paper, Charles sighed with completion and bowed his head to the desk as he peacefully fell asleep for the last few hours the night had to offer.

❊ ❊ ❊

"Good morning, Charles," said Susannah as she drew back the silk curtains and tied them along the edge of the wooden window frame, allowing the dawn to crash through the darkened study. Her voice fell sweet as the morning dew. "My dear! You slept at your desk again?"

"Wifey, I simply couldn't keep my eyes open long enough to make it to the bed." Charles ran his fingers through his messy black hair, and lumbered from the desk to embrace Susannah. "How did you sleep, my love? Are you in pain this morning?"

"Sure. There is always pain. But it is not for you to worry about now," she said meekly as Charles slid his hand along her back, then gently felt her stomach, still swollen from childbirth.

"I would take the pain from you if I could." His eyes set towards hers. They were narrow and pretty, and the corners of her eyelids hung like kingly curtains, slowly opening and closing to reveal the sunshine he thoroughly enjoyed peering into.

"You must not take the pain away, even if you could. The pain is the measure of grace by which God is choosing to endure me today. The Spurgeons cannot flee from pain. No more than a bride flee her very own groom." A calm smile crawled across her face as she caressed his beard.

"Well, I'd still insist to try."

"Tell me. How are you feeling about the music hall today?"

"Anguish," he replied without thinking.

"Anguish?"

"Anguish, dear."

"Well, Charles. Your grandest and most fruitful sermons are those which cost you soul-travail and spiritual anguish, are they not?" she asked, dropping her hands and resting them on her hips.

"I don't speak of my sermon. I am confident in it. I mean, I feel as though I am locked up in chains about today, in general. I know that has no sense about it." He paused, then continued, "I simply cannot put the right word to it. I have an unsettled spirit today."

"Yes, love. And still, you must not fear."

Susannah placed her hand under his chin once more to pull his eyes towards hers. Where they met, there was peace. "Today, the music hall will be holy ground. And God has chosen you to be the herald of Good News. So, speak now. Speak to your Lord. Tell Him of your fears and doubts. Then, wait and watch for Him to fill you with a spirit of freedom and confidence."

Like an arid wind from the sea, a brush of calm blew through Charles's heart. Susannah kissed Charles on his forehead then turned to leave the room. "And don't forget to bid Charles and Thomas a good day before you leave."

CHAPTER 10

MORE DEAD
THAN ALIVE

London, England 1856

When Charles arrived at the Surrey Gardens Music Hall at six o'clock on the third Sabbath of October, his breath was stolen away. The roar of a million locomotives could not compare to the volume of the nearly twenty thousand people that assembled in the gardens to wait for the doors of the music hall to open.

While only twelve thousand could fit inside, the magnificent crowd gathered under rows of beech trees, up and down the banks of the fish pond, and under the wide porches and foyers that surrounded the exterior of the magnificent concert hall. The four spires that cornered the edges of the building reached to the sky, casting elegant shadows over the crowd and the garden's lush green landscape. The building's modern architecture and yellow brick exterior could have overshadowed the natural beauty of the gardens, but oddly, the mingling of ancient and modern proved to be breathtaking.

The music hall was filled once the doors of the great entrance were opened at five minutes after six, although the process of packing the hall was a terrible mess. The crowd rushed and pushed towards the entrance, squeezing their shoulders through the tiny doors, and once they finally burst through, they ran in every direction to find a seat, or at least a place to stand. The people had a violent excitement about them; there was an every-man-for-himself mentality, nothing like a normal place of worship. In a city where houses of worship were often orderly and calm, the Surrey Gardens Music Hall was a contrasting house of chaos and clamor.

As Charles's carriage made its way through the mass of people on Manor Street, he noticed the diversity of the crowd. Women, children, men, grandparents, youth, black, white, rich, poor, aristocrats, and common folk—all doing their best to make it into the already-packed concert hall. Charles, who was accompanied by two of his elders, held to his leather seat and shook his head in wonder.

"Who are all of these people?" Charles asked one of the elders, as he peered through the window. Neither of the elders answered.

As Charles continued to inhale and exhale, over and over, he tapped his knuckle on his front teeth and thought, *Prove Yourself tonight, God.* He was overawed and felt faint. This wasn't the first time he had preached to a sizeable audience, yet the magnitude of the evening caught him by surprise. As his carriage passed through the gardens, a place men and women had assembled for entertainment and wild exhibits, he begged the Lord to impose a magnificence that would echo for generations. His heart leapt within his wide chest. He closed his eyes, and remembering the bottomless pit, he silently pleaded with God to save every single person that attended this sacred gathering.

"Charles, right this way to the entrance," said one of his elders, startling Charles from his prayer. "We'll go through this door to take you to the platform. But, we still have ten minutes before it's half past six, so you can wait here if you'd like."

"No, we will start early tonight, gentlemen," he said confidently. "They've been waiting long enough."

A sting of reverence and awe shot through him as he climbed the steps towards the orchestra level that perched at the end of the long rectangular hall. Three balconies, each holding three thousand people or so, circled the entire room and overlooked the main seating area in the middle, giving perfect view of the spacious platform and pulpit. Large, golden chandeliers regally hung from the ceiling of every balcony and provided a kingly appearance to the music hall. Even the design of the flooring was given special attention, as it was patterned with blue and white porcelain tiles that seemed to hug the long rows of chairs. Every wall was laced with silver and ember splotches of paint, while slender pillars extended from the floor, attached to each of the balconies, then reached all the way to the ceiling, and held the entire structure like strong towers. Several hundred feet above the center section, the ceiling was adorned with iron studs and square windowpanes, allowing both day and evening to invade the room.

On this evening, the air was unusually bright as the falling sun cast its final rays through the windows that lined the ceiling. It was a modern marvel—a work of art—and never had there been a building that felt so heavenly, so wonderful. Charles thought of the Heavenly City and was sure there was a similar palace with a similar brightness—except there, only Jesus would shine brighter and more beautifully.

The hall, filled to the brim, began to settle as Charles made his way to the pulpit, and then a great hush filled the room as he placed his notes on the pulpit and opened his Bible. He pulled his long, black hair behind his ears, cleared his throat, and glanced down at the second row to see if Susannah had taken her most prized seat. He met her eyes, took a deep a breath, then prayed loud enough for every single person to hear.

"God, Most High. Prove Yourself tonight. Prove Your glory. Prove Your goodness. Prove Yourself tonight." After he prayed, Charles led a hymn with force and feeling, and as they sang with the voice of a thousand oceans, he swore the windowpanes were rattling loose from their hinges. It was a volume fit for Heaven and he was sure it was enough to garner the attention of angels. Men, women, and children sang with fervency, and once the hymn was complete, those who had chairs sat, and those who did not simply stood—all with eyes and ears peeled towards Charles.

"The voice of God rings in my ears tonight, my friends," began Charles. "Why should we be unbelieving? Have we one thing to make us not believe? Are we not strongest in our God when we are weakest in ourselves? We are weak, but God hath chosen the weak things of the world to prove Himself now!" Most of the crowd nodded their heads, some scribbled notes on slices of paper, others simply listened with intrigue. "Hear the Word of God tonight. Our text is from the book of Proverbs, chapter three." With a curious combination of tenderness and boldness, Charles read from Proverbs, loud enough for every ear to discern—even the ones he could not see, propped against the back walls.

Nearly every person in the back of the music hall was glued to Charles, unable to take their eyes and ears from him. Charles appeared tiny from the back of the room, his head the size of an acorn, his broad shoulders seeming an inch wide. Women squinted and pressed their elbows to their knees, while men leaned backward in their seats and stretched their eyes wide. Still, his voice was burly and boisterous and filled the hall without any amplification. It was strange that one could sit or stand along the furthest walls—nearly one hundred meters from the pulpit—and hear the voice of Charles with absolute clarity. In the sanctity of the moment, even the back of the room was experiencing the wonderful work of the Spirit of God.

But, there was another spirit at work in the back of the Surrey Gardens Music Hall. In an age when God was reviving a city, igniting souls to know Jesus, and gathering unprecedented flocks of people, darkness and evil contrived a plan to disrupt the assembly. Darkness is always plotting and scheming, but when a man stands before twelve thousand souls, anxious to speak the Word of God, the devils snicker and sneer, rub their grimy hands together, slither along the floor between shoes and skirts, slip through balconies and slide along bannisters, swinging from chandeliers and rafters, carefully whispering to every listener, "Don't believe."

In this instant, the hardened hearts of a few men, desperate to undermine the work of God in the sacred assembly, yelled with malicious intent, "Fire! Fire! Fire!"

Another shouted, "Yes! The galleries are giving way!"

And another joined, shouting from beneath the grand entrance stairwell, "The place is falling! The building is falling! Run!"

Hundreds jumped from their chairs in the back of the music hall and rushed towards the opened doors under the grand stairway. Like a disturbed ant mound, men, women, and children burst towards each other in all directions, shoving and scrambling, pushing and pulling. In a moment of panic, the force of the crowd broke the wooden bannister that trimmed the first balcony, and people fell from the second floor to the first. Hurling themselves headlong, they trampled over each other as they tried to flee a fire that didn't exist.

Those who fell to the floor, either by force or fainting, were crushed to death on the stone steps of the northwest staircase, stampeded by feet pressing upon them. It was a dreadful panic, a horrible panic.

Charles, unable to comprehend the distant commotion from the pulpit, and unaware of its severity, continued to preach.

Susannah turned her head towards the back of the music hall, curious about the commotion, and a sinking feeling turned her stomach. A few of the elders on the platform ran towards the back of the room to see what was happening, and slowly, whispers of the tragedy trickled throughout the room, row by row. After a few attempts to recapture the attention of the massive crowd, Charles knew it would be impossible to continue preaching. He did his best to stay calm and bring a quietness to the people, but a deep sense of confusion and distress came over Charles. He knew the Enemy was doing what the Enemy does best—steal, kill, and destroy.

Charles pressed his lips together, gritted his teeth, and thought of the many years of his childhood that darkness had haunted his own story. He remembered the whispers of the Enemy, how loud they seemed to ring, and then all at once the powers of darkness seemed to press on Charles like a stack of bricks. Charles was no stranger to the Devil, and the Devil was no stranger to Charles Spurgeon. His entire soul wreaked of a curious blend of sorrow and outrage. His eyes welled with sorrowful tears, and he choked back the desire to burst into shouting. All he could do was belt out a hymn of praise, because when the Enemy tries his best to win, the child of God knows that a song of victory is most necessary.

"Praise God from whom all blessings flow," he began to sing.

"Praise Him all creatures here below," a few others began to whisper-sing from the platform.

"Praise Him above ye heavenly hosts," another hundred or so joined.

"Praise Father, Son, and Holy Ghost." By the fourth line, the front half of the room bravely sang along, but Charles somehow knew that something terrible had happened in the back of the great room. He clenched his Bible, held it up to the crowd still rustling around, and shouted louder than the chaos in the room.

"My friends, there is a terrible day coming," his voice cracked and his hands trembled, "when the terror and alarm of this evening shall be as nothing. My friends! Even if you are the chief of sinners, believe that Christ died for you, and you shall be saved. Do you not know that you are lost and ruined, and that none but Jesus can do you any good? Jesus can heal you; and He will, if only you trust Him." Charles struggled to finish his last words, as a knot grew within his throat and his knees faltered behind the pulpit. No dam could hold back the well of tears that grew in his eyes, and as he glanced at Susannah who sat with solemnity, his face was quickly drenched.

As hundreds continued to pour out of the hall in fear, a river of sadness poured into his own heart. He placed his Bible back on the wooden pulpit, gripped the front of its edge, and leaned towards his flock with the final words of the night. "My brain is in a whirl, and I scarcely know where I am. I suspect that many persons have been injured by rushing out." His head slouched from his shoulders and his face hung somberly towards his now-closed Bible. "May God Almighty dismiss you with His blessing, and carry you in safety to your homes. Pray, my friends, that some good may, after all, come out of this great evil. Do not, however, be in a hurry. Let those nearest the door go first."

Charles once again started singing, "Praise God from whom all blessings flow," and as the crowd somberly sang along and migrated towards the exits, Charles ran towards Susannah and wrapped his quivering arms around her. They shared no words, only a common sadness. Her strong hands slipped into his as they made their way to the private exit near the platform and climbed into the carriage, where one of his elders recounted the dreadful events of the back of the music hall.

Charles never saw the seven corpses that were neatly laid on the lush grass of the gardens outside the grand entrance, under the shadows of the beech trees. He never had the chance to hold the hands of the twenty-eight that were carried to nearby hospitals, seriously bruised and injured. He never saw the terrible scene of hundreds who sat along the edges of the fish pond, faces buried in their hands, dizzy with fright and sadness. Truthfully, it may have been too much for Charles to bear, for the memory from behind the pulpit on October 19 in the Surrey Gardens Music Hall was enough to cripple him with a depression and sorrow that he would hold to his grave.

Gently, the carriage crawled forward and carried Charles to his home on New Kent Road, more dead than alive.

SECTION 3

CHAPTER 11

An Oak Tree in Clapham Common

London, England 1859

There still stands, within an expansive city park in south London, an ancient tree with splintered limbs and coal-black edges. Its roots have long withered, and it has not sprouted a crisp oak leaf in a hundred springtimes. The wind no longer swirls around its branches, weary birds find no comfort within its vacant offshoots, and the brilliant colors of new life have turned a darker tone. Everything has a beginning, and everything has an end. Still, everything has a purpose. This tired tree in the center of Clapham Common revealed its purpose in the stormy summer of 1859, and stands today, without regret and without doubt.

Although three years had passed since the awful tragedy at Surrey Garden Music Hall, Charles carried the memory everywhere he went. It plagued him—worse than a virus, more painful than disease. There remained a bitter sting every time Charles's carriage approached the edge of the Surrey Gardens on Sundays, every time he glanced at Proverbs 3:33, and every time he closed his eyes at night and woke with the morning. He often wished himself dead. He refused to be comforted.

The memory, paired with the vicious attacks in the newspapers, were unceasing daggers to Charles's heart, hurling him into a stupor of grief. He wondered what he could have done differently on that tragic Sunday, questioning whether his own popularity had caused the death of seven innocent lives. The mere thought that he had, in some sense, caused the death of men and women on an occasion that should have been marked by peace and hope, absolutely devastated him.

The newspapers had slandered him, filling front pages with fabricated accounts of the tragic evening. "Mr. Spurgeon is a preacher who hurls damnation at the heads of his sinful hearers," accused the *Daily Telegraph*. "We would place in the hand of every right-thinking man, a whip to scourge from society the authors of such vile blasphemies as, on Sunday night, above the cries of the dead and the dying, and louder than the walls of misery from the maimed and suffering, resounded from the mouth of Spurgeon in the music hall of the Surrey Gardens."

❊ ❊ ❊

Charles rested from preaching and public ministry, seeking solitude in the New Forest, a few hundred kilometers west of London. He found his heart to be in a strange land, one with muted colors, and darkened sunrises. He told his grief to the flowers, and wept with the dew of the morning. His mind, like a wreck upon the sand, was incapable of its usual motion. His intelligence and ration, once a cup of tea to delightfully draw from, were pieces of broken glass that pierced and cut him. His

Bible, once his daily food, was now a barren cupboard with only stale bread. Prayer yielded no balm.

After a month of solitude, Charles finally returned to his pastoral and preaching duties, though the tragedy had prostrated and drained him to near death.

London also seemed to be spinning out of control. Quickly becoming the largest city in the world, its population had increased by three million people since Charles made his first trip to the British Empire's capital. Queen Victoria oversaw an aggressive expansion of the Empire, which now reached into India, Africa, and Southeast Asia—causing London to become a safe haven for immigrants and refugees. As the city grew in populace, it also grew in problems. Millions were living in overcrowded and unsanitary slums. Nearly half of the population found themselves in the lowest class, barely able to find work, food, or shelter. For years, the city's sewage had been dumped into the Thames River, overwhelming all the city streets and alleys with the stench of excrement, sickness, and death. The rich called it a mistake, the newspapers called it "The Great Stink of 1858," but the ones living on the streets and alleyways simply called it a disgrace. Low wages, high unemployment, poor public safety, high crime rates, overcrowded boroughs, terrible sanitary conditions, rampant homelessness, and every corner of London seemed to spin out of control.

"Wifey, I'm tired," Charles said to Susannah from behind a book.

"Of course you are, Charles. You very well ought to be." Her hand perfectly fit into his, and she loved the opportunity to distract him from his work by sliding her silken palm into his. Holding his hand made her feel safe, loved, and treasured. Susannah was perfectly happy on the few nights a week they could sink within the thick cotton sheets of their bed, reading books by candlelight, listening to the sweet snores of their boys at the foot of their bed. As Charles's influence in the city increased, so did the demands of his schedule. Most nights, Charles was away from his house—preaching, writing, serving the poor, visiting the sick, or counseling a weary church member. As a busy week of ministry had finally calmed, Charles enjoyed the company of his best friend and a quiet book.

"What are you reading?" whispered Susannah, soft as the moonlight that seemed to stick to the walls of their simple, quaint bedroom.

"Dickens," he said plainly, setting his eyes back on the slender book.

"Tell me about it."

"Stop talking, wifey," he whispered from the corner of his mouth.

"I will not stop talking, Reverend."

"You know I have a souring in my soul when you call me 'Reverend.'"

"Of course I do, Charles." She rolled towards him, still clasping his strong hand. "That's precisely why I call you *Reverend*."

"Wifey, call me something different. And, stop talking this instant." Charles turned the page and continued to read.

"Call you something else?" she asked as she closed her book and gathered her thoughts. "Alright. I shall call you—Tirshatha." She whispered it again, this time close to his ear, and much slower. "Tir—sha—tha. You want me to call you something different? I shall call you Tirshatha."

Charles, a lover of language, brought his open book to his chin, then rolled towards Susannah and asked with delight, "Tirshatha? What does it mean?"

"Your excellency," she said sarcastically.

"Hmm. I do like that, wifey. Tir—sha—tha. I like the sound of that, indeed." He offered a gruff chuckle, then rolled back towards his book.

"Tell me about your book, Tirshatha."

"It is the second novel by Charles Dickens, *The Parish Boy's Progress*. And I must say it has frozen my soul. It is a story of an orphan slave with an unfortunate life. He is just a boy, but he is sold and purchased, as one would do with a possession. He lives in London, in the worst of slums. The city is decrepit. And darkened. Poverty seems thick as a wool coat, and everyone seems to wear it. It drapes over their lives and holds them to the ground. And Oliver—he's the orphan boy—although he has a sturdy spirit, I can't help but read this as more than fiction. I think the Lord may be using it to stir the waters of my heart—to rile me up to see what's in plain view. Does that make any sense, Susie?"

"God often uses simple things to captivate our hearts. Your heart is a tablet, Charles. Perhaps He is trying to carve something within its edges," she said reassuringly.

"Yes, perhaps."

"Tell me more," she said.

Charles inhaled and exhaled deeply, then stroked his long beard that had nestled its way perfectly between the open book and the white sheets. "I find myself grieving. Grieving over the darkness that pervades and persists. Grieving over poverty and starved children. Grieving for those enslaved and imprisoned. I think of London, and America—oh, the awful things happening in America—where men have imposed a bitter prison on fellow image-bearers of Christ. And wifey, I simply cannot bear it. And, if were honest, I find myself grieving with my own lostness. My heart wrestles with its own bondage—those old shackles of depression and sadness that I have carried since a child."

"I see it, Charles. You are a strong man, but you carry more than most," she replied tenderly.

"Do I? Do I carry more than most? I hardly think so, Susie. I think the burden I carry is simply different, as it is invisible in its nature. No one sees it. In my study yesterday, I fell to my knees as a knot seemed to grow in my throat, choking my breath. There was no reason for it. But I felt an agony of grief beyond explanation," Charles stared at the ceiling as his heart vented with raw emotion. "At times, I feel as though I am as mire in the streets, the laughingstock of fools, the song of drunkards. And yet, in the same breath—even as I verbalize these things—I know I am more useful to the cause of Christ in my brokenness. And I desperately want to prefer Him to all the applause that man could ever give."

Charles, overcome with emotion, wiped his eyes with the cotton bed sheet under his book. "Ah, wifey. I am afraid it is much more than Charles Dickens at work here," he laughed. "Perhaps the Holy Ghost is stoking a fire in my bones I cannot look away from. It is as if the entire world, including my own, is being attacked by the grimy hands of evil. I have never hated that old Devil more than I do in this moment." He pulled the sheets to his eyes once again and waited for Susannah's reply.

"The people . . ." recited Susannah slowly from memory, "which sat in darkness saw *great* light. And to them which sat in the shadow of death—light is sprung up," she whispered.

"Matthew chapter four," smiled Charles.

"Yes. And, light *will* spring up, Charles. Perhaps our God is allowing you to *sit* with darkness for a moment, so that you may crave the springing of light even more. Light cannot be caged. It cannot be held or imprisoned."

"Light is sweet beyond expression, is it not?"

"Incredibly."

"I recall with such detail—when I was a boy—how all the world seemed against me. I wondered if the heavens were falling upon me, or the earth opening her mouth to swallow me up. I felt as if I were in a condemned cell, and all creation were the walls of my dungeon. And while deep in the shadows of death and darkness, the Lord showed me something that moved me unexplainably. I remember a man—Mr. Tagley—he showed me a beautiful baby fox. It was bright with red and orange, brilliant fur. It was wild and perfectly created by God, but it was trapped in a very tiny metal cage. And there was an iron lock on the door."

Silence hung in the air as Charles stared at the ceiling and Susannah patiently waited for the story to unfold.

"I—I just remember being so very confused as to why Mr. Tagley would cage something that should have been free. It *should* have been free. And to this day, I wish I could have burst into that cage, opened it, and freed it! I don't even know why I am recalling it. It was so long ago. When I asked my grandfather about Mr. Tagley's fox, he said something I've never forgotten. He said, 'Charles, sometimes the Lord shows us something that seems so wrong so we can *change it*. Other times, He shows us something that seems so wrong so it can *change us*.' I suppose, I desperately want both. I am chilled through my very marrow as I consider the great darkness of sin and evil that invades our world, and I want to break into every single brothel, kick in the doors, and free every soul that is in bondage to darkness."

"Yes," said Susannah confidently. As she wiped a bulging tear from the corner of his eye, she was grateful for the opportunity to be the only woman in the world to lay beside him in moments of weakness. The world knew Charles Spurgeon as a great orator, a man of other-worldly talents and abilities, but she knew him as a country boy from Essex—vulnerable, and in need of the love and support of a good woman.

In the silence, Charles thought of Jesus and His interaction with the oppressed, poor, and lowly. He was intensely moved as He knew Jesus was not *only* the Bread of Life, but also the man who literally passed out pieces of baked bread to hungry men, women, and children.

Charles was very aware of the social ills that seemed to plague his city and his people, and he had learned to assume a fatherly posture in his pastorship. Although he was primarily concerned with people's salvation, he was secondarily becoming more concerned with their redemption. The redemptive work of Christ had all kinds of social implications for him, as pastor. To him, the proper imitation of Christ meant having a deep love and empathy towards those in the city, especially those in desperation, poverty, and bondage. *If the hands of Christ had the audacity to reach towards the hurting,* Charles thought, *then surely must I! The Christian must always be a helper, one that reaches his hand out.*

"Charles," whispered Susannah, breaking the silence, "zealous saints are usually the ones who have experienced the greatest darkness before basking in the sweetness of light. They see all that Christ has done for them, so they *cling* to Him, and they never may have done so if they had not *sat* in the shadow of death."

As Charles's hand continued to envelop his bride's warm hand, he felt a rush of wind blow through the bedroom window, and the two began to shiver in the sheets.

"You are most right, wifey. And, goodness! It must have dropped ten degrees outside," said Charles as he rose from the bed to close the window. "There is a storm brewing tonight. I feel it." He gently closed the iron window frame, latched it, then stared into the darkened city street that barely glowed from nearby gas lamps cornering the intersection.

"Come to bed, Tirshatha." Susannah smiled, blew across the candle on her nightstand, then crawled between the sheets. By the time he kissed his two boys and patted the rise and fall of their chests, Susannah was fast asleep. With a final movement, Charles blew out his candle and wandered towards sleep.

❈ ❈ ❈

Above the city of London, hovering beyond the social storms of poverty and war, another storm began to cycle and brew. A deep fog fell upon the city, and a cool wind chased through her streets. Lightning scattered across the sky and ignited flashes of light that pierced the blackness like a dagger. Rain, hard as stones, pelted against rooflines then poured into the city streets of London. The entire city did its best to brace the terrible storm, but as each minute passed, more lightning scattered, more rain fell, more wind howled. Like war cannons from a nearby ship, thunder shook houses and rattled cathedral windows. The rain was loud enough to drown all the normal sounds of the city—the clanking of horse hoofs, the pub singing in midnight bars, the snoring of children, the trains that ran through the city center. As the war cannons continued to fire, one after another over the bow of hell's furious ship, the heart of London trembled.

Those without homes, the thousands of homeless in London, experienced the worst of the storm's fury. They climbed into garbage bins and frantically sought shelter beneath porches and exterior stairwells. Some huddled with shivering neighbors under cardboard boxes and tattered umbrellas, while others sought refuge under the strong oak trees of Hyde Park, the Crystal Palace Gardens, and Kensington Gardens. Beneath the shelter of an enormous oak tree in the corner of Clapham Common, twenty homeless children held tightly to each other— damp with summer rain, drenched in nervous tears. Hundreds of homeless children lived in the vast expanses of Clapham Common, and on this dreadful night, shelter had never been a more dire need.

Suddenly, a sound of great might cracked from the heavens and shot a thick bolt of lightning to the highest branch of the oak tree above the children. The tree burst into a ball of fire, and all of Clapham Common seemed to radiate from its ghastly glow. The children screamed in reverence, but compared to the volume of the storm, their voices seemed too small for most to notice.

"Children! Run! You must run!" yelled a man from a nearby sidewalk who often walked a different path on his way home from work, but on this stormy night had chosen to walk through

Clapham Common, under the covering of tall trees. "You must run! The tree will give way!"

He flapped his hands in the air, wide as an eagle, as he ran towards the terrified children under the blazing oak tree. With one swooping motion, he gathered the children and pushed their backs towards the open common area of the park. "You must run! Now, run!" Their tiny feet spattered against the mudded ground as they ran in all directions. "Now, keep running! You must run!"

The fiery tree above the man could no longer hold its heavy branches, and all at once they broke off, raced to the ground, and crushed the fragile body of the man below. Thunder cracked. Lightning pulsed. Cannons fired. Children ran. But, there in the middle of Clapham Common, during a terrible storm in the summer of 1859, laid a brave man who gave his life to save twenty homeless children from death.

The terrible storm eventually passed, and the bright sun reappeared to drain the flooded grounds of Clapham Common. The city streets resumed their bustling noise, and what was left of the oak tree finally cooled. When Charles heard the news of the man's death, and the salvation of twenty orphaned children, he was deeply moved. And though he didn't know the man personally, Charles was intrigued by the man's willingness to spare his life for children that most in London had long forgotten.

❇ ❇ ❇

"I am deeply saddened by your loss, madam," said Charles to the man's widow, as he held a cup of warm tea. "I can only imagine the pain you and your children must feel." He *could* imagine it, actually. He often thought of what it would be like for Susannah to deal with his death. He knew that God was faithful and would certainly be enough, but he frequently imagined what would happen after he died, who would take care of his wife and sons and his church.

"Mr. Spurgeon, I am under a great debt of gratitude that you and your elders would visit my house to offer your condolences," said the woman, showing little emotion. She was a simple woman who lived in a simple home, decorated with simple beauty, and since the death of her husband two weeks ago, the deacons of New Park Street Chapel had consoled her several times.

"My husband—he was a good man. He took great care of our sons and me. Ever since I became sick, he tirelessly cared for me. I am very sick, Mr. Spurgeon. Sick with the same disease that lives in many of us here in London."

"Yes—*cholera* is what they call it," said Charles with empathy.

"Yes. It is terrible. Before William died—that was my husband's name—my sickness was the worst thing I've ever known. But, now, the pain of his departure overshadows it all."

"Christ, have mercy," Charles whispered beneath his breath.

"I worry for our boys. We—I—have three. And, they are orphans now, Mr. Spurgeon. Orphans with a sick mother. And I don't know how we will get on. Or where we will get money. I do not know how we are to live—or if I want to. I cannot bear to live without my husband." She held her shaking hands close to her bosom and kept her eyes to the arms of her chair, barely able to move from the pains of cholera and sadness.

"I can say from the deepest recesses of my soul, that I think I have sorrowed—at certain periods this week—almost as much as if I had been myself the real mourner," he said as he placed his cup of tea, now cool, onto the table between their chairs. "It is a good thing for us to be sad, because when the springs that bind heart to earth are cut—then we soar." The woman nodded and glanced towards Charles who smiled tenderly. "The heart is made better by sorrow because it becomes more sensitive. In the house of mourning, we can hear every whisper of God."

"I desperately need to hear those whisperings, Mr. Spurgeon."

"Sister, hear me. In the darkest of darks, the light of Christ shines the brightest. And in the quietest of quiet, you hear the Savior say, '*I am with thee.*' He certainly is with you. And we—the Church—are with you. You mustn't raise your children alone. This is why you have the Church. Tomorrow, after services at the Music Hall, let me preach on that fatal spot in Clapham Common. Let me preach of the hope we have in Christ. And let us collect an offering for your family. Will you allow us?" he asked.

"Yes, Reverend. Thank you."

The whole incident sounded too much like the gospel of Jesus, and with a desire to see Jesus glorified and the man honored, Charles planned a memorial service in Clapham Common following next Sunday's service. They announced the memorial service in the city newspaper as well as from the pulpit, and on the afternoon of the memorial service, nearly ten thousand people gathered in Clapham Common. They placed a wagon beneath the tree to serve as a platform, and a small pulpit on the edge for Charles to give his sermon. There was a quiet anticipation as Charles made his way to the pulpit to address the crowd.

"It is not often that men are struck dead by lightning," preached Charles. "It is very rare that lightning strikes the earth, and one of our fellow creatures is launched into eternity. When such a solemn event occurs, we ought to hear the voice of God, and listen to what He says to us."

Charles turned to see the tree behind him, and pointed to what remained as he continued. "I thought, as I passed this tree a short time ago, what a sermon *it* might preach if *it* could speak. How the rustle of its leaves would forewarn us of the stealthy footsteps of death. And, as it towered to the skies, how it might be regarded as a finger directing us to look towards heaven and seek the Lord." He placed his hands upon the pulpit and continued. "We have much grief and sorrow today as we mourn the loss of a brother, willing to lay down his life for another. And, there is no solace for our griefs like the gospel of Jesus Christ. What sorrow has brought on a midnight . . . *grace* can transform it into noon.

"I wish I possessed the power to convey the great hope of Christ Jesus into the mental eyeballs of all my hearers today. But, I cannot, for I am also a man of great sorrow." Charles paused to take a deep breath and swore he could hear the cries of the trampled saints from the dreadful evening at the Music Hall. After shaking off the dark memories, he began again, "Today, on this sacred ground beneath this oak tree, I wish to point all who mourn—all of us—I wish to point us towards Heaven.

"To you, who are oppressed, to you, who are weary, pressed down, burdened, and hopeless. To the sick, the orphaned, the forgotten—this gospel of Christ is for you.

"Some of us were brought very low before we found the Savior. We were emptied like a dish that a man wipes and turns upside down. We had not even a drop of hope left in us. But, we rejoice in Christ today. Christ has caused light to shine on those who sat in darkness. He can do the same with you. Be of good courage—there is hope for you."

A warm brush of breeze blew through the Common as the crowd remained silent and still. As they listened, some of their darkened and sorrowful hearts began to lighten with the brightness of the Good News of Jesus being preached. Charles, full of empathy and full of boldness, continued to preach to the mass of people.

"Jesus of Nazareth—He is bone of our bone and flesh of our flesh. He touches you with the hand of His humanity, but He touches the Almighty with the hand of His Deity. He is man, and feels your needs—He is God, and is able to supply them. When

the Lord Himself—the One that made the heavens and digged
the foundations of the earth, comes to be your Savior—there
remains no difficulty in your being saved.

"What a solemn spot this is, here in Clapham Common.
It is said that we often walk over our own graves without ever
knowing it. There . . . in that tree . . . stands the monument of
the awfully sudden death of a fellow-creature. And let it so be
remembered.

"May God bless the widow. May He bless the orphans. May
He bless the sick and diseased. May He bless those enslaved to
every sort of bondage. You want no other light than that of Jesus!
Dream of no other! Give up self! Give up self-hope! Whether you
sink or swim, throw yourself into the sea of Christ's love. Rest
in Him and you shall never perish—neither shall any pluck you
from His hands."

Charles closed his eyes and bowed his head beneath the
brightness of the sun overhead before he said his last word,
"Amen."

At the close of the sermon, an offering was gathered. Within
a hundred wicker baskets, the crowd had given twenty-seven
pounds to the widow and her children—nearly two years of a
common man's salary. On that day in Clapham Common, in
front of an oak tree with splintered limbs and coal-black edges,
the heart of Charles Spurgeon was reignited once again to
preach the saving news of Jesus—the news that had the power
to comfort, heal, and free any man who believed.

CHAPTER 12

THANKSGIVING

Virginia, USA 1859

Mr. Bennett grunted and sighed as he slowly lowered himself into his leather-backed chair. The parlor, his favorite room in the old plantation house, was a cozy sitting room near the grand entrance of the Old House, just next to the dining room. Cherrywood panels lined the four walls, each with ornate carvings of flowers, hills, and trees, crafted by Richmond's finest artists, giving the room a sense of masculine elegance. In the center of the longest wall, a stone fireplace reached from floor to the ceiling, dwarfing the room with its wide stone facade. On the oak mantle, a loaded shotgun and a leather satchel of shells perched in front of a tattered Virginia State flag that hung from the ceiling. A fire had been started earlier in the evening by one of the servants, and the crackle and hiss of the flames soothed Mr. Bennett as it cast a warm, soft light into the cold, darkened parlor.

The room typically smelled of cigar smoke and brandy, but on this festive evening, the faint aromas of Thanksgiving turkey, corn stuffing, and pumpkin pie still lingered from the afternoon feast. The parlor, more than any other room in the house, was Mr. Bennett's sanctuary. When he wasn't drinking on the porch, he spent his evenings slouched in the chair of the parlor, far from the noise of the plantation and the nagging of his wife. A crystal decanter of brandy sat on the small wooden table next to his chair, and on most evenings, served as his only companion.

At first glance, Mr. Bennett seemed to be a happy man—one with every earthly comfort money could buy. But, unbeknownst to those around him, he possessed a broken and lonely soul. Like a man who tells ghost stories just to scare an old lover into his arms, he would say anything just to keep people near him. He craved friendship above all things, yet it was the one thing his money could never afford.

There was a faint knock on the door.

"Come in," belted Mr. Bennett above the crackle of the fire.

The door slowly opened as one of the servants stepped through the door, stopping just to the side of the entrance, standing at attention. Following close behind him was the Reverend Humphrey H. Kuber, the only Baptist preacher in Matthews County. Kuber was a man of wealth and influence, and he had joined the Bennetts for their annual Thanksgiving dinner on the plantation.

"Come in and sit," said Mr. Bennett, his hand motioning to the lonely leather chair next to his. "Would you like a drink?" Mr. Bennett held the decanter of brandy, and slowly poured the brown liquid into his own glass.

"No. Thank you," said the smiling reverend as he reclined in the chair. "Unfortunately, my religious convictions will not allow me the pleasures of strong drink. I *am* a man of conviction, after all, Mr. Bennett. Especially, on the day we give *thanks* to the Almighty."

Mr. Bennett nodded politely, and placed the decanter back on the table. "I've never understood the Baptists' misgivings with the creature comforts of the world," Mr. Bennett said with an exaggerated southern drawl. "Seems to me, men of the cloth could use a respite from the difficulties of this life."

Kuber laughed boisterously, placing both his hands on the top of his round belly, becoming painfully aware that he had eaten more than his share of pumpkin pie. Kuber did not want to offend his host by declining expensive brandy, but his convictions toward alcohol ran deep. He had seen more than one of his Baptist brethren fall prey to the sin of drunkenness, so for him, it was better to avoid it altogether.

"Before I leave," Kuber quickly changed the subject, "I wanted to extend my gratitude for a lovely evening. It has been quite some time since I've eaten such a wonderful meal. My dear wife . . . bless her soul. She is a wonderful woman, charming and lovely, with many abilities. But the art of cooking is not a gifting the good Lord saw fit to bestow upon her."

The two men chuckled and continued chatting around the dwindling fire as Thomas stood stiffly next to the door of the parlor. He listened, absently, to the two men's idle banter. He was fully prepared to stand there for the rest of the evening, if necessary, to offer assistance to Mr. Bennett and his guest, if the need were to arise. And although his legs hurt from standing since breakfast, Thomas didn't mind his evening responsibilities. There were many worse assignments that Quentin Ellis could have given him.

Life had been different on the plantation since that fateful night in the summer of 1857 when Thomas had been found by Jesus. Thomas spoke to anyone who would listen about the peace and love that had replaced the hate and torment of his heart. The best way Thomas knew how to describe it was that a great burden had been lifted from him. Since childhood, his constant companions were fear, grief, and loneliness—but all of those had been replaced by the sweet love of his Lord and Savior. Through Jesus, Thomas had been given the greatest gift a man could ever be given—peace in the midst of whatever circumstances life may bring. Although Thomas was still bound by the fetters of servitude and the evils of slavery, his soul was free. He had found peace.

Thomas often thought about freedom from Mr. Bennett and Quentin Ellis—what it would be like to be his own man, free to go and do as he pleased. But unlike his childhood, he was no longer consumed with hatred towards the men that held him in chains. Thomas had memorized a verse of Scripture that he had found to be more real and true than the plantation air he breathed.

When the Son sets you free, you are free indeed.

"I have an important question for you, Reverend," Mr. Bennett asked loudly, as he leaned to the front of his chair and stared intently at his guest. "Something has come to my attention that concerns me greatly, and you might be the man to calm my anxieties."

"Alright. Do tell."

"Well, I have heard about a pastor in England. I believe his name is Spurgeon." Mr. Bennett continued as Kuber listened and nodded his head. "He pastors a large church in London—a very popular man. And it seems that his sermons are published and read by thousands, even here in the southern states. Have you heard of him?"

Rev. Kuber sat forward in his chair and grumbled, "Yes. I have heard of that pompous, hell-deserving Englishman." He shook his head with disgust. "Reverend Spurgeon . . . well, he used to be a hero of sorts for me. I even had the poor judgment of preaching one of his sermons on the doctrine of Calvinism in my own pulpit some years ago."

"Tell me then, have you heard of these blasphemous sermons he preaches?" wondered Mr. Bennett. "Sermons and articles where he preaches *against* slavery? Calling it *evil*?"

From the edge of the room, Thomas continued to remain still, but listened to the gentlemen's conversation with intrigue.

"I have. And, I received an anonymous letter containing a copy of the deceitful nonsense just a few days ago," said Kuber. "Turns out, Mr. Spurgeon preached an entire sermon, protesting the deaths that occurred at the slave uprising at Harpers Ferry."

"The United States Marines did us a favor by killing those vile abolitionists," said Mr. Bennett with disgust in his voice. He slid back in his chair and took a giant slurp from his nearly empty glass.

"Precisely," replied Kuber. "I read the sermon in its entirety and I was appalled at its utter audacity. Spurgeon claimed that it would be better for a thousand unions to be dissolved than for *us* to own a few slaves in the peace and quiet of the southern states of the American Union. What in hell's fury would cause a *white* preacher to take the side of colored people?"

"It's nonsense!" screamed Mr. Bennett, slapping the table next to him, knocking over his brandy, and nearly knocking the decanter to the floor. Hurrying towards the table, Thomas wiped the spilled drink from the table, and poured a new glass for Mr. Bennett. "I've got it, boy," he yelled at Thomas, shooing him back to the edge of the parlor.

"What's more egregious," interrupted Rev. Kuber, "is that people are listening. Lots of people. Spurgeon is deeply respected in America, and I fear that his satanic drivel might find its way into the hearts of the naïve and uneducated people of Virginia. I simply don't understand how any true Christian or follower of our meek and humble Savior could for one moment entertain, much less give utterance to, such heresy that prevents me from owning a black man."

"Indeed," Mr. Bennett agreed heartily. "That sort of incendiary language will most certainly prove more dangerous than any uprising led by men like John Brown at Harpers Ferry."

Thomas was anxious to his bones as he listened to the gentlemen in the parlor. *Who is this Reverend Spurgeon?* he thought. His exposure to white people had been limited to the ones on the plantation and the handful that he had met on his supply trips into town, but every white person he had ever met owned slaves. Most of Thomas's friends were of the opinion that few white people would even make it to Heaven, so Thomas tended to agree.

However, this preacher sounded very different, for Thomas had never in all of his life conceived of a white preacher with the conviction to stand for the black man.

"What time is it, boy?" yelled Mr. Bennett as he stoked the wood in the stone fireplace. Thomas leaned into the hallway to count the numbers on the wooden clock that hung on the wall. It took him several times to make sure he read the time correctly. "What time is it?" yelled Mr. Bennett a second time.

"Sir, seven thirty-three, to be exact." Thomas responded, leaning back to his silent post next to the door.

"It's about time for you to get going, Reverend Kuber. You do have a long trek home," Mr. Bennett said plainly.

"It is. But what do you say about you and me riding over to the town square for a few minutes?" asked Kuber as he stood to his feet and pushed his arms through his winter coat.

"Right now?"

"Something there you'd probably enjoy seeing, my good friend."

"You've piqued my interest." Mr. Bennett turned to Thomas and said, "Boy, get my coat. And get the carriage ready. You're taking us to the town square."

"Yes, sir." Thomas handed Mr. Bennett his coat from the hook near the door, then hurried to get the horse and carriage ready.

❊ ❊ ❊

It was a fifteen-minute carriage ride to the center of town, and as soon as Thomas turned the corner of the square, the blazing brightness of the fire warmed his face and caused his eyes to squint. There in the center of the town square, a bonfire was built on the public lawn that sprawled between the courthouse and the city jail. Nearly as tall as the two-story courthouse, the fire raged and soared relentlessly. Several hundred men, women, and children stood around the edge of the lawn, their shadows prancing like turkeys as the blazing fire continued to erupt. All the buildings that surrounded the lawn were brightened by the bonfire. As Mr. Bennett and Rev. Kuber exited the carriage, they, too, were lit with an orange radiance.

"What is this, Kuber?" asked Mr. Bennett with wide eyes. Thomas, who had just slid from the top of the carriage, also stood with wide eyes towards the fire.

"This? This . . . is what we do with European propaganda that tells good Christian-folk they can't own a slave." Rev. Kuber held Thomas by the elbow and whispered into his ear, "You'll probably need to see this too. Come with us."

The three men slowly walked across the street towards the bonfire in the center of the public lawn, as the horse and carriage fell into the darkened Virginia night behind them. Once closer, Thomas noticed the townspeople were not merely watching the bonfire, but they were throwing things into the fire. Men carried stacks of newspapers, then hurled them to the fire, and shouted with joy. Women carried pamphlets and flyers, along with books and other publications, and threw them into the fire

as well. The crowd cheered every time another stack of papers
and books ignited in the bonfire.

They continued to walk all the way to the edge of the fire,
then stood just a few feet from its edge. The warmth scorched
their faces, and they cowered their heads from the heat. An
anxious knot grew in Thomas's gut as he stood between his
master and Rev. Kuber, only a few feet from an intensely raging
fire. In earlier years, Thomas may have taken the opportunity
to push Mr. Bennett into the fire. But since the peace of Jesus
had overtaken him, the ugly thought merely crossed his mind
and quickly fell aside. He wondered if the men had brought him
there to push *him* into the fire. Perhaps this was their plan the
whole time. Thomas took a deep breath and stared into the leaping flames in front of him.

"You brought me to a book burning?" Mr. Bennett asked
Kuber.

"A Charles Spurgeon book burning!" Kuber laughed and
smiled with satisfaction. "They are happening all over the
South. On plantations, outside of courthouses, in front of
schools. Many of us have had enough! His writing is no longer
welcome here. And we're not just burning books. We're burning
anything that he's ever written." He pulled a newspaper clipping
from the inner pocket of his coat, then turned to Thomas and
asked politely, "What's your name, boy?"

"Johnson. Thomas Johnson, sir."

"Well, Thomas Johnson. I believe you should have the
honor."

Kuber slid the folded newspaper article into Thomas's hand
and nudged him towards the fire. Sweat began to seep through
Thomas's coat, as he was only a few feet from the raging flames.
"Go on, boy. Read it. Then, toss it into the fire with the rest of
them."

"He can't read!" said Mr. Bennett with disgust. "Give me
that, boy." He pulled the article from Thomas's hand, unfolded

it, then read aloud the heading in big black print. "The Rev.
Charles Spurgeon," he yelled over the volume of the fire and the
cheering crowd, "condemns American Christians for tolerating
slavery in the southern states."

Thomas was truly astonished that a preacher could cause
such an outrage from so far away. His sermons were bold enough
to spark a two-story fire in the middle of the town square in
Richmond, Virginia. His written words were provocative enough
to stoke the anger of a hundred townspeople in the late hours of
a holiday evening. The ink of his pen was mighty enough to fill
books, newspapers, articles, sermons, and pamphlets. Thomas
couldn't believe that this preacher's message of freedom—physical freedom from institutional bondage—made it all the way
from Spurgeon's desk in England to Thomas's cold hands in
Richmond, Virginia.

"Throw it in, Thomas," said Mr. Bennett, shoving the newspaper article back into Thomas's hands.

Mr. Bennett and Rev. Kuber watched Thomas crumple up
the newspaper article and toss it into the raging bonfire. The
paper erupted into flames, and almost immediately turned to
ash. Filled to the brim with gratitude, Thomas silently thanked
the Lord for the white preacher who had the audacity to con-
front slavery from the other side of the world.

The crowd continued to throw sermons and books into the
fire, pausing only to warm their hands with its comfortable heat.
The three men turned away from the fire, silently making their
way back to the horse and carriage, and as Thomas turned to
look at the bonfire once more, he realized the profound beauty
of a cold Thanksgiving night brightly lit and tenderly warmed
by sermons on fire.

CHAPTER 13

THE FOULEST BLOT

London, England 1863

Few ministers of the gospel undertook a workload comparable to that of Charles Spurgeon. He was always on the move, always growing and learning, always reading, always listening. Waking at six o'clock every morning, Charles tried his best to drink from the Scriptures, but was often distracted with the many tasks that seemed to overwhelm him. He lived with the constant tension of knowing all that had to be done, and his need to posture himself before God with patience and submission. The task of pastoring and the weight of ministry were too much for a mortal to bear, and on the days that Charles led with his own energy, he buckled under the burden.

New Park Street Chapel found the means to invest in their own permanent building, and although Charles missed the grandeur of the Surrey Gardens Music Hall, the church continued to flourish at their new location in Elephant and Castle in Southwark, London. Charles and the congregation voted to rename the church Metropolitan Tabernacle, and in March of 1861, his congregation filled the newly constructed six-thousand-seat auditorium, with several services throughout the day. Its appearance was not extravagant, but it was beautiful. Charles insisted the design be influenced by Greek architecture, as the New Testament was written in Greek, and the exterior consisted of a massive portico, lined with six soaring columns. Although it contained fewer seats than the music hall, the large construct was substantially bigger. The project was paid for in cash, and when completed, no building in London surpassed its beauty or height.

Charles found himself exhausted after overseeing the critical move from the music hall to the Tabernacle. "Kill yourselves with work, and then pray yourselves alive again," he often told the men he discipled, laughing from deep within his gut. Anyone who heard Charles say this knew he was hardly kidding, as he often allowed overworking to lead to physical decline. Still, Charles pressed on and dealt with the tension. Charles firmly believed that an easy life of ministry surely led to a different kind of death, so he chose to spend every ounce of his life doing what he was created to do—labor for the kingdom of God—even if it killed him.

Throughout the years, Charles had grown in his love for discipling young men, and rarely a moment passed when he wasn't surrounded by two or three, telling them stories of revival and Christ's atoning work. Every meal was an opportunity to invite a younger fellow into his home, and Susannah never refused the opportunity to host students, as she also loved to mentor and teach younger women.

As Susannah warmed pots of potatoes and beef with young English girls, Charles would often sit at the dining room table, with either of his sons bouncing on his knee, answering questions from those he discipled and placing bits of wisdom within their teachable minds. "Young men that are strong—overcome the wicked one and fight for the Lord while you can! You will never regret having done all that lies in you for our blessed Lord and Master." The younger men listened, nodded, and jotted down notes as Charles continued to press further into their souls. "And, crowd as much as you can into every day—postpone no work until tomorrow."

As focused as Charles was on teaching young men, he never once neglected the discipleship of his two sons, Charles and Thomas. He loved them with a fierce affection, second only to Jesus and Susannah, and in that order. He knelt by their bed every night and prayed, "God, may these boys increase in wisdom and stature and favor with God and man."

While he preached, his boys often sat behind the platform in the large plush chairs previously reserved for deacons. Now that they were old enough, Charles took joy in kicking the deacons off the platform in order that his children could sit in the seats closest to him. He always wanted them near, so with silver pencil case and pocket book in hand, they wiggled and squirmed through long sermons, scribbling notes and drawing cartoons of their father preaching in Metropolitan Tabernacle. After the final hymn was sung, they stood at the back of the music hall and waited for their father to rub their heads and ask the same question he asked every Sunday.

"What did you learn today, boys?"

"Not I, but Christ," they said in unison.

"Good boys!" he said with a glee only a proud father could possess.

"Father," asked young Charles one Sunday, "what is the *secret* of your magic powers?"

"Magic powers?" asked Charles with a look of puzzle. "What on earth do you mean—*magic powers*?"

"Father! You're the Prince of Preachers! The Prime Minister of England!" said young Charles jumping up and down. "Yes! You have *magic* powers! All of London knows it, Father!" joined

Thomas. "Won't you tell us this instant? What are your magic powers?"

Charles knelt to the ground, gathered his boys to his broad chest, and whispered in their ears, "Not I, but Christ." Charles kissed their cheeks and soared with gladness as they ran off towards their mother with a newfound discovery.

Neither of Charles's sons ever wondered if they were loved and treasured by their father. His example, his consistency, his generous love, his fearless devotion to God and His Word— they were all on par with his fatherhood. And although young Charles and Thomas would not be able to articulate it until much later in their adult lives, they understood the secret of his power: he had been with Jesus, and Jesus lived in him.

❊ ❊ ❊

The more Charles spent time with Jesus, the more concerned he became about every single man and woman on the planet coming to know Him as Savior. With the expansive use of the printing press in the nineteenth century, Charles's words had the ability to reach eyes and touch hearts of those who had no opportunity to visit his church. Charles sincerely loved the use of printer's ink, and realized it was an untapped avenue for catching the eye of readers and striking their hearts with the life-giving words of the gospel. Men would scribble notes from his sermon as he preached it, then Charles and Susannah would edit the manuscript before sending it off to the printers to duplicate. Soon, sermons and tracts were scattered throughout the United Kingdom as his congregants went from house to house, selling if they could make a sale, giving them away if readers were unable to afford them.

On one occasion, while Charles was preaching, a man who was supposed to transcribe the sermon didn't show up. After preaching, he was disappointed and angry, feeling as though his sermon had been wasted.

"Susie, there was no one to record the sermon!" he said with frustration after the conclusion of the service. "How will others hear?" His eyes roared and his head shook with dismay.

"But, Joseph Harrald was here, Charles," she whispered calmly.

"Harrald? Who is Harrald?" he asked.

"William Joseph Harrald. He's a young man—can't be over twenty years of age. But he never misses a word when you preach. He's at nearly every service. Writes it all down." Susannah slid her hand into his, pulling him towards a crowd of people still mingling near the back of the Tabernacle. "Come, let's go and meet him."

As they walked closer, Charles noticed the young man sitting next to a leather satchel, plump with sheets of white paper.

"Mr. Harrald?" asked Charles as he pulled his hand from Susannah and extended it towards Joseph.

"Yes, Reverend Spurgeon." Joseph stood, smiled, and greeted his hand warmly. "I appreciated your sermon today, Pastor." Joseph's appearance was neat and tidy; his hair groomed and properly greased. Charles appreciated tidiness, and was struck by Joseph's seemingly put-together countenance.

Charles tipped his head at the young man, respectfully, then set his eye towards the leather satchel. "My wife tells me you write all of the sermons on paper? Word for word?"

"That's correct," offered Joseph as he nodded his head and revealed his perfectly straight teeth through a proud grin. "I've found it the best way to retain the information. I can hardly remember the text unless I write it all down. Would you care to see?"

Charles carefully untied the leather strap and, to his amazement, every single word from his sermon had been perfectly transcribed onto the bright linen paper. As he flipped through the pages, Charles saw sermon notes from weeks and months prior, each perfectly written as he had preached. Charles laughed with an excitement that chased his anger away, then closed the satchel and embraced Joseph with a bear-like hug. "I need a secretary to stand by my side, Mr. Harrald. Would you be willing?"

Without thinking, Joseph replied with a sturdy, "Yes!" The seemingly random encounter after a church service soon became a necessary relationship in helping the sermons of Charles Spurgeon make their way from spoken word to printed text. Thus, Harrald became one of Charles's most trusted helpmates.

❋ ❋ ❋

"Charles, what do you think of the increased sales of your sermons in America?" asked Joseph from the corner of Charles's study in the Tabernacle. Every Monday, Joseph transcribed sermons while Charles studied and wrote at his desk.

"I suppose it's a very good thing," mumbled Charles as he continued to spill ink onto a half-written page. Without lifting his pen, he continued. "The printing press is the mightiest agency on earth for good or evil," answered Charles.

"Do you really believe that?" inquired Joseph.

"Absolutely."

"When you say that the printing press is the mightiest agency on earth, what do you mean?" asked Joseph, pressing further.

Frustrated by the distraction, but eager to give a proper answer, Charles set down his pen and pushed the paper to the center of his desk. "Listen. God has made the printing press to be a great agent in the world's evangelization. And, the great final battle of the world will be fought—not with guns and swords—but with types and presses."

"You know that some are burning your sermons in America. We should continue to print, and print more?" Joseph asked,

innocently. At the time, his sermons sold almost a million copies every year in America. At book shows around the world, one
thousand copies of his sermons were sold every single minute.
But, the more Charles wrote about slavery, the more books were
burned in the bonfires outside jail yards, plantations, and book
stores throughout the Confederacy.

"We must keep printing, Joseph," he answered with a curious grin. "America is in as great of a need for the gospel as
the United Kingdom—perhaps more. With the evils of sin and
slavery still persistent, God speed the cylinders of the Christian
printing press!" Joseph rose from his tiny desk in the corner of
the study and sat in the armchair next to Charles's desk as he
listened. "The gears of the printing press must never stop churning, printing sermon after sermon, releasing the truths of the
gospel to every corner of the world. Including the United States
of America!"

"Are you prepared for more criticism?"

"I can only prepare for what is in front of me, Joseph."
Charles gathered the paper and pen and continued to write. As
Charles became more outspoken against slavery in the southern
states, he was attacked with more criticism than he could have
ever imagined. He never strategized, plotted, or schemed to be
an advocate for the freedom of American slaves, but the more
love he had for the Good News, the more hatred ensued for
American "Christians" who justified it.

For months, Joseph had read stories from American newspapers covering the war between the northern and southern
states. It seemed violence and war infected every story coming
from America. Joseph had also received hundreds of letters and
articles personally sent to Charles. There were stacks of similar letters on Joseph's desk, and although he read every one of
them, he only shared a few with Charles, shielding him from the
most vicious of verbal attacks.

"Mr. Spurgeon is a beef-eating, puffed-up, vain, over-righteous pharisaical, English blab-mouth," wrote the *New York Herald.*

"Mr. Spurgeon, you are a fat and vulgar man with sleek hair and soiled teeth. You ought not to meddle in the affairs of the good and godly Baptists of the Southern States of America, and should tend to your own matters in England," one letter read.

"We invite all persons in Montgomery, Alabama, who possess copies of the sermons of the notorious Spurgeon, to send them to the jail yard to be burned on next Friday, this day of the week. A subscription is also on foot to buy of our booksellers all copies of said sermons now in their stores, to be burned on the same occasion," wrote an Alabama newspaper.

Charles, noticing that Joseph was at war with silent thoughts in the armchair, set down his pen, pushed the paper once again to the center of his desk, then interrupted the mysterious silence.

"Joseph, let me tell you a story." Charles adjusted his chair and turned to Joseph, lighting the end of a fresh cigar. "Do you remember, just a few months ago, when Susannah and I traveled to Switzerland?"

"Yes. For a moment of rest and vacation."

"Ah, yes." Charles puffed from his cigar, then continued to talk as swirls of white smoke crept from his lips and twirled along the thick hairs of his beard. "The mountains of Switzerland are simply majestic. They seem to loom over everything, like an endless watchtower. And these mountains stand along the edge of a swiftly flowing river that cuts through the country—the Meuse River, they call it. The river was so narrow and shallow, that as our steamboat floated along, it drove up great waves upon the banks on either side. In some parts, along the river, there were people washing ironstone at the water's edge to separate ore from the earth."

Joseph reclined in his chair, deeply interested in the story. Sometimes when Charles told stories, he told them with such vivid detail that one could easily imagine themselves being right there next to him. "Susie and I, there on a steamboat, were *wildly* fascinated with the beauty of the mountains, and the river—it was all very delicious. But there within the brilliance of it all, I must say I saw the most prevailing of evils my eyes had seen. When the barges of ironstone came to the shore to unload, *slaves* bore the heavy baskets on their backs. Men and children, but mostly women. It was an awful sight, Joseph."

Charles cleared his throat and dropped his eyes to the ground.

"If there were coals or bricks to be carried, the slaves did it. They carried everything, and their masters sat perfectly still, and seemed to *enjoy* seeing them work. When we came to a landing place, if the rope was to be thrown off so that the steamboat might be secured, there was always a slave woman to run and seize it. And nearby, there stood a big, lazy fellow to give directions as to how she should do it. They were worn, working as slaves, as their masters stood on the edge and smiled with delight."

Joseph remained silent.

"Slavery is to be *absolutely* deplored. What barbarity dooms someone to the whip, to till the fields, carry heavy burdens, *and* be the drudges of civilization?" Charles shook his head in contempt and tapped the end of his cigar onto the ashtray on the corner of his desk.

"And, what do you say with slavery in America, as most slave owners would also say they are Christians? How can a man be *'Christian'* and own slaves? I cannot understand this," Joseph sat forward in his chair, leaning towards Charles.

"Some who claim the name of Christ in that awful Confederacy—" Charles's voice loudened with a more serious tone, "seem to regard slavery with a wonderful *complacency*. They have so accustomed themselves to wrap it up in soft phrases that they lose sight of its real character."

"How do you mean?" Joseph was a sponge, soaking up every bit of wisdom and knowledge as Charles continued to unpack the issue.

"They refer to slavery as simply a 'peculiar institution.' But, they forget of what its peculiarity consists. It is *indeed* a peculiar institution! Just as the Devil is a peculiar angel! And his demons are peculiar villains. As their hell is a *peculiarly* hot place!"

Charles slammed his fist on the desk and a spark of righteous anger ignited from his eyes. It was a posture that few saw, as most of the time he tempered his anger with charm. But sometimes righteous anger is the only appropriate reaction for a man of conviction who sees something so profoundly evil right in front of him. Charles paused, took a deep breath, then pushed himself from his chair and walked towards the small bookshelf in the adjacent corner of the study.

"For my part, Joseph, I consider such miserable tampering with the 'peculiar institution of slavery' to be the most *scandalous* of sins, and I will hold no communion of any sort with those who are guilty of it."

Running his fingers along several spines of books, he finally stopped at a worn Bible and pulled it from the shelf. It was heavy and cool in his warm hands. "For centuries," he continued with a quieter and more somber tone, "men have tried hard to make these Holy Scriptures support their villainous and disgraceful acts. But human slavery is the *very thing* which defies the great kingdom of God. And it is *unknown* to the Word of God. When you've been with Jesus, you find it impossible to justify. The men who *dare* find Scripture to justify the buying and selling of souls ought to be damned."

Silence once again filled the small study, as Joseph leaned backward in his chair and pressed his hands over his teary eyes. Charles neatly returned the Bible to its place on the bookshelf and walked to the desk to pull another mouthful of smoke from his cigar.

A perfect marriage of holy anger and incredible sadness filled Charles as he slumped into his chair, slid it forward, and picked up his pen. He slid a blank sheet of paper from the edge of his desk, and Joseph watched the pen of Charles Spurgeon inscribe three impassioned sentences.

Slavery is the foulest blot that ever stained a nation.

America is in many respects a glorious country, but it may be necessary to teach her some wholesome lessons.

It would be better that the North and South should be rent asunder, and the States of the Union shivered into a thousand fragments, than slavery should be suffered to continue.

With that, Charles neatly folded the paper in half and placed it into Joseph's hands. He stood from the desk, tugged his cotton vest into place, extinguished his cigar, then pushed the chair to the desk before walking to the study door.

"What should I do with this?" Joseph asked with wide, curious eyes.

Charles gripped the doorknob and turned to Joseph, "We have no magic power, Joseph. But we have Christ and His gospel. *It* has the power to break the vilest of darkness. Send it to the printing press. May it reach anyone in the southern states of America who dare listen."

CHAPTER 14

EMANCIPATION

Richmond, Virginia 1865

Sunset came unmercifully to a city caught in the violent throes of death. Richmond, Virginia, the capital of the Confederate States of America, was on fire in the spring of 1865. The light of the sun, fading above the hills of the city, mixed ominously with the glow from the flames that leapt above the tobacco factories and mills set on fire earlier in the day. Defeated men, hell-bent on the Union Army never receiving the spoils of their life's work, would rather light their property on fire than ever hand it over to the North. The news that General Grant's army had taken St. Petersburg spread like the Black Death through the city, and the evacuation of Richmond, Virginia, had begun in earnest.

Pack mules, wagons, and horse-drawn carriages, driven by some of Richmond's finest citizens, lined the bridge that crossed the James River. People were desperate to leave the city, preferring exile into the unknown rather than captivity and imprisonment by the army of the North. Smoke from the inflamed city covered the river like a grey cloud, making the escape all the more difficult. The once proud and defiant people of Richmond covered the faces of their children with blankets, partly to protect their lungs from the grey smoke, but more important, so they would have no memory of the fateful day when the evil Union Army invaded their beloved city.

Atop a hill just north of the city, Thomas and Ezekiel sat quietly inside the opening of their army tent, fire crackling at their feet, watching the chaos and listening to ever-growing sounds of cannon fire echoing in the distance. Through the clouds and smoke that covered the valley below them, great explosions of light erupted over the city, followed by seconds of silence. Then, to their surprise, the sound of another factory—Richmond's lifeblood—came to a booming, explosive end.

Earlier in the year, Mr. Bennett's son volunteered for the Confederate Army, and Thomas and Ezekiel were sent with him as personal servants. Their days and nights were exhausted at the whim of their new master—cooking meals, cleaning weapons, and returning the buttons of the young man's grey uniform to a brassy shine. Mr. Bennett's son was adamant about the appearance of his uniform. Even though the grey wool of his jacket was torn and dirty, at least his buttons shined. Thomas spent many evenings with turpentine and an oily rag, ensuring his master looked his best when reveille was sounded the next morning.

Over the course of the year, Thomas had seen and experienced more horror than he ever imagined possible. On numerous occasions, his master's unit had gone into the heat of combat, so Thomas became intimately acquainted with the realities of what the South called "The War of Northern Aggression." Thomas and Ezekiel never saw the battle themselves, but worse, they were eyewitnesses to the carnage caused by cannons and bullets when the soldiers returned to camp. Thomas's quarters were only a few yards from the unit's hospital tent, and on many nights he fell asleep to the sound of men screaming in agony as Confederate surgeons sawed at the tender bones that would cause limbs to disappear forever.

The screams of these young men, many of whom were teenagers, haunted Thomas for the rest of his life. Years later, lying peacefully in his bed but unable to sleep, Thomas still heard their screams for relief. The source of their haunting came, not from the agony itself, but from the impetus of their suffering. He could not fathom what would cause a young man to suffer such great loss for a cause as unjust as the preservation of slavery. Why would these men, many of whom had never owned slaves, sacrifice their lives to maintain an institution that had caused him a lifetime of pain and indignity?

During calmer days, Mr. Bennett's son tried to explain the Southern motivations for the war to Thomas. "The North," he said with a condescending voice, "has no right to impose its will on the southern states. We're not fighting a war to preserve slavery, as much as we're fighting for sovereignty. Ain't nobody gonna tell us what we can or cannot do. That's why we fight," he said emphatically.

Thomas remained unconvinced. As a follower of Jesus, Thomas abhorred the violence that led to so much human suffering on both sides of the conflict, but on the other hand, Thomas hoped the North would prevail in granting him the earthly freedom he had longed for since his youth.

"It won't be long now," Ezekiel said to Thomas, staring at the raging fire that was once Richmond. "The sounds of cannon fire are getting closer. That means the Union Army ain't far away." Years of hard labor and long days had taken their toll on Ezekiel. His eyes sagged towards his strong cheekbones, while grey streaked through his hair and beard. A nervous excitement welled up within Thomas as he listened to Ezekiel explain what was going on. "We are near the end, boy."

Since the beginning of the Civil War between the northern and southern states of America, Thomas had anticipated, even imagined this exact moment. The sights and sounds of Richmond's demise were unfolding right before his bewildered eyes.

As darkness continued to fall, a hurried rush of activity began to envelope the Confederate camp. Horses shifted nervously at their posts, neighing and crying, adding to the sounds of hurried chaos around them. Officers moved about franticly, shouting orders to their men, calling for their units to ready themselves for one last stand against the Union forces. Other soldiers, filled with fear, spoke in hushed whispers to plan their escape from the impending invasion of Grant's army. There was a general sense among the camp that all was not well.

"Should we make a run for it?" Thomas whispered, drawing close to his friend. His face, dirtied from weeks in the camp, revealed a curious mixture of fear and excitement. "Ain't none of these white folks gonna even know we're gone. I ain't seen the master in hours. He might already have skee-daddled as far as I know. Let's slip off down this hill and cross those ramparts right down there." Thomas pointed into the valley at the wall of wooden spikes and twisted metal that lined the banks of the James River, serving as Richmond's last line of defense. He knew the terrain well, since he and Ezekiel spent several weeks of the winter digging ditches and building wooden barricades to protect the city from invasion.

"Calm yourself, boy. It ain't our time just yet," Ezekiel firmly spoke to Thomas, still looking through the opening of the tent, nervous that the conversation would fall upon the wrong ears. Even though Thomas was by now a full-grown man, Ezekiel still called him "boy." It was a term of affection, not condescension, for Thomas was the closest thing to a son that Ezekiel would ever have.

"Nope, it ain't our time just yet." Ezekiel stood and walked towards the back of the large canvas tent that had been their home for months. Faint light from an oil lantern cast a warm, orange glow on the inside of the tent, illuminating Ezekiel's path to a trunk that lay at the foot of his bed. The old wooden box contained all of the old man's worldly possessions and its metal hinges creaked as Ezekiel opened it. Reaching inside and shifting its contents, Ezekiel finally found his well-worn and tattered Bible. Ezekiel carried the Bible to Thomas, who still sat at the entrance of the tent, and without speaking, Thomas quietly opened its pages to the Old Testament, to the book of Daniel.

The eleventh chapter of Daniel was a section of Scripture that both men treasured at the end of a long day of service, as it held within its verse hope—a hope that only a man in bondage could appreciate.

Light from the nearby fire and the gas-lit lantern illuminated the Bible's pages as Thomas murmured the verses, just loud enough for Ezekiel to hear.

"'Now in those times,'" he read methodically, "'there shall many stand up against the king of the south: also the robbers of thy people shall exalt themselves to establish the vision, but they shall fall.'"

"That's right," groaned Ezekiel as he listened.

"'So the king of the north shall come, and cast up a mount, and take the most fenced cities: and the arms of the south shall not withstand, neither his chosen people, neither shall there be any strength to withstand.'"

"That king of the north sure does sound a whole lot like President Lincoln," laughed Ezekiel from the corner of the tent. The men didn't know the original intended meaning of the verses in the book of Daniel, but they couldn't help but see Abraham Lincoln as a similar sort of person that they read in the Bible. Throughout the years of war, they had heard many stories of Lincoln—heard him to be a man who had the courage and wisdom to challenge the ruin and disgrace of slavery. After all, he was willing to shed the blood of a nation to see the demise of slavery in the South. To them, these verses held the promise that President Lincoln, the "King of the North," would over-throw the forces of the South and bring freedom to the millions of men, women, and children who were bound in chains.

"'And the arms of the south shall not withstand,'" Ezekiel repeated quietly, as he looked towards Thomas and stared past him into the smoky distance.

"That's the Word of the Lord," Thomas said, closing his Bible and placing his hand on the shoulder of his friend. "Our God has been faithful to us all these years, so let's just wait and see if the Lord shines bright for us tomorrow morning."

With that, the two men closed their tent and crawled onto their cots, unaware that this was the very last night that either of them would ever spend as a slave.

Thomas's sleep was fitful and restless, and after what seemed like minutes, he arose to the sound of a young Confederate cor-poral yelling his name. "Thomas! Wake up!" The young soldier kicked his cot, shaking him from sleep. "Get up! The Union forces are right outside the city. President Davis himself done took off last night. Ain't no reason for any of us to stay any longer in this godforsaken place."

The soldier turned and ran out of the tent, continuing to yell as he went from tent to tent. "Wake up! Get up! They're here!" he yelled. The camp quickly grew from chaos to utter panic. Young Confederate soldiers ran in every direction, desperate to escape from the haunting reality—the Confederacy had fallen. All was lost.

Ezekiel and Thomas sat up quickly in their cots and stared at each other for a long moment. As their eyes met, slow smiles crossed both of their faces as both men jumped to their feet to put on clothes, like two little boys who had just awoken to the magic of Christmas morning.

They had spent their entire lives waiting and hoping for this moment to come, disbelieving that it ever would. Neither of them knew how or when a door to true freedom would swing open, but suddenly and unexpectedly, on the third of April in 1865, it had.

In a rush, they grabbed what they could from the tent that had been their home for so many months. As they left the tent, they ran down the hill and into the haze and smoke of the Richmond streets. Chaos reigned as the last Richmond citizens fled their property, hoping to make it to the hills before all was lost.

Peering past the chaos, Thomas noticed a unit of soldiers riding into the streets, several hundred feet in front of him. But, there was something peculiar about these soldiers. They weren't wearing the gray-brown uniform of the Confederacy; instead, their coats were blue, and their horses strong and well-fed.

"Ezekiel!" Thomas shouted pointing ahead of him down the streets of Richmond. "Those soldiers down there in the street. Those ain't Confederate soldiers! That's the army of the North!"

A fierce wave of emotion welled up in the pit of Thomas's stomach. Hot tears of joy puddled in his eyes as a sound began to form in the back of his throat. It was soft at first, then it grew, and built with intensity until it finally burst from his mouth like fireworks on the Fourth of July.

"I'm going to praise God 'till I die!" Thomas screamed with all his might. The two men embraced, almost knocking each other over. They held each other with all their strength, circling and dancing, hugging and cheering—a kind of celebration that only free men can truly enjoy.

"Look!" Ezekiel shouted, grabbing Thomas's arm and turning him towards the town square. Between the smoke and fire that raged through the city, Thomas saw another group of Union Soldiers standing at the flagpole at the base of the capitol building. Two of the soldiers had lowered the Confederate flag, taking the tattered cotton rag from its hinges and replaced it with the stars and stripes. Meticulously, hand over hand, the soldiers raised the American flag to the top of the pole. The wind caught the flag and it grew taut, flapping in the breeze. Richmond, Virginia, once again belonged to the United States of America.

Thomas didn't know what to do next. An unfamiliar mix of excitement and fear held his feet to the ground like invisible chains that no longer existed. In all of his dreaming and hoping for freedom, he never thought about what he should actually do when and if this moment ever arrived. As they stood, men and women of color began to slowly walk from the houses and stores that lined the streets. Timid souls, young and old, gathered in mass, staring and pointing at the new red, white, and blue flag that flapped above the capitol building. Within seconds, an unseen force fell upon the throng of former slaves that increasingly filled the streets of Richmond. It was joy—joy like they had never experienced. Timidity soon disappeared, and as the church bells began to ring in the distance, the city streets were overcome by the shouts and whoops and celebration of a freed people.

"The plantation," Thomas said to Ezekiel with conviction. "We need to go tell everybody back at the plantation. The Lord God Almighty done freed us all."

❋ ❋ ❋

As Thomas and Ezekiel rode their horses from Richmond to the plantation, a palpable tension hung in the air, as thick as the fog that blanketed Turkey Creek on a wet summer morning. Neither men spoke. The restless sleep of the previous night and the utter exuberance of the morning had left them tired. For Thomas, his first morning of freedom had been exhilarating, but still, a nagging sense of uncertainty followed him to the plantation. Neither had known what to expect or what they would find when they made it back to the place that had been both home and prison for the two men in their lives before the war.

What will it be like to return as a freed man? wondered Thomas. *And where will we all go next?*

A myriad of thoughts raced through his head.

At best, all the slaves may already be gone—each starting on their own individual journeys of freedom. But at worst, there was the unspeakable fear of mass murder—Mr. Bennett and Quentin Ellis, hearing the news of Richmond's demise, could surely lash out with gun and sword, dealing hot retribution for the loss of all that they held dear. After all, it had been very clear, for all of Thomas's life, that Mr. Bennett's slaves were not people, but property. Thomas knew in his heart that the events of the morning would not change the way Mr. Bennett viewed his slaves, and he feverishly worried that instead of freeing them or treating them as equals in the sight of God, that his anger and hatred would lead to the death of hundreds on his plantation, for he would much rather kill them all than see a single member of his property become free.

Thomas and Ezekiel turned the corner and crossed the entrance of the tobacco plantation, then made their way down the long road that splintered from the main road to the big house. Moss-covered trees guarded the edges of the white fence that lined the long dirt road, swaying gently in the breeze and casting long afternoon shadows onto Thomas and Ezekiel's anxious faces. The calm wind and soft rustling of leaves brought an eerie cadence as they continued down the road.

When they approached the big house, Thomas tied his horse to a post near the barn. Ezekiel dismounted his horse and followed suit. The plantation was quiet—far too quiet for Thomas's comfort. The land that had contained the sum of his youth had always been a land of bustling noise—the clanging of pots and pans being cleaned in the big house, the flapping of cotton dresses hanging on laundry lines, the shouts of the foreman, the incessant talking of Mrs. Bennett, the labor of his people in the tobacco fields—all combined to form a symphony of noisy rhythms that was quite normal on the tobacco plantation.

But in the quiet of the afternoon, none of the familiar sounds were played. The silence unsettled Thomas, causing his pulse to quicken and beat with fire in his neck and chest.

Where is everyone? he thought.

Thomas stopped just short of the front porch, and as he looked across the grassy lawn towards the slave quarters, he saw no one. Usually at this time of day, the tobacco fields contained a flurry of labor. They stood quiet—empty and lifeless.

"Ain't nobody here," whispered Thomas to Ezekiel. "Maybe word already made it here that Richmond fell? Let's head to the quarters to see if anybody's still around," Thomas turned towards the small clapboard shacks that lined the opening of the big house's courtyard, just beyond the grassy lawn. As they turned, a faint sound emanated from the second-floor window above the porch. Both men stopped in their tracks. Not daring to move, they listened intently.

"What was that?" whispered Thomas, eyes widening with fright. Ezekiel didn't say a word. He slowly and without sound, raised his fingers to his lips—a silent gesture for Thomas to be quiet.

The noise sounded again, louder this time, longer in duration. Both men heard it clearly—the sound of a woman crying. Ezekiel motioned his head towards the house and both men walked quietly up the steps of the front porch. The wood boards of the porch creaked and moaned as the weight of the two men fell upon them. Their approach to the front door sounded like claps of thunder compared to the silence of the plantation. All at once, the crying stopped.

The front door to the big house was wide open, and Thomas was the first to step into the spacious foyer that lay just inside the door. It was dark and damp. No candles were lit, and the gas lamp that usually cast light on the ornate decorations of the foyer, lay on the ground—shattered into a thousand pieces. The large oil paintings that once lined the walls were gone, hastily torn from their frames. Pieces of broken china scattered on the ground under Thomas's feet, and on the dining room table, half-dead flowers limped from thin pools of water. Even the vases were gone.

The sound of a woman's cries began again, much louder, clearer, and more forceful in intensity. A soft whimper grew, swelling into the hard, guttural sound of wailing. Thomas looked up from the rubble of the foyer and recognized the source of lament—it was Mrs. Bennett.

Without saying a word, Thomas turned towards the stairs and began walking upstairs, towards the cries.

"What in the name of God are you doing, boy?" Ezekiel hissed, trying in vain to keep his voice unheard.

"It's Mrs. Bennett, Ezekiel," Thomas whispered with com-passion. "Sounds like she might be in trouble."

"Boy, from the looks of this house—she probably is. Don't mean we gotta go gettin' ourselves involved, though."

"Let's just go take a look. From the looks of this place, Mr. Bennett done took off," Thomas said as he continued up the stairs.

Ezekiel followed, and when they reached the top of the stairs, Thomas heard Mrs. Bennett's cries from the master bedroom. The door was pinched opened and a sliver of light shown through the opening, casting a glow into the landing of the stairwell. Thomas pushed the doorknob and gently opened the door, allow-ing his head to lean slowly to the left, surveying the bedroom. When his eyes adjusted to the soft white sunlight that filled the bedroom, Thomas found himself face-to-face with the barrel of a shotgun.

"You better get out of here!" Mrs. Bennett screamed at Thomas with both barrels of the gun aimed squarely at

Thomas's head. She stood trembling violently with anger and fear. Her hair was disheveled, and she still wore her white night-gown from the evening before. Tears stained her cheeks. Her eyes were red, wild with fright. Her countenance was starkly opposite from when Thomas last saw her, as she pranced around the plantation barking orders. He wondered how she devolved into such a mess.

He gently raised his hands, palms facing toward Mrs. Bennett in a gesture of peace. "Hold on now, Mrs. Bennett. Put the gun down. I don't mean you no harm." Thomas spoke with assurance and slowly inched towards Mrs. Bennett. "I'm here to help."

Mrs. Bennett's arms stiffened, raising the gun eye-level with Thomas. "You move one more step closer, boy, and I'm gonna empty both these barrels," said Mrs. Bennett through clenched teeth.

Thomas thought briefly about charging the woman, and wondered why he was helping her at all. He still recalled seeing her, from the whipping post, turn away and offer no help as he begged for mercy. He had thought of her with such hatred, and was confused by his willingness to now help her in her own distress.

"Mrs. Bennett—it's me, Thomas. Thomas Johnson. Me and Ezekiel came back from Richmond. Ma'am, it has fallen," he said. "The whole town is on fire. The Union Army is coming. We came back to tell everybody. Please, Mrs. Bennett, lower that shotgun. I don't mean you no harm."

For what seemed like an hour, she didn't move. Their eyes locked and held in the silence. Finally, Thomas spoke again.

"I don't know what happened to you, ma'am, but I swear I won't hurt you. Please ma'am, put down the shotgun."

As she burst into tears, Mrs. Bennett began to lower the gun. Suddenly, her body gave way to her mourning, and the gun fell from her hands as she collapsed to the floor. Thomas ran to her and gently held her in his arms. Her skin was cold, and her eyes were hollow. As she looked up at him with terror and fear, Thomas felt an emotion for this first time in his whole life. He felt for this woman an overwhelming sense of compassion.

"He left me, Thomas," she cried. "He's gone. He took every-thing . . . except me."

"Mr. Bennett left you? Where'd he go?" Thomas asked.

She gathered her strength, and sat forward, wiping the tears from her swollen eyes. "This morning we got word that Richmond fell. The rumors had been reaching us for weeks that it was possible. We had planned to go further south together. We have family in Alabama. We talked of going there. We thought of going to Texas, maybe starting a new life. But this morn-ing, when the news reached us that the Union Army was in the streets of the city, he filled a wagon with as much as he could, and just left. I don't know where he is, Thomas. I don't know what to do. He took everything."

The woman sobbed and heaved into Thomas's arms. He felt helpless to offer any real comfort to her, but as he held her, he remembered the words of Scripture where the Lord asked His followers to weep with those who weep, and to mourn with those who mourn. So, he did the only thing he knew to do. He held the frail woman, like a child in his arms, and wept.

※ ※ ※

Ezekiel, still standing near the door of the bedroom, slowly moved towards Thomas and Mrs. Bennett. As the scene of a master and her slave—arms wrapped around each other in familial love—played out before the old man's eyes, a mixture of fear and resolve filled him. He gently crouched on the floor next to Thomas and Mrs. Bennett, laid his old and tired hands on the woman's arm, lowered his head, and began to pray. Fear no longer held her face, only sadness. She trembled as she listened to Ezekiel pray.

"Dear Father, I pray now for Mrs. Bennett. I pray that in these trying days that You would protect her, watch over her, and give her peace. And Lord, I forgive—" Ezekiel choked on the words, but did his best to push them forward, "I forgive Mr. Bennett. And I forgive Mrs. Bennett. I pray that above all else, Lord—that she would turn to You, and know Your forgiveness, too. I pray that she would know You as her Helper . . . her heavenly Father. We ask these things now of You, Lord, in the mighty name of Jesus. Amen."

With his prayer completed, both men stood and quietly left the room, walking down the stairs, through the front door into the sunlight of the porch. The long road that had brought them to the big house lay before them. It had always been for them a boundary—an untouchable barrier between them and the outside world—but now, it stretched as a pathway to a life yet lived, a life where they were no longer slaves, but now men unchained by the yoke of evil.

Side by side, Thomas and Ezekiel walked down the steps of the big house and began the process of putting behind them, forever, their identity as slaves. As they traveled the long road to the plantation entrance, Thomas turned to look behind him, one last time, at the home he had longed to leave since childhood.

In the courtyard of the big house, next to the well, was the old broken-down wagon that had served as the place all the slaves received their morning assignments. Thomas squinted through the sunlight, and there he saw a man with red hair and a tobacco-stained beard, lying on his back, lifeless and pale. Quentin Ellis's pistol was still in his hand, gripped by his cold, dead fingers.

For a brief moment, Thomas mourned. Then, he turned his eyes towards the gate at the end of the road, where uncertainty lay on the other side.

CHAPTER 15

GREAT MERCIES

London, England 1869

I t is a great mercy to be able to toss and turn, changing sides during the night in a bed. It is a great mercy to set one's head on a pillow for an hour of sleep, interposed between long stretches of pain. It is a great mercy to press eyelids together to catch a glimpse of reprieve, as brief as it may be. We call those things mercies, because like the span of blue between a mass of thunderclouds, so is rest in the midst of suffering.

Charles pulled the linens towards the foot of the bed and carefully arranged the pillows as Susannah preferred, then walked across the small room to her chair, which sat in a darkened corner. Slowly, and with caution, he lifted her flimsy legs to his chest with one hand while placing the other behind her softened back, then carried her to the bed. Her fragile body hung limp in his strong arms. As he slid her body into the sheets, they shared not a word, only a smile—the kind that only lovers know.

It is difficult to say when Susannah first realized she was
devastatingly ill. With constant attention given to mothering her
household, as well as serving at the Tabernacle every Sabbath,
she often pressed through tremors of pain in her abdomen, hoping it would simply pass. The strength of a woman is perhaps
most easily seen, not in her ability to carry large stones, or shout
loud words from a platform, but in her ability to endure silently
while still holding everyone else up. This is the kind of strength
that was hidden in Susannah Spurgeon since she gave birth to
Charles and Thomas, but by the spring of 1869, she could hide
it no longer.

"Has the pain worsened, my love?" Charles caressed her
smooth face as he kissed her forehead.

"It does seem quite worse today," she said.

"If I could take it from you, you know that I would," Charles
spoke gently.

"I know. But you mustn't." Susannah smiled, but her smile
soon dissipated as her eyelids slowly drooped like heavy curtains, and she sank to a restful sleep.

Charles knelt to the floor and wept. He traced his finger
along vibrant patterns of the wool rug beneath his knees, and
thought of the thread of suffering that was slowly being woven
into the tapestry of their lives, their marriage, their friendship.
He found himself on his knees often, but when he knelt beside
the bed of his broken bride, he yearned for Heaven in a way
only sickness can incite. "Oh, God," he whispered in the shadows, "the sick bed is soft when You are there. The furnace of
affliction grows cool when You are there. Oh, God be *there*." He
rose to his feet, kissed Susannah's face once more, then quietly
closed the door as he left the room.

Their new house on Nightingale Lane, in the quiet nook near Clapham Common, was the perfect safe haven for a sick wife and a busy pastor. By the time they were in their mid-thirties, Charles and Susannah had experienced more than most do in a lifetime. Once the doctors had diagnosed Susannah with an incurable illness that affected her physical body in a paralyzing manner, the need for a comfortable home with ample room for live-in nurses and full-time help for the children became necessary. One man who became a permanent member of the Spurgeon household was George Lovejoy, or "Old George" as Charles referred to him. The witty Englishman in his fifties with dark hair and a light beard, was proud to serve the Spurgeon family as butler, valet, and comic relief. Every morning when Charles asked, "Well, George, how are you this morning?" the inevitable answer was, "First-rate, sir. As fresh as a salt fish."

The Helensburgh House, as they called it, stood on the outskirts of London, just south of the Thames River. The high cost of the four-thousand-square-foot home was paid by a few families of the Metropolitan Tabernacle; it was a token of their appreciation for Charles and Susannah's public ministry and private friendship. The yellow brick home—founded in love, walled with sincerity, and roofed in with generosity—was something Charles never took for granted. He considered it a blessing of immeasurable value.

The exterior of the two-story house boasted thirteen windows, each arched and perfectly set within cement headstones that surrounded them. Each window's edge held a planter box, filled to capacity with fresh flowers and herbs. A set of stone steps led to the front porch, where a wooden door stood beneath a four-story spire reaching almost double the height of the house. Atop it, an iron weather vane spun as the country breeze chased along the metal roof and flew past the four chimneys that stood on every corner of the house.

It could hardly be called a *private* residence, as most days every bedroom was filled with a traveling preacher, a student in need of a bedroom, or young men from the Pastors' College that Charles started some years ago. Upon arrival, every visitor was struck with the Helensburgh House's charm and hospitality.

Lining the front porch was a beautiful garden, and when you entered the house from Nightingale Lane, the front door opened to a galley where paintings of Essex and the New Forest lined the white plaster walls. Portraits of the Spurgeon twins hung neatly between bright windows—a new portrait for every year they were alive. Next to the galley was the large kitchen with a countertop that surrounded the perimeter, and a wooden table in the center for preparing meals. The kitchen was managed by women from the Tabernacle, and they frequently prepared family meals for the homeless and hungry in the city, as well as any out-of-town guest that found the house to be a place of respite. From the kitchen, a spacious dining room opened into a conservatory where Charles smoked cigars and drank sherry as the setting sun cast orange rays through the tall and open glass windows and ceiling. Nothing was excessive or decorated with finesse, but comfort and warmth filled the hallways and crawled from the wooden floors to the high ceilings trimmed with dark-stained oak beams.

The interior and exterior of the Helensburgh House added tiny specks of pleasure to the Spurgeon family's life, but no grandeur of a home could overcome the sting of sickness that lay in the small bedroom next to Charles's study.

❋ ❋ ❋

Charles did his best to brighten her bedroom with as many charms as he could find. In one corner of her bedroom he placed a cupboard, and filled it with her favorite books and treasures from their travels in earlier years—a wooden box from Switzerland, a pocket watch passed from her grandfather, ceramic figures of her favorite animals, photographs of her family, and an opal ring.

Several years ago, Charles had asked Susannah, "Is there anything I can get for you while I am out today, Susie?"

"I should like an opal ring and a piping bullfinch!" she squealed with delight.

Charles was surprised and amused by her request, but simply answered, "Oh Susie, you know I cannot get those for you. Where on earth would I find an opal ring and a pet *bird*?" A few days later, on his way home from the Tabernacle, Charles peeked through the window of a jewelry store and spotted an antique opal ring. He carried the tiny ring home and slid it on the finger of his wife, "There is your opal ring, my darling."

"And—my bullfinch?" she delighted as she peered at the ring.

"A pet bird is *much* harder to come by, Susie!" he whispered playfully.

Nothing had been forgotten which could bring any extra comfort to his invalid wife, who was now almost entirely confined to her bed. He had thought of all the things that might please her, and there were such tender touches of devoted love upon all the surroundings of the little room that no words can describe her emotion when she gazed upon them.

Charles warmed his hands by the fireplace in his study as he thought of tomorrow's sermon at the Tabernacle. The wood crackled and popped as it burned, and although the fire was tiny, its gentle heat was enough to push all the cold from the spacious room. He slumped into the couch and sat in silence for what seemed like hours, thinking and praying, thinking and praying. His plump cat, Old Dick, slithered into his lap and purred, begging for his master's touch. "Old Dick—you fat cat," he mumbled, breaking the silence. He was never fond of Old Dick, swearing that cats were too mysterious. He much more preferred the company of Punch, his little brown pug. Punch was always a good source of amusement, since Charles had taught it several impressive tricks—all of which brought a delirious chuckle to Charles.

He shoved the old cat to the floor, then moved to his desk to finish the sermon. His desk was scattered with newly written letters—encouragement to acquaintances, wisdom to students, and correspondence to complete strangers from all over the world whom had sent him a letter. Charles loved the art of letter writing. Some of the ink on the letters still sparkled with wetness, too fresh to place in an envelope.

On the opposite side of the desk were printer's proofs of sermons, awaiting the process of editing and amending, with handwritten commentary from Joseph along the edges. *This needs more work. This section is confusing. This needs more of the gospel!*

The deep desk stood in the very center of the room, and was surrounded by floor-to-ceiling bookshelves richly furnished with books, new and old. Over the years, Charles had collected hundreds of books, and it seemed nearly every houseguest brought Charles a new book to add to the bibliophile's collection. There was a section for the Puritan writers, several shelves for commentaries, and rows of old Bibles and hymnals. Charles pulled his chair from the desk and thought of the first meal he ever shared with Susannah Thompson in Mrs. Onley's kitchen so many years ago. Volumes of life had been written in their thirteen years of marriage—great triumphs and terrible tragedies. He remembered telling her of his desire to someday own a library with bookshelves just like these, an entire room devoted to the study of books, and he couldn't help but mourn the fact that she seldom had the energy to enjoy the study herself. A feeling of aloneness sank deep within Charles as he sat in his chair, his mind as scattered as the desk top in plain view, his heart as weary as the nearly extinguished fire in the corner of the room.

No one knew the private anguish with which Charles lived. Many knew of Susannah's sickness, they knew of his many responsibilities, and the strain of a public life. But, none knew the depth of an inner turmoil that had been creeping toward Charles since he was a child in Stambourne, Essex. As an adult, he seemed to juggle his numerous responsibilities with ease—preaching several times a week, marrying and burying, often answering five hundred letters every week, teaching at the Pastors' College, caring for Susannah, fathering his twins, and personally taking on the financial responsibility for most of his ventures.

Added to that, Charles continued to war with the hidden struggle with depression and unworthiness. It might seem the easiest thing in the world for Charles Spurgeon to preach and write, but as he grew in age, the signs of weariness moved from internal to external. He grew weary of large crowds. Charles hated being in a crowded room; it made him claustrophobic, as if everyone needed something from him. But, he also despised being alone; it made him paranoid, as if no one would ever need something from him again. And, like the rise and fall of the tides, one moment of confidence seemed to follow another moment of anxiety—over and over again.

Punch lazily moped from the couch to Charles's desk and patiently waited for a pat on the head and a scratch beneath his belly. "Not now, Punch." The pug's wrinkled skin scrunched against his short legs as he sat, eager for Charles to pay attention. Charles fumbled through his coat pockets and desk drawers, unable to find a cigar. "Punch, fetch me a cigar," Charles ordered his dog. Punch immediately scrambled off to the small armchair next to the fireplace and fetched a half-smoked cigar from the seat. With pride, Punch sat at Charles's feet, wagging his knobby tail, holding a now-slobbery, half-smoked cigar in his mouth. "Good boy, Punch!" Charles laughed heartily. He pulled the cigar from Punch's mouth and wiped it on his trousers before lighting the end with a match. The flame seemed to light his entire face as he drew the warm air into his mouth and turned the cigar in circles to light it evenly.

As he tasted the subtle hints of cocoa and cardamom, a strong pain immediately rushed from the corner of his back to the center of his stomach. Like a sharpened sword thrust to his body, this pain was more intense than any he had ever felt. It turned his stomach and soured his mouth. His hand trembled, causing his cigar to fall to the ground. Beads of sweat formed across his face, then ran along the back of his neck, and began to roll down his back. He braced himself with the desk, enough to stand from the chair, then slowly lumbered toward the couch near the fireplace. The walls of the library crept towards him in unison as the floor beneath turned to ripples of water. All at once, the entire room spun forward, clockwise, slowly at first, then faster and faster, now counterclockwise.

Charles gripped the leather covering of the couch, holding on for dear life. As the walls continued to spin, the back of his throat began to water. His stomach rumbled and roared then spewed vomit from his gut to the floor beside the couch. He desperately wanted to cry for Susannah to help, but resisted the urge, knowing she would be unable to leave her bed without help. Heat rushed from Charles's bones as the room slowly turned darker and darker, until nearly black. His ears rang, sharp and piercing, then all at once, everything turned to blackness.

"Mr. Spurgeon! Mr. Spurgeon? Are you alright? Can you hear me?"

Charles winced as he opened his eyes to the now fully-brightened study. The Sunday morning sun lit the room with radiance, but the pain of brightness roiled his eyes. "Oh my! Dear God—it's the Sabbath! And I have not prepared my sermon!" He spoke, barely opening his lips, "What happened, George?"

"I don't know, Mr. Spurgeon. I found you lying here this morning on my way to Mrs. Spurgeon's bedroom. You are soaking with sweat, sir. Here, place these wet towels on your face and arms. You have a raging fever!" He carried a pile of wet towels intended for Susannah, and slowly placed the towels on Charles's forehead, under his chin, and on top of a clammy arm.

"I must get to the Tabernacle. They will be waiting for me." For a second, Charles tried to sit up, but pain shot through his entire body, and he found himself without the strength to move. He slumped back into the couch and sighed.

"I do not think you will be going anywhere today, Mr. Spurgeon. I have summoned the doctor. She will be here in thirty minutes. Rest, sir." George placed the final towel on his left arm, and when he stood to leave, Charles closed his eyes.

"Reverend Spurgeon," Charles woke to the familiar and sweet voice of Dr. Anderson, the wonderful doctor to Susannah. She was the second female Englishwoman to qualify as a physician in Great Britain, and a frequent visitor to the Metropolitan Tabernacle. She specialized in treating women in London with all sorts of gynecological issues, but she was also a fine physician and surgeon—one of the very best. "Mr. Spurgeon, I need you to drink some water and tell me what has happened," she said as she pushed a lock of mouse-brown hair behind her ear.

Charles drank an entire cup of water, then sat forward, the room still slowly spinning. "I—I was at my desk. Sitting to work on a sermon. All of a sudden—a pain, unbearable, and a fever so warm. I couldn't stand. So—I lay on this couch and I only recall waking here to the sunlight."

"I am going to take your temperature, and I want to hear your breathing." Dr. Anderson measured his temperature and listened to his lungs as he inhaled and exhaled. "Tell me about your pain. Where is it? And what level would you say it is?"

"My entire body aches. More than flu. Deeper. All the way to the bone."

"Yes? And how would you describe the intensity?"

"Some of the worst pain I have known."

"Have you seen any markings on your body? Any red bumps?" she asked as she opened his shirt and scanned his skin.

"No."

"Well, I suppose you will soon, Mr. Spurgeon. You have *variola*. And, I'm afraid your symptoms will only worsen over the next twelve days, give or take."

"Worsen? What is variola?" He buttoned his shirt and squirmed as more pain shot through his bones.

"Variola is a condition also known as smallpox," she said plainly.

"*Smallpox?*" said Charles, feeling a tinge of fear crawl through his chest.

"Yes, and I'm sorry to say—it is *incredibly* painful."

"And how is it treated, Doctor?"

"Well, Mr. Spurgeon. If only you would have been alive in the *seventeenth* century—the common treatment was twelve bottles of beer every twenty-four hours," she answered through a laugh.

"Only twelve?" he asked sarcastically.

"Your body must rest. I can prescribe medication to help with the pain, but in a few days you will start to notice lesions all over your body. They will seep and ooze, but you must not touch them. They will pass, but most likely scar your body. In fourteen days, you should be back on your feet. This is not an enjoyable sickness, Mr. Spurgeon. I truly am sorry." Empathy and compassion were easily seen on Dr. Anderson's pale-white face as she always rocked her head back and forth as she spoke, as if to say, *Goodness—I feel it with you.*

"Thank you, Dr. Anderson."

❊ ❊ ❊

It took Charles nearly three weeks to recover from smallpox. Throughout those three weeks, he groaned and growled as the sores spread over every inch of his body. There was an epidemic throughout the United Kingdom, and the "speckled monster" of smallpox showed no bias—it infected young, old, rich, and poor. Still, as terrible as the pain of smallpox was, nothing compared to the next arrow aimed at Charles Spurgeon.

In winter of the same year, Charles suffered from his first experience of gout. Those who experience it, never rid themselves of it, and seldom recover fully. The term "gout" is derived from the belief that drops of pain-creating material originating in the blood stream fall into the joints, crystallize there, and produce symptoms which may only be described as hellish agony. The feet are most commonly the first of the body to become prey to the horrendous disease. Knobs swell within the joints and turn the toes inward, and upward. The skin reddens and stiffens. Like an extreme version of arthritis, the affected foot becomes too painful to touch, much less stand on. After an episode of gout flares up, its effects may last for days or weeks before the swelling subsides. Worse, the disease tends to recur—flaring up over time, worsening with each episode—until the whole body eventually buckles under the tyranny of the disease.

Another painful side effect from gout—perhaps the most terrible—is unseen, tucked beneath layers of psyche and emotion. Many who suffered from gout found that it was accompanied by depression, and since Charles already wrestled with depressive thoughts, gout was a bitter enemy without rival.

"How are you today, Mr. Spurgeon?" asked George as he stoked the winter fire in Charles's study.

"First-rate, George."

"As fresh as a salt fish?" said George, peering from the fireplace and winking at Charles.

"Fresh as a salt fish," answered Charles with a sarcastic grin.

"What do you need from me today, Charles?"

"Will you ask Joseph if the letters are being responded to? And if the everything is set for Sunday at the Tabernacle?"

"Yes, Mr. Spurgeon. Of course."

Charles, wrapped in a blue blanket, lay completely still on a cot in the corner of the study. Since he could barely climb the stairs and didn't want to be too far from his study, George set up a make-shift bed so that Charles could lie flat during most of the day while continuing to work. Under the blanket, both of his feet were wrapped tightly with cotton bandages to compress the swelling. He dared not move his feet or wiggle his toes, as it would stir a pain that would then shoot to every corner of his body. His knees were also wrapped in white bandages, and the severe swelling looked as though bundles of chestnuts were buried beneath his skin. Charles gritted his teeth and massaged the temples of his forehead with his palms. His hands, fortunately, were his only extremities unaffected by gout. He was thankful to be able to move them freely, pick up a book, and hold a pen.

"One more thing—beg your pardon, sir," said George as he finished tending the fire. "A few of the church elders and deacons are here and would like to come up to speak to you. Are you fine to see them now?"

"Yes. Send them in."

Seven men and three women gathered around Charles's bedside, then pressed their knees to the ground. Eye-level with Charles, they each spoke a blessing and begged God for healing. Their voices cracked and their eyes watered. They each carefully laid one hand on Charles's broken body and extended their other to Heaven. They prayed for Susannah, begging God for healing and peace, and for Charles Jr. and Thomas, asking God for an increased measure of grace on their lives. Charles lay perfectly still, eyes and teeth clenched, surrounded by the warmest display of affection and concern.

"Amen," sighed Charles as they finished praying and rose to their feet.

"Charles," said Mrs. Bartlett, a faithful deacon of the church for nearly ten years. "We are going to lay hands on and pray for Mrs. Spurgeon. But before we do, we want to discuss something with you."

"Yes, Charles," added Brother Woollard, an elder and long-time friend.

"Alright—what do you want to discuss, my friends?" Charles asked through a painful groan.

"We are all in agreement today, Charles," continued Brother Woollard. "You must trust we have your greatest interest in mind. You are the heart and soul of the Metropolitan Tabernacle—our respected leader—and our trusted pastor." All ten men and women nodded along, some offering verbal cues of agreement. "But . . . your health is of the utmost priority."

"Charles," Mrs. Bartlett whispered sweetly, "you *must* take a break from ministry. You must rest. The Lord wills it."

"You can *trust* that the work of the Lord will continue, Charles," said another elder in the circle, as he nodded his head.

Charles's lips began to tremble as tears filled his eyes and spilled onto the blue blanket that wrapped around his chest. His heart burst with sadness as he feared the worst for his health, the well-being of his two sons, and the health of his invalid wife. He fought to gain his composure, then muscled the energy to barely mutter a request.

"Brother Everett," he spoke slowly to the elder nearest to his face, "bring me a pen and paper." Brother Everett gathered a pen and a clean sheet of paper from Charles's desk, then carried it to the bedside. "Transcribe this. And please read it aloud at the Tabernacle on Sunday."

"Yes, Charles. I shall write as you speak."

"Dear friends," Charles muttered as Brother Everett wrote every word onto the paper, "the furnace of affliction glows around me." He paused between each sentence, allowing Brother Everett to write exactly as the words were spoken. "Since I last preached to you, I have been brought very low. My flesh has been tortured with pain, and my spirit has been prostrate with depression. Yet, in all this, I see and submit to my Father's hand. The peace of God be with every one of you, my beloved! My love in Christ Jesus be with you all! I write these lines in my bed . . . mingling them with the groans of pain . . . and the songs of hope. And I ask for your prayers. The Lord be with you, evermore."

Brother Everett finished the last line and placed the sheet of paper neatly in the inside pocket of his coat. "I will make sure the congregation hears these words, Charles. Now, you must *rest* in the midst of suffering. Godspeed, brother." They filed out of the room, one by one, and quietly shut the doors of the study behind them.

Charles forced his eyelids together, and for just a few hours, experienced the great mercy of peaceful sleep.

CHAPTER 16

WHAT FREEDOM FEELS LIKE

Chicago, Illinois 1875

He sat at the desk of his study, as he did every evening to painstakingly work on his Sunday-morning sermon. A peculiar nervousness returning to his chest and belly every week about this time, for Sunday morning was coming. Since becoming the pastor of Providence Baptist Church in Chicago in the spring of 1873, most of his thoughts were occupied by two all-consuming thoughts. First, he constantly wondered when the day would unfold that God finally allowed him to return to his homeland of Africa to bring the Good News of Jesus to his own people. He thought of it every single day. Second, and only slightly less taxing on his mental constitution, the ever-present and looming reality that every Sunday morning required a new sermon—a fresh word for the people of Providence.

As one could assume to be true for most pastors, Thomas Johnson experienced an odd concoction of emotion when Sundays finally arrived. It was both a sincere joy, and a nagging feeling that he wasn't nearly qualified for the job God had given to him. He loved the feeling of standing in the pulpit, telling all who would listen about his beloved friend, Jesus. But, every time Thomas spoke, he was vividly aware of his lack of education and grasp of the English language.

Back on the plantation, he was a learned man—a master of many things. Thomas understood the complexities of planting and harvesting tobacco. He knew how to cook large meals, and properly serve the delicacies of southern cuisine—skillet-fried steaks, pot roasts, and buttermilk biscuits, to name a few. He even mastered sewing, and could easily mend torn clothes, stitching them back to their original condition. Still, none of these skills helped Thomas when he stood behind the old wooden pulpit of Providence Baptist, peering out at the hungry souls of his congregation, teaching God's Holy Word.

During most Sunday sermons, he delivered his speech without much incident, but every once in a while, his old dialect from the plantation would spill out of his mouth without warning— a word of slang or a mispronunciation of a common phrase. All the while, his congregation reacted with polite smiles and hearty head nods, because his love for Jesus and his care for them as his flock simply overshadowed any lack of eloquence in his speaking.

A door opened behind him, and Thomas turned to see the face of his beautiful wife, Henrietta, beaming with joy.

"Time to put up that sermon, my love, the Smiths will be here in a few minutes," she said in a gentle tone.

In earlier years of marriage, as Thomas was first beginning to preach, an interruption from his quiet study would have frustrated him. He was often short with Henrietta if she walked in during sermon preparation, startling him from his focus. But years of living with this wonderful woman had taught him that there are some things more important than a perfect sermon— one of which is a happy wife. He found that Henrietta thrived under the kindness of a patient and calm husband.

"Come in, sugar," Thomas spoke with endearment, wrapping his hands around her waist and pulling her to his lap. He kissed her round cheeks and neck as she squirmed and giggled, play-fully trying to get away from him.

"Stop it, Thomas!" she paused to look at him, then gently kissed his cheek. "Our guests will be here any minute and I got a goose in the oven."

Thomas lifted his wife off of his lap, then turned to look out the frosted window to the streets of Chicago, Illinois. It was dreadfully cold outside. Ice crystals formed in the corner of the window frame, inside and outside, and a deep snow blanketed the Chicago streets as far as Thomas could see. A few yards down the road, a tall street lamp flickered against the raging cold and revealed a heavy downfall of fresh winter snow.

"I hope the Smiths make it okay," said Thomas with con-cern. "They only live a few blocks away, but Santa Claus himself wouldn't venture out on a night like tonight."

※ ※ ※

Thomas and Henrietta met each other shortly after the war had come to an end. He first saw her while serving dinner for General Weitzel of the Union Army, shortly after the fall of Richmond. Thomas and Ezekiel, not knowing what to do or where to go after leaving the plantation, had joined themselves to the Union Army and found employment putting on grand dinners for the General and his staff. Henrietta and her mother had served in the same capacity for General Robert E. Lee of the Confederacy before the fall, so they, too, quickly offered their services to General Weitzel upon his occupation of Virginia.

As long as Thomas lived, he swore to never forget the first
time he set his eyes on his beloved Henrietta. She wore a clean,
white cotton dress that shined like the sun against the contrast
of her smooth, ebony skin. Just above her shoulders, her hair fell
soft, like the corn silk of the summer.

On the night of General Weitzel's party, they found themselves working together in the kitchen. Henrietta attentively prepared a plate of hors d'oeuvres to be taken to a table of Northern
dignitaries, carefully placing tomatoes inside mushroom caps,
then topping them with a sliver of tarragon. Her hands moved
gracefully and neatly.

On the other side of the long, wooden counter, Thomas
stood with a mound of uncut onions, and pulled each one to
a cutting board where he chopped them into tiny squares. As
hard as he fought to keep his eyes from dripping with tears—too
prideful to allow a pretty woman see him cry—they were soon
overwhelmed. They began to itch and burn, then tears poured
from his eyes and fell down his cheeks as he quickly tried to
wipe them away, fearful that the other cooks would think he'd
lost his mind.

Thomas heard laughter from across the counter and looked
up from his chopping, only to see Henrietta holding her belly,
laughing the most beautiful laugh he'd ever heard.

"Looks like those onions are getting the best of you," she
said without a hint of malice in her words. Her voice was gentle
and kind, like rain on green fields in the spring.

Thomas couldn't speak. He just stood looking at her, unable
to move, for he truly had never seen that kind of beauty in all of
his life.

Thomas raised his hands to his face to wipe away the tears,
embarrassed that this beautiful girl had noticed his struggle. As
his fingers wiped away the wetness from his face, juice from the
onion splashed back into his eyes, causing him pain and making
the tears come even harder. Eyes shut and grimacing, Thomas

laugh-cried and blindly began searching for a towel to end the suffering of both his eyes and his pride.

As he groped and fumbled about the kitchen, he suddenly felt a cool and damp cloth touch his cheek. The beautiful young woman had seen his plight and mercifully wet a towel, crossed the length of the kitchen, and brought it to his face. He raised his hand to touch the cool towel but instead, and accidentally, caressed her hand. Then, he opened his eyes—red, irritated, and still streaming with tears—to see up close for the first time, Henrietta's enchanting face.

"You already trying to hold hands with me?" Henrietta said playfully, her warm smile melting places inside Thomas he didn't know existed.

"No—uh—I'm sorry, ma'am," Thomas said awkwardly, "I promise I didn't mean to hold hands with you." He suddenly lost control of his ability to speak or utter a coherent sentence, as he was dumbstruck by her beauty.

"Well that's a shame," she grinned, exposing her beautiful smile, then let go of the cloth and returned to her side of the counter.

Thomas loved her instantly. In that very moment, he determined to do whatever it took to spend the rest of his life making her smile. She had been a great gift from the God, for after the death of his lifelong friend Ezekiel, Henrietta had filled a void in him that could have only been filled by a good woman who loved the Lord. Since they had married, she had been his best friend, his lover, and most important, a constant source of encouragement in his walk with Jesus.

Suddenly, there was a knock at the door. Henrietta clapped her hands together and let out a playful squeal at the noise, for she always loved when company came to their modest home. The

knock came again as Henrietta danced across the wood floor of
their house. A brutal northern wind snuck into the room as she
opened the door to the smiling faces of Mr. and Mrs. E. Stroud
Smith. Snowflakes flurried into the house as Henrietta quickly
closed the door behind their houseguests.

"I smell roast goose!" shouted Mr. Smith as he put his arm
around Henrietta and hugged her with the warm affection of an
elderly father.

"It's in the oven, kind sir," said Henrietta with her best imitation of the King's English.

"And that is a very good thing my dear, for I am famished
and my wife has not fed me *once* this glorious day." Mr. Smith
cast a nervous glance at his wife of forty years.

"Where is your beloved husband—the honorable, bishop,
priest, and reverend Johnson?" said Mr. Smith, peering his head
into the study across the living room.

"I'm here, Mr. Smith," said Thomas, standing from this desk
motioning to his good friend to join him.

Mr. Smith walked slowly across the room to join his friend
and pastor, then embraced him with a warm hug. The Smiths
had begun attending Providence Baptist Church earlier in the
year when they had heard that a young black man had taken the
pastorate. Spending most of their lives in England, the Smiths
hadn't fallen prey to the prejudices of race and color the same
way many were so prone to in the United States, and as a child,
Mr. Smith had been taught to measure a man on his ability and,
more important, his character.

When first hearing the young Thomas Johnson preach, Mr.
Smith had been surprised, not by his mastery of speech, but by
the preacher's obvious yielding to the Holy Spirit. He possessed
an authority and power in his preaching that didn't come from
education or talent, and Mr. Smith recognized it instantly. Soon
after, he and his wife and their two daughters joined the small

congregation, as Mr. Smith knew that much could be learned from the Reverend Thomas Johnson.

"Ah, my good lad! I see that you are working on your Christmas sermon," said Mr. Smith, standing over Thomas's small desk. "I love your passion for God's Word, Thomas. May you never lose it."

"I've been working hard at it since this morning. Christmas sermons are sometimes the hardest. You have to preach on the same subject every year," Thomas laughed and sat back into his chair.

Mr. Smith sat into the small sofa next to the fireplace. It crackled behind him, warming him and the entire room.

"And how is it coming together, my friend?" Mr. Smith asked, gesturing his hands towards the pieces of paper that lay upon Thomas's desk.

"It's coming together fairly well. I've struggled, as I often do, making sure I don't sound like a buffoon," said Thomas laughing again.

The subject of the mastery of language was a familiar topic between the two men. After Mr. Smith began attending Providence Baptist, their friendship began easily and the older man met almost weekly with Thomas, helping him learn to read, write, and speak the English language.

"You are much better than you give yourself credit for, young man. Think about how far you have come. You were not educated at Harvard or Oxford, or any other school for that matter. But look at you now, Thomas. God has brought you very far, son," said Mr. Smith with his voice becoming firmer and more animated.

"You are the pastor of a church. People come from all over the city to hear you preach. You have something better than an education—you have the power of the Holy Spirit!"

"It's true," Thomas said, only half believing the words that came from his mouth. Thomas stood, staring out the window at some unseen place in the distance, trying to muster the courage to tell his friend something that had consumed much of his thought for months.

"All this talk of the Holy Spirit brings me to something that I've been wanting to tell you for some time." Thomas changed the subject.

Without warning, a loud and boisterous laughter erupted from the two men's wives who were working in the kitchen.

"Are you alright in there?" shouted Mr. Smith to his wife, without leaving the comfort of his sofa.

"We are indeed!" Mrs. Smith yelled from the kitchen. "I'm simply telling embarrassing stories about you to Henrietta!"

Thomas and Mr. Smith smiled and chuckled.

"She probably told Henrietta that I remind her of that plump Christmas goose!" Mr. Smith said, grabbing his belly, heaving with laughter.

Thomas joined in the belly laugh and thought of how much he truly enjoyed time with the enlivened Smiths. Sadly, trust for a white man had been a casualty of his youth. His encounters with white people during his days on the plantation had been singularly one-sided, as he existed solely for them, their pleasure, and purpose. But the Smiths and his Chicago congregation were radically different. They were good people that never viewed him as unequal; instead, they propped him up and elevated him as their leader, and their pastor. Slowly, much of the old baggage of distrust for white men slid to the waste.

"Forgive me, young man—you were saying something before my wife so inconsiderately called me a goose."

"Ye—Yes, I was." Thomas gathered his thoughts.

"Over the years I've spent untold hours scouring my mind as to what good might have come from the oppression of my people. Four million souls were bound in chains by the southern states. Four million souls, Mr. Smith—their lives stolen away at the end of a whip. And—after many years of thinking—I might have found the answer as to why God might have allowed *me* to go through all that." Thomas paused, looking into the fire as if to summon the courage to say the words now gathering in his heart.

"Africa," he said, lifting his head from his gaze into the fireplace. "The only possible good that I can see from my years spent in slavery, is that I was found by Jesus in the midst of slavery. And now—because of that—one of her own sons can go back to Africa and tell her people of my Lord and Savior. I can't stop thinking about this one truth, Mr. Smith. Even in the middle of that godforsaken tobacco field, God didn't forsake me. I was an angry young man, full of despair and utterly hopeless, but one night, like a bolt of lightning from a clear blue sky—I didn't see it coming, but Jesus showed up. He found me, and saved me, and gave peace and freedom to my heart. And now, Mr. Smith—I love Jesus more than life itself. So, I can't think of any endeavor that I would rather give the rest of my days to, than to go tell the people of Africa about Jesus."

Mr. Smith rubbed his freshly shaved chin, and listened patiently as Thomas finished.

"But—you think your lack of education is a stumbling block to these ends," stated Mr. Smith, knowing instinctively what Thomas was thinking.

"Unfortunately," Thomas said, as he squirmed in his seat, apparently nervous, "my lack of education is but one of the *many* barriers that I might stumble on." Thomas's eyes widened with passion.

Mr. Smith noticed the reflection of the fireplace in the young man's eyes. It crackled and danced as Thomas spoke. Mr. Smith could see it clearly, and it brought a small smile to his face, as he had always known Thomas to have fire in his eyes. The old man loved him for it.

"Africa," continued Thomas, "is a land of venomous reptiles, cruel fevers, and cannibal tribes. But, those do not concern me near as much as my lack of ability to present the gospel to my people in a clear way, not only through my speech—but through written word. Both of which I have begged the Lord to open some door through which I could enter and learn. But, I have found little help, other than your teaching, Mr. Smith—which I am thankful for."

Mr. Smith sat back in the sofa and sighed. The clock in the corner of Thomas's study clicked and tocked as the old man carefully chose his words.

"Alright. There is something I've been wanting to tell you, Thomas," said Mr. Smith as he sat forward in his chair, closer to the fire in Thomas's eyes. "One of the reasons I accepted your invitation for goose tonight was to inform you that in February, Mrs. Smith and I will be returning to England. My business here in Chicago has run its course, and my company has demanded my immediate return. I received the letter but a few days ago. It seems that London is experiencing quite an industrial revolution and my services are required."

With those words, a disappointment instantly enveloped Thomas's heart.

"But, there is something I want to present to you—an opportunity for you. I've hesitated to tell you—too afraid that you might seize upon the opportunity and we would lose you as a pastor, but now that we are leaving—well, it's a good time to tell," Mr. Smith said, standing up from the couch and placing his arm upon the young man's shoulder.

"You need schooling, Thomas. And, I have heard of a place in London that would suit you very well."

"What is the name of the school?"

"It's called the 'Pastors' College,' and it is the educational arm of a church called 'Metropolitan Tabernacle,' whose pastor is—"

"Charles . . . Haddon . . . Spurgeon," Thomas slowly finished the sentence, interrupting Mr. Smith.

"Why, yes son. How do you know of Mr. Spurgeon?" asked Mr. Smith, raising a hairy eyebrow towards his silver hair.

"You wouldn't believe—but, I first heard his name when I was a younger man on the plantation. He preached against slavery. I was even present when some of the pastors in Richmond were burning his sermons."

"Really?" sighed Mr. Smith as he sunk back to the couch. "I would never have imagined!"

"I've read much of his writings. That man has caused me to love the Bible more. Do you honestly believe this to be a real opportunity? To study at Spurgeon's college?"

"I do, Thomas."

"Well—I—I mean, I don't know how that could work." Thomas shook his head.

"Listen son, I have a good friend in England. His name is Mr. Hind Smith." He rolled his eyes as he said his name. "Yes, I know he shares the same last name as me, but I assure you he does *not* share my charm or ravishing good looks." He laughed, bringing merriment once again to the room.

"He serves as a pastor at the YMCA in Manchester, and I have already informed him of your desire for further education. He hopes that Pastors' College may be willing to accept you for further training in preaching and theology. As it turns out—I've taken the liberty to ask Mr. Hind Smith to write a letter to Mr. Spurgeon."

"A letter? To Charles Spurgeon? What for?"

"To ask him for your acceptance into the school, son! To train you for mission." His impish smile returned to his wrinkled face. "And—I have taken it a step further. I have begun preliminary discussions with the good people of Providence Baptist about funding tickets for you and Henrietta to travel by sea to England, should you feel that the Good Lord is directing your course."

Thomas could not believe what he was hearing. He and Henrietta were happy in Chicago, but the call to Africa was one he could never seem to shut off. The only barriers to his saying, *Here I am Lord, send me,* were now crumbling at his feet. Thomas stood, leaned over the couch, and grabbed Mr. Smith tightly around the neck, hugging him with all of his might.

"Thank you, Mr. Smith—from the bottom of my heart—thank you." He loosened his grip on Mr. Smith, then shouted towards the kitchen, "Henrietta!"

"Yes, darling!" she responded.

"It's time to start packin' your bags. We're going to England."

※　※　※

Dinner was delightful, as the two couples talked for hours around the small dinner table in the Johnsons' kitchen. Once the goose was consumed and the conversations of England and Africa dwindled, Mr. and Mrs. Smith braced for the cold and left for home. It was Henrietta's custom, when facing a difficult decision, to retire to her bedroom to pray and seek the Lord, so as soon as the Smiths' carriage marched from the street, she closed the bedroom door and fell to her knees.

Thomas sat alone at his desk. The wind howled through the crooked window frame, rattling the pane of glass, and the snow continued to stack against the sill next to the fireplace. As he stared at his almost-complete sermon, his eye was caught by his old journal that he kept on the corner of his desk.

Its cover was worn and the pages were yellowed. As he opened the front cover, the glow of the fireplace illuminated the first page. It revealed words that Thomas had written a lifetime ago, and he snickered at the handwriting, wobbly and frail.

Out loud, almost as a soft prayer, Thomas read the words—

born august 7 1836—a human
born again june 1857—a child of God
born into human liberty april 3 1865—a free man

Ten years after those words had been written, Thomas now sat at his desk in a house in Chicago, Illinois, with a steady hand, and a new fountain pen, and a bold mission for God burning within his bones. He began to write, adding a fourth line:

Called to missions in Africa, December 1875—a bondslave to Christ

CHAPTER 17

LET THE MAN COME

London, England 1876

Scarcely a year passed without one kind of illness or another confining Charles to his bed, sometimes for weeks, oftentimes for months. They were hard times, to say the least, spent out of the pulpit, either suffering, convalescing, or taking precautions against the return of illness. Susannah continued to remain in her bed on most days, but spent many nights writing entries in her journal and helping Charles craft sermons by candlelight.

On some mornings—on his better days—the swelling in Charles's joints would dwindle, allowing him to step out from his bed onto firm feet. These mornings could stack together like diamonds on a string, giving Charles weeks and months at a time of reprieve from the suffering. He was always grateful for those diamonds, and sprung up from his bed with a delightful sense of freedom. He and Susannah read together on those mornings. Then, Charles would kiss her forehead and fill his day visiting the sick, orphans, and other members of his congregation who needed their pastor.

But, on other mornings—on worse days—the swelling in Charles's joints would form into knots the size of golf balls, keeping him from standing. These mornings brought an immense sadness, and stoked the fires of depression within his heart and soul. He would lay in his bed, staring at the ceiling, wondering if the strength to stand would ever return. He worried about his wife, his children, and his church. The emotional and spiritual pain often overshadowed the physical pain of the gout, and although Charles trusted God, it still hurt.

❋ ❋ ❋

"Sing when you're in trouble, Charles! God loves to hear songs from His people—*especially* when they're in the storm," said George as he squeezed Charles's bicep and placed a cup of warm tea beside his bed.

"True, Old George. How is Susannah today?"

"She is having a good day." George brought Charles a wooden tray with his Bible, a few sheets of blank paper, and an ink pen, and placed it on the corner of his bed. "But Mrs. Spurgeon has noticed you have not read the Scriptures in a few days. She *insists* you make time this morning before anything else." Charles spawned a sincere chuckle and sipped his morning tea.

"Are you feeling well enough to work in your office today?"

"I am, George. Let's leave in one hour."

At once, George placed another piece of wood into the burning fireplace before leaving the study and quietly closing the door. Charles embraced the silence and stillness of the room as the morning sun peeked through the shades of the windows that lined his study. Just beyond the windows, his balcony overlooked the unattended garden in the backyard. Charles rubbed

his hands together, warming them, reminiscing of better days
when his knees sunk into the cool dirt of the garden, and his
muddied hands pulled stray weeds and caressed new buddings
that dared to rise from the soil.

Surely those days will return, Charles thought. But as he saw
the morning light illuminate his garden, he longed for the Better
Garden—the one that contained no thorns, no weeds, and certainly no gout. He thought of Heaven every day, and longed to
sink his knees into the fertile soil of that Celestial Garden, just
beyond the Crystal Sea.

"Tirshatha." Charles heard the familiar whisper from the
study door that opened to Susannah's bedroom.

"Susie!" exclaimed Charles, sitting taller in his bed.
Susannah radiated with beauty, even though her body was rid-
den with pain. She limped towards Charles's bed, and sat on
the edge next to the Bible. She slid her smooth hands over his
wrinkled cheeks, past his ears, then into his messy hair. Their
breathing slowed, and their eyes locked perfectly. "You look
beautiful today, Susie."

A meek smile rose from her face. "How I wish I could say the
same thing about you, husband."

Charles's laugh was always one of Susannah's favorite
things. Both belly laughs and reluctant chuckles were prizes
for her. She loved seeing his eyes squint with delight, his teeth
peek from his mustache and beard, and his round belly jiggle
as he laughed with childish glee. In sickness and in health,
Charles and Susannah continued to find space for laughter and
enjoyment of each other. While others may have soaked in their
misery, neglecting one another, Charles and Susannah were
determined to find those little sparks of joy—no matter how difficult it proved—every single day.

"How are your hands and feet feeling today?" she asked.

"Not as bad as they were yesterday." He opened his clenched hands. They trembled as she ran her hands across his swollen knuckles and jagged fingertips.

"It looks so painful," she whispered. "I wish I could take them from you, Charles."

He forced a smile onto his face, squinted his eyes, and let out a deep sigh. The wrinkles on his face surprised Susannah, as it seemed there were more than the last time. They stretched like a spiderweb from the corners of his eyes towards his graying hair. From the edge of his dried lips, they cornered his smile and buried themselves into his beard. Charles exhaled deeply and continued, "I am a torn soul, wifey."

"What do you mean?"

"I mean that I know the truths of God. That He is our treasure . . . and that He is enough . . . even in the midst of suffering. And yet, I am a torn soul."

"Because you wish for a smoother path?" she asked concernedly.

"Perhaps I do," he spoke slowly as he pressed his eyelids closed. "I—I simply do not *want* to be confined to this bed. I do not *want* your body to be ravished with pain. I do not *want* for our lives to be marked with sickness. I do not *want* it. And yet, if this is what God has for us—I want to *want* it! Does that make sense?" He lowered his head in frustration and opened his eyes to the tattered leather cover of his Bible, still sitting unopened atop the wooden tray on his bed. "I want to *want* this hard path we are on."

Susannah spoke not a word, breathed deeply, then reached into the cabinet next to his bed to retrieve a glass jar of cream and a roll of gauze that Dr. Anderson had left for Charles. Pouring a small amount of cream into the palm of her hand, she rubbed her hands together, then carefully applied the ointment to his shaking hands. Charles rested his head on the headboard of his bed and closed his eyes as Susannah meticulously ran her hands along each finger, through the cracks and bends, over the knobs and open sores. As she traced the deep lines within his palms, she thought of all that these hands had held throughout his forty-three years of life—wooden pulpits, leather Bibles, the hands of sinners and saints, his two sons, her, their household, the Tabernacle, the pen that had composed life-giving sermons to so many souls.

"Our Father," she delicately prayed as she wrapped each of his hands in the clean, white bandage, "would you please, by Your kindness and in Your mercy, keep these blistered hands to the plough." When she was finished, she closed the jar and returned the items to the cabinet, then opened his Bible to Psalm 119 and pushed it close to his chest.

"I love you," she whispered. "And perhaps the *worst* thing that could happen to our family is to have our path made too smooth. We are on the harder road, Charles. The one less traveled. May God keep our hands to the plough on this rough road."

"Yes," he said confidently. "And, the further we are on the road, the less there is of it to bear."

"George will be in soon to take you to the Tabernacle. You have much work to do. And I must lie down." Once again, she kissed his forehead, then gracefully left the room and sank into her bed.

Charles, filled with courage and gratitude, whispered Psalm 119:50: "This is my comfort in my affliction: for Thy Word hath quickened me."

※ ※ ※

When Charles arrived at the Metropolitan Tabernacle, just a few kilometers from the Helensburgh House, it was already noon. Tuesdays were busy days in the church office. Nearly twenty men and women were necessary to assist with the task of running all the ventures outside the normal scope of the Metropolitan Tabernacle's routine, including the Pastors' College, *The Sword and the Trowel* (a weekly publication), an orphanage, and the Colportage Association (an entity that distributed Christian books and literature through the world). The work of the ministry had stretched far beyond Charles's hands, and he was delighted by the bustling ministry that was affecting people far from the borders of the United Kingdom.

Joseph Harrald was joined by several other secretaries at the office of the Tabernacle, as the heavy load of ministry work demanded many hands to make it lighter. Joseph handled most of the correspondence with mail, Mr. Keys helped oversee *The Sword and the Trowel*, Mr. Wigney managed the Colportage Association, and his brother, James Spurgeon, ran most of the day-to-day operations of the church as the associate pastor. His best deacon, Mrs. Bartlett, cared for young women studying the Bible, and saw nearly seven hundred women attend Bible classes throughout the week.

Though Charles was a strong leader, the secret of his pastorship was in his vulnerability. He never tried to hide his bandaged hands and feet, he rarely hid his depression, seldom shielding people from his weariness. Instead, he made it a rule to include his office bearers in the journey. His honest nature was attractive to people—his closest elders and deacons frequently called him "the dear governor," a term of endearment and respect. In fact, it was his vulnerability that allowed him to be such a great comforter to the sick and oppressed. He empathized in the deepest way possible, drawing them into the depths of his heart, where he shared the healing balm of the gospel for which he had become so desperate.

"There are many letters for you here today, pastor." Joseph met Charles at the door of the study, carrying a basket spilling with letters of different sizes and shapes, from all over the world. He held it towards Charles and waited for him to receive the basket. "I've separated them into a few sections, based on what part of the world they are coming from, and I've sorted out the ones that do not require a reply."

Charles grinned at Joseph and held out his two bandaged and unusable hands.

"Mr. Spurgeon . . . I'm sorry. I—I didn't realize . . ." said Joseph, embarrassed by his lack of discretion.

"It's quite alright. Just set it on my desk."

Joseph blushed and carried the large basket to the desk.

"Thank you, Joseph. Are there any that must be answered today?" Charles sat in the wooden chair at his writing desk in the corner of the room, in between the desks of Mr. Wigney and Mr. Keys. His rotund body instantly dwarfed the chair and desk. Through the years, he had gained weight, but his appearance still remained neat and sophisticated. "Will you kindly remove my hat?"

"Of course, Charles." He hurriedly removed Charles's hat from his plump head and hung it on the coat rack near the door of the study. "There are a few that should be answered today. One from a minister in Manchester, Mister William Hind Smith of the Y.M.C.A., Peter Street."

"Let me see it." Joseph placed the letter on the desk as Charles read it quietly.

Dearest Reverend Spurgeon,

I am writing as a brother in Christ, and a fellow pilgrim on the journey homeward. I have recently given a portion of my home to a lovely man and his wife, as they have traveled all the way here from the United States of America in search of a course of study before going to Africa as missionaries. Thomas Johnson and his wife, Henrietta, both found their freedom after President Lincoln's Proclamation in 1865, as they were both enslaved to the terrible institution of slavery in the Confederate Union. Mister Johnson has no money, and no way to afford the

Pastors' College, only a sharp mind and a dangerous aspiration to reach Africa with the gospel.

With sincerest urgency, I beg of you to admit Thomas Johnson as a student to your Pastors' College.

Warmly,

Rev. William Hind Smith

Charles rose to his feet and reread the letter, this time out loud to Joseph and Mr. Keys. The three men were completely stunned, as they had not heard a similar or more profound story than a freed slave seeking education through the Pastors' College.

"Gentlemen, are there funds available in the school fund to provide this man a scholarship? I cannot imagine a better suited use for the Lord's resources than a former slave desiring to take the news of Christ's freedom to the land of his fathers."

"We will find the money, Charles," Mr. Keys replied with authority.

"Joseph—at once—send a reply to Mr. Smith."

"What should it say?"

"Write this." Charles cleared his throat, then spoke as Joseph anxiously scribbled.

Dear Mr. Hind Smith—Yes, let the dear man come.

—C. H. Spurgeon

SECTION 4

CHAPTER 18

WHISPERINGS

England 1876

When Thomas's feet hit English soil for the first time, it was an exhilarating experience. After a grueling trek across the Atlantic Ocean on the *SS Spain* of the National Line, Thomas and Henrietta arrived in Manchester in the winter of 1876. England was much colder than he expected, but the warmth of the English people—their kindness, hospital-ity, and warm tea—assured Thomas that God was taking care of him, just as He always had.

After being accepted into the Pastors' College, Thomas and Henrietta moved from the Smiths' house in Manchester to Mr. Wigney's cozy apartment near the college. Mr. Wigney was kind enough to offer his extra bedroom to the Johnsons, free of charge, and they soon came to love the man dearly. Every morning Thomas knelt at their bed frame, asked the Lord for wisdom and guidance, and then walked to the college to attend classes. Thomas often shook his head in disbelief as he sat behind his desk in the classroom, listening to professors and frantically taking notes; he never imagined he would experience the privilege of school, much less a college. This sense of overwhelming gratitude spilled out into every conversation he had with people—believing and unbelieving. Thomas couldn't help himself from telling every person he came in contact with about the goodness of God.

※ ※ ※

"Tonight should be a good night, Henrietta," said Thomas as he unpacked his school bag onto the tiny table in the corner of their bedroom.

"I'm nervous, actually," Henrietta said as she sat at the table and thumbed through Thomas's notes titled "An Introduction to Hermeneutics."

"Yes—I'm nervous too. But, I guess that's alright," said Thomas.

"What is her—men—owl," she paused, unable to finish reading the strange word.

"Hermeneutics. It's a funny word for how to read the Bible," he smiled, removing his coat, settling it on the back of his chair.

"Why are you nervous about tonight?" asked Henrietta earnestly. "I thought you'd be excited."

"Oh, I'm excited. I'm *very* excited." Thomas sat in the c on the opposite side of the table and continued, "Before the . . . when I was still a slave in Virginia . . . I heard my ow talk of Mr. Spurgeon. I was a nobody. A piece of somebody property. So, there was no idea of me ever *seeing* Mr. Spur though I dreamed of hearing him preach one day."

Henrietta placed her elbows on the cold metal table as Thomas continued, "Well, I supposed the Lord knew this. And, He has granted me more than my desire. I guess this is the way the Lord treats His children, doing greater things for them than they ask or think. So, I *am* excited. I'm also just a little nervous. He is a hero to me, and I worry if I have the right words to say. Who knows? He might talk the whole time! What do I have to say to Charles Spurgeon, anyway?"

"Will his wife be there tonight?" she asked.

"Susannah. Yes. Mr. Wigney said she will be there."

"What will you talk about?" asked Henrietta, revealing a nervousness of her own.

"I—I want to tell him—how much of an encouragement he has been to my faith."

"How are you gonna tell him that?" she asked with a puzzling look.

Thomas fumbled around his bag until he found a tiny pamphlet and set it on the table in front of Henrietta. She picked it up and read the title, "'The Preacher's Prayer.' Did Mr. Spurgeon write this?"

"Well, sort of. This was sent to me a long time ago from the American Bible Society. It was called 'Preacher's Prayer' because it was an address that Mr. Spurgeon gave to his students."

"What's it about?"

"In this little book, Mr. Spurgeon wrote that if a preacher wishes to reap in the pulpit, he must plough in the closet." He paused and nodded his head. "I prayed before I preached *many* times before, but I never saw the matter of prayer in the same light as this little book put it. No book—other than the Holy Bible, of course—has ever given me such help and encouragement."

"I see," Henrietta nodded as she flipped through the pages of the pamphlet. "You should tell him those very words."

"I do plan to do that. Maybe that'll keep me from being nervous." Thomas smiled and gently pulled the pamphlet from Henrietta's hand and slid it back into his bag.

The carriage ride from Thomas's apartment to Charles's house on Nightingale Lane took nearly an hour, since London's traffic had continued to worsen over the years. When Charles and Susannah first moved into the Helensburgh House, it was surrounded only by rural countryside, but by 1876, the expansive city had crawled its way from the River Thames, down Clapham High Street, and into the Spurgeon family's once-quiet neighborhood near Clapham Common.

As the carriage rolled to a stop, the driver bounced to the ground to open the iron gate that bordered the entrance of the Helensburgh House. Along the brick fence, several gas lamps flickered in their glass cases, but were unmoved by the strong winter wind that sailed through the front yard.

"My goodness . . . that's a nice house," Thomas said as he buttoned his coat and checked to make sure his hair was in order. Combed down from the middle, it stood tall out around his ears and almost appeared as a dark triangle atop his well-groomed face. He was of solid build—lean and tall—and his facial features were weatherproof from the years of hard labor in the fields.

As Thomas and Henrietta exited the carriage, Thomas placed a few silver pounds in the hand of the driver and thanked him for his service. The size of the Helensburgh House always surprised visitors, with its massive tower in the middle section and rows of candlelit windows along the front. Henrietta held Thomas by his forearm as they made their way up the steps to the small front porch.

"I can't believe I'm here," he whispered excitedly to Henrietta. "I know he's just a man. But, he is a very good man."

"He's just a man," Henrietta reassured him.

Thomas knocked gently on the door, and to his surprise it opened almost immediately. As it creaked into the darkened entryway, Thomas was met by a smiling Old George.

"Welcome, welcome," whispered George. "I am so very glad you are here, Mr. and Mrs. Johnson. Please do come in. My name is George." He extended his hand and shook both Thomas and Henrietta's somewhat vigorously.

Thomas was surprised by George's enthusiasm, but even more surprised by the darkened house and the whispered welcome. George closed the door behind them and took their coats, hanging them gently on the rack next to the window of the foyer.

"We are delighted to be here, George. Please do tell Mr. and Mrs. Spurgeon how grateful we are they would invite us into their home," Thomas said, keeping his voice as low as George's.

"Well my friends, you can just do that yourselves." George turned towards the empty hallway, paused, then turned back towards them. "Follow me, and I'll take you to the conservatory. Would you care for some evening tea?"

"Yes, please," Thomas and Henrietta said in unison.

"I've kept the lights very low in the conservatory. And, please keep your voices just above a whisper. Sometimes, light and sounds are very difficult on Mrs. Spurgeon's headaches."

Thomas was caught off guard by the strangeness of the encounter. He had heard that Mrs. Spurgeon was sick from time to time, but didn't realize the gravity of the situation until he saw George's concerned eyes and the three nurses that passed them in the hallway, on their way home for the night.

"Good night, ladies. God speed," said George as they quietly squeezed the doorknob and closed it behind them. "God has been good to give us these women. They are a godsend in caring for the Spurgeons."

"The Spurgeons?" asked Thomas in surprise. "Is someone beside Mrs. Spurgeon sick?"

"Aye, Thomas," whispered George, wrinkling his nose and biting his upper lip. "Mr. Spurgeon has been very sick for some time. Were you not aware?"

"No. I was not, sir." Thomas slumped his shoulders, as a rush of genuine grief rose from his chest. "Is it a serious illness?"

"It has affected Mr. Spurgeon in ways I cannot explain. And yes—it has always been serious."

"Mr. George, perhaps we should return on another evening? Perhaps, a better day?" asked Henrietta, still gripping Thomas's arm.

"No, no, no—he has been looking forward to meeting you both for quite some time. He would not dare miss the opportunity to welcome you to London—and to the Pastors' College."

George continued to reassure them as he led them down the hallway, through the dining room and library, and into the glass-walled conservatory near the back of the house. The walls and ceilings of windows glittered as they quietly reflected the tiny gas lamps around the room. Thomas stepped down into the conservatory, then waited for his eyes to adjust to the shadowy room. As the darkness changed to muted light, Thomas released a quiet sigh of sadness as he saw Charles sitting on the corner of a couch, covered in a blue blanket with a bandaged head, his quivering and bandaged hands neatly placed on his lap.

"Mr. and Mrs. Johnson," whispered Charles, "please, come. Come, sit." Charles's bleary eyes remained steady and focused, but it was obvious to Thomas that he was in pain. Thomas and Henrietta quietly gazed toward the center of the room where Charles sat across from Susannah. Her body lay slouched in a large comfortable chair, and she was wrapped in a beautifully patched quilt made of cotton and silk. Her hair, slightly greying at the roots, was pulled neatly behind her ears, revealing her simple face and warm smile. The Spurgeons seemed tired, worn from years of pain.

"We wish we could stand to greet you, but please do come sit with us," whispered Susannah.

Thomas seated himself on the couch next to Charles, while Henrietta sat in a wooden chair next to Susannah. A sober silence filled the room as they welcomed the moment and refused to rush it forward.

"Thomas," started Charles, "you must know how honored I am to meet you."

"Sir—I," started Thomas before he was interrupted by Charles.

"No, you must hear me say it, Thomas. When we first received word of your coming to England . . . and the story of God releasing you from bondage . . . and your desire to preach the Good News to Africa . . . we at once knew we must make a way for you to attend the Pastors' College. I do hope everyone is treating you properly."

"They are, sir—I—I—"

"Charles. You must call me Charles," he insisted, leaning towards Thomas and ever so slightly, smiling through his wiry beard.

Thomas quietly laughed and nodded, agreeing to Charles's request, "Alright, sir. I'll call you Charles."

"And you . . ." Charles said, directing his attention to Henrietta who was perfectly poised in her chair, "you must be Henrietta."

"I am. And it truly is good to meet you both," she said.

"Tell us. What do you think of England?" whispered Susannah, stretching her eyes open and lifting a polite smile.

"It has made a lasting impression on us," Thomas cleared his nervous throat and continued. "Just after we were settled in Manchester, earlier this fall, I preached at the Jackson Street Ragged School. Are you familiar with it, Charles?"

"I cannot say that I am. Tell me about it," Charles said, interested.

"My sermon was nothing worth talking around," Thomas said, "but there was something that stuck as one of my first memories of England. In the entrance of the school, I saw a *beautiful* painting. It was the queen. And she was giving a Bible to an African prince who was on his knees with his hands open to receive it. So, there I was, staring at this painting, when one of the professors saw me staring. And, do you know what he told me?"

The listeners shook their heads and leaned in, listening intently.

"The African prince had come to England to ask the queen a question. 'What's the secret of England's greatness?' the prince asked. The queen, without hesitation, handed the prince a Bible. And as she put it in his hands, she said, '*This* is the secret of England's greatness.'" Thomas paused and looked around the small circle of friends. "From that day, I have not been able to shake that painting out of my mind. It has been confirmed again and again—the secret of anyone's greatness is the *Bible*."

"Amen, Thomas," said Charles, much louder than a whisper. He was immediately struck by Thomas's ability to tell a great story. Noticing his charisma and charm, he realized the young preacher had the rare ability to draw a listener into his world, even though he didn't have a robust vocabulary, as his passion made up for any he lacked.

As Thomas continued to tell the story, Charles and Susannah listened intently. "And do you know what else has stuck in my memory?" he asked. "As I looked into that painting, I remembered the first time I realized the queen wasn't a black woman!"

"Why on earth did you think the Queen of England was a black woman?" asked Susannah with smiling curiosity.

"Well, ma'am, when I was a little boy, I heard that the queen had given a very large amount of money to free slaves in the West. So, of course, I imagined her to be a black woman. Who else would have enough kindness to buy the freedom for slaves they'd never met? I simply couldn't believe that a great ruler— one so kind to colored people—could be *anybody* but a black person." Thomas settled into the couch.

"I have brought tea," interrupted George as he entered the conservatory, placing a piping cup of chamomile tea beside each guest.

"Tell me, Thomas," said Charles with a somber voice, "you were a slave for how many years?"

"Twenty-eight, sir."

"Twenty-eight years?" Charles said each word slowly, separately, then leaned forward from the couch and placed his bandaged hands on his knees.

"It was all I ever knew," Thomas continued. "And, I still can't believe I am free."

"Did you know Jesus when you were a slave?" asked Charles.

"Yes. Jesus found me on a tobacco plantation in Virginia when I was a much younger man. And when I met Him, He changed everything." Thomas took a sip of his tea and continued, "See, when Jesus found me, He was all I had. After a long, hard day of work, and sometimes during beatings at the whippin' post, I knew that Jesus was there. He was right there the whole time."

"What was it like to worship Jesus on the plantation?" asked Charles with genuine intrigue.

"Our nights of worship were much like this night. We huddled inside a candlelit room long after the master and foreman went to sleep. It was always just a few men and women, sometimes a few children, and first thing we did—we just sat and talked about Jesus. We talked about our struggle, our day in the fields. Then, somebody would open a Bible and read it. Usually it was my friend, Ezekiel. He had such a way of talking about Jesus that it made you want to love Him more."

The memory of Ezekiel, the outline of his face and the warmth of his voice flooded Thomas's memory, bringing a rush of nostalgia to his senses. "We tried to meet every night. Other times, we'd have to crawl on our hands and knees to make it to the little clapboard shack in the middle of the plantation.

Sometimes, if the moon was too bright, and the foreman was out, we couldn't meet. But on most nights, once we got to Ezekiel's quarters, it was like *Jesus* was right there with us. Right there in the darkness. I always knew He was there."

"Praise God," whispered Charles sincerely.

"Charles—if I may ask—what is yours and Susannah's—" Thomas struggled to find the right words.

"What's our sickness?" Charles helped him finish the question.

"If I may ask?"

"The doctors have not been able to assess my dear Susie's condition. After the birth of our twins, Charles and Thomas," Charles paused and thought of the irony of their names.

"Charles and Thomas are their names?" asked Henrietta, forgetting Old George's polite request to whisper.

"Well, I must say it is indeed an incredible twist of fate," Charles continued. "After the birth of Charles and Thomas, Susannah noticed a horrible pain in her abdomen, and since then, it has held her to her bed."

Susannah nodded and pursed her lips together.

"As for my illness, it is called *gout*. Some days, it merely causes my hands to ache, but other days—worse days like this one—my joints swell, and my skin cracks."

"My goodness. I'm very sorry," whispered Thomas, full of compassion.

"No—no. My pain is *nothing* compared to what yours has been, Thomas," Charles raised his voice slightly, as his indignation for the old way of American slavery still riled him. "The evils done to you were terrible, Thomas. And they were done by the hands of men with no regard for human dignity. Mine and Susannah's suffering is much shallower."

"What do you mean, Pastor Spurgeon?" said Thomas, once again forgetting to call the revered man 'Charles.' It was difficult for him to view as an equal a man he had so long admired and respected.

"I mean that I cannot complain. I should rejoice in these sufferings." Charles leaned backward into the couch and used his bandaged hands to help illustrate the story as he talked, "A few years ago, after a long period of painful illness from gout, I was starting for a short drive in my carriage, in the hope of gaining a little strength, when this gentleman came up to the carriage. And pointing to my bandaged hand and foot, he said, with all the scorn and contempt he could compress into the words, 'Whom the Lord loveth, He chasteneth. But, I would not have such a God as that.'" Charles took a pause, then raised his bandaged hands and held them up as he finished, "I felt my blood boil with indignation, and I answered, 'I rejoice that I have such a God as this. And if He were to chasten me a thousand times worse than this, I would still love Him.'"

"Ah, yes Charles. I'm sure you would."

"But my bandaged hands and feet still seem very shallow compared to the depth of sufferings you both experienced for so long," he said looking at Thomas and Henrietta.

Turning his body towards Charles on the corner of the couch, Thomas extended his hands forward, then motioned for Charles to place his hands within his. Carefully, Thomas held the trembling hands of the weakened pastor. Choosing his words with caution, Thomas immediately felt the power of the Holy Spirit give him words beyond his own wisdom, beyond his own vocabulary.

"These bandages," he whispered slowly, "are the sufferings we *can* see. They are on the outside. They are flesh. They are blood. But, they are *only* the physical, my friend. What about all of your sufferings that nobody can see?"

Charles tilted his head back and exhaled deeply. His hands continued to shake as they rested on Thomas's strong hands. He squished his cheeks towards his eyes, then shut them tightly to hold back a river of tears. Throughout the years, no one other than Susannah had ever attempted to peer into the depths of his sufferings in such an earnest way.

"Charles," continued Thomas, "you say my suffering as a slave was somehow worse than yours. If my *only* sufferings were seen in the beatings—*only* seen in the bloody scabs and the tender scars—then maybe you can say I had it worse than you. But my suffering wasn't just the things on the outside, and neither is yours." He steadied his eyes on the old pastor's face, now drenched in tears. "Your suffering ain't just bandages and sores and pain. That's a part of it, for sure. But, that's just the stuff on the outside. What about the spiritual wounds?" Thomas asked. "What about the wounds that live in your mind?"

Charles took a deep breath and wiped tears from his eyes with one of his bandaged hands. The tears soaked into the gauze, and he felt their cool waters touch his skin. "No one living knows the toil and care I have to bear. I ask for no sympathy, Thomas."

Thomas nodded his head and placed Charles's hands back onto his knees. "I rejoice that I got a God that puts me in moments like these," said Thomas, nodding his head from the edge of the couch. Within the candlelit room, Thomas's face glowed with compassion and understanding.

"Pastor, you got burdens on you that no muscle of your own can hold up. And then, you also got the Devil—the old foreman on the plantation of your soul—and he's gonna do whatever he can to keep your spirit low, to pile burdens on your shoulders that are too heavy to bear. That's what the *Devil* does. That's who he is. It's all he knows how to do."

"Yes," muttered Charles. "I can—I can recall as a child, feeling so overwhelmed by the powerful darkness of the Devil. I tried so hard to push him away, but at times it seemed like darkness was choking me by the throat, and beating me down. Then, after I met Jesus—I thought that would all flutter away. But, if I'm honest, I still wander into murky seas of depression and sadness. It's unexplainable, I know. Sometimes, it feels as though the entire room narrows, and time slows down, and all I can see is shadows, and total darkness."

"And that's why we worship an *all-sufficient* God, whose burden is light, and whose yoke is easy. He's the Light of the World. And He ain't like no Devil—the old foreman who whips us with leather straps and shackles us with iron chains. He ain't like that," said Thomas with a rhythmic, sermon-like cadence.

Charles spoke no words, but nodded his head in agreement.

"Does God chastise us?" asked Thomas rhetorically. "Sure He does. But He chastises us with tender love. Does He bruise us? Sure. But only with gentle kindness. He might even crush us to the ground, but only with His fond affection. Think about your suffering, Charles. Not the bandages or the sores, but think about the brokenness underneath. It's a burden, yes. But a gentle burden. And it's meant to stir up more faithfulness in you. I know that you know this, pastor. But, have you forgotten?"

Charles remained speechless. He continued to wipe tears from his face, as he nodded and continued to listen, soaking up every word from the Holy Spirit, who was speaking powerfully through this new and unlikely friend, Thomas Johnson.

"Your depressive thoughts aren't meant to press you down. No! They are meant to fly your soul *up*. Up to the arms of the Good Master. Charles, you count up your crosses, as bitter as they might seem. You count up your diseases, pains, and sorrows, as many as they might be. Then, you see that Jesus put 'em all there. He put them there so you'd run to Him faster than you've ever run. He might not ever take them away. Even if Jesus had never taken slavery away from me, I still think it would have done just what it was supposed to—make me run to Jesus over and over again. *That's* when you see how sweet He is. He's right there. Has been the whole time. Sharin' in that suffering. Weepin' with you. Why? Because He's *that* good."

"I suppose He is *that* good," choked Charles through tears. "When you—when you finally made it to the shack at night to worship, were you able to sing?"

"Oh, Charles—did we ever! Now, we couldn't sing out loud. If the foreman heard us, he'd pull us out and beat us. So you know what we had to do? We *whispered* our songs. Sometimes, during the hardest of seasons, all you can do is whisper songs of hope in the night. But I'll tell you—God always hears."

Charles sank back into the couch and covered his face with his bandaged hands. "I—I'm not sure I've ever thought about singing in the darkness in such a . . . in such a real way." Charles rarely struggled to find the right words, but in the moment, he was overtaken by the parallel of Thomas's story of slavery and his own enslavement to depression and suffering.

"What did you sing?" whispered Susannah, plainly.

"Oh, ma'am, we used to always sing one of my favorite songs. It's one that has settled in my mind and buried itself into memory. It's the one they were singing when I met Jesus for the first time. I remember the night so well. We all knelt in a circle, held hands, closed our eyes, and then whispered the song to the Lord."

"Would you sing it, Thomas? As you did on the plantation?" asked Susannah, tenderly.

"Oh dear, yes. Would you sing it?" asked Charles, as he did his best to hold the flood of tears in his eyes. "I'd very much like to worship in this darkness with you."

Thomas knelt to the floor and held an empty hand towards Charles, the other held toward Henrietta. Charles carefully pushed himself from the couch, pressed his knees into the hardened floor, and placed one hand into Thomas's and the other into Susannah's. Forming a circle, they each held the hand of the person next to them, and as they did, a gentle warmth passed from finger to finger, palm to palm, flesh to flesh, spirit to spirit. Thomas's warm eyes and calm smile focused on Charles's face, then swung to Susannah's where it met her teary eyes. A sting of pain rushed through Charles's swollen knees, but there within the stillness of the glass conservatory, the pain was welcomed— for, it was the sting of sweet surrender.

The kind light of the silver moon shone brightly through the glass ceiling and overwhelmed the candle flames and overpowered the darkness. The wintry wind blew around the conservatory, but no one moved or shivered, for the warmest and most soothing worship time they had ever experienced was underway.

The circle of friends bowed their heads, closed their eyes, and breaking the silence of the night, Thomas, in a whisper, began to sing—

> *My Lord. He calls me.*
> *He calls me by the thunder.*
> *The trumpet sounds within my soul.*
> *I ain't got long to stay here.*

He took a deep breath, then continued—

> *Steal away.*
> *Steal away.*
> *Steal away to Jesus.*

Susannah smiled fiercely as she thought of Jesus, and swore He was sitting right there next to her. Charles kept his eyes closed as tears continued to erupt, even through his tightened eyelids, and as Thomas held Charles by the swollen hand, he thought of Heaven and Jesus, confident that all of Heaven was joining in the worship of the Good Master. Thomas took another slow, deep breath, then started the second half of the chorus as the faint whisperings of Charles Spurgeon sang along—

> *Steal away.*
> *Steal away home.*
> *I ain't got long to stay here.*
> *Steal away home.*

CHAPTER 19

THE NEW FOREST

England 1878

By the time Thomas Edison completed his design of a filament lightbulb powered by electricity, excitement and curiosity spread across America and Europe. Some were quick to make the change from traditional gas-lit lamps to trendy lightbulbs, but Charles scoffed at the idea. He was a man who enjoyed the simple things in life and couldn't conjure a reason to clutter his Helensburgh Home with odd-shaped bulbs that hummed and glowed an unnatural glimmer.

He had always been a simple man, and simple men love simple things. From the early years of roaming the hills of Essex and enjoying the cool winds that chased through Stambourne, Charles tried his best to avoid modernity by surrounding himself with as many natural things as possible. On sickly nights, he loved sitting on the stone patio that stretched toward the garden in the backyard, tracing the summer stars with his fingers, trying his best to count as many as he could. When Charles felt well enough, he hurried to work on his many beehives near the wooden fence, just behind the garden. He watched their hives grow and expand, and was mesmerized by their single-mindedness and firm devotion to the production of sweet, golden honey. Ever so gently, he lifted bursting honeycombs from their hives as he licked his lips and smiled with delight. The beauty of God's creation seemed to peel Charles away from the constant stirring of London, offering a healing to his depression.

Charles also found that brotherly friendships were a powerful force in the war against darkness, and when Sabbath rest was paired with the company of a beloved friend, the days were brighter indeed. One of those beloved friends quickly became Thomas Johnson. In the two years since their first meeting in the conservatory, Charles and Thomas effortlessly dove into the depths of kindred friendship, far below surface-level chats or small talk. Charles was deeply intrigued with Thomas's past experiences as a slave and his future hopes for ministry, while Thomas was genuinely attentive to Charles's own wrestling with sorrow and grief. The company of a good friend proved more appealing to Charles than any modern entertainment found in London, much more soothing than fine possessions that the nineteenth century could afford, and certainly stronger than the light of a filament lightbulb.

Whether it was a starry night on the patio, a morning in the garden, an afternoon with bees, or a week in the countryside with a friend, Charles did his best to surround himself with things that felt natural, real, and truthful. Because, when a person wars against depression, and tries with all their might to push away the haunting darkness that always seems to shout lies and whisper deceit—that person pays very close attention to the things that illuminate truth. Like sunshine after a weeklong shower, truth is wonderfully bright to a depressed heart.

⊠ ⊠ ⊠

"Old George," Charles said as he placed his arms into his long coat, "What time will Thomas arrive?"

"He should be here any moment, sir," said George.

"Have you packed the carriage?"

"Of course, sir," George replied as he arranged a pile of suit-cases near the front porch. "I've also packed your books, your writing utensils, and a nice bottle of Sherry."

"Thank you, George. Is Susannah settled for the week while I am away?" Charles asked.

"She knew you would ask, sir. And—insists you stop worry-ing about her, and get on your way. She knows that a week of rest in the New Forest is, for you, better than a month by her side." George winked, then began to stack the luggage at the rear of the carriage that sat in the front courtyard of the house.

Charles recalled the thrill of purchasing the old carriage— some years ago—as well as Susannah's uncontrollable laughing at its rugged and grotesque appearance. Its inelegance was wors-ened when Charles asked George to install a wooden platform at the rear—just above the bumper—to support a wobbly stack of luggage with leather straps and silver buckles. Charles affection-ately named the old carriage, *"Punch's Coach,"* which bewildered and amused Susannah every time she saw Charles awkwardly climb into the door with his pug in his arms.

"You'll be taking Punch with you, I suppose?" yelled George from the other side of the carriage.

"Of course, George. It wouldn't very much be a proper trip without Punch, now would it?"

"No sir. And—you couldn't call it *Punch's Coach* if that beast was not gnawing on the furniture and urinating on the floor during the length of the trip," he joked as he kicked the iron wheels of the trustworthy carriage. George whistled, calling for

Punch, then at once the squatty pug ran from inside the foyer, sat just beneath the open door of the rickety carriage, lifted his leg, then marked his territory on the wheel of the carriage.

"Well done, Punch. Well done," George said, gently placing the pug inside the seating area, as both men roared with laughter.

Charles and Punch adored each other, and nestling into the cozy seats of the carriage on long journeys. Charles appreciated comfort in most things, but amusingly cared nothing of his carriage's appearance. And old shabby carriage and an old horse—inappropriately named Peacock—were matters of perfect indifference to him, so long as they were safe and trustworthy, and carried him out of the noise of the crowded world, into the stillness and beauty of nature's quiet resting places.

Charles placed his leather satchel next to Punch, scrubbed the top of the dog's head, then made his way to the horse at the front of the carriage.

"Peacock—you devil, you! Strong as an ox . . . gentle as a kitten. Are you ready to drive us over the hill and dale and into God's *real* creation?" Peacock flickered his ear as Charles patted his head, scratched behind his ear, and ran his hand through Peacock's long, brown mane. "You know Susie always laughs at my affection for you, Peacock?"

"Susie laughs at *many* of your affections, Charles. Especially your affection for animals," wheezed George, overhearing. "Look, sir, Mr. Johnson has arrived."

With suitcase in hand, Thomas walked—nearly skipping—towards the carriage and embraced Charles as a long-lost brother. "Charles, it is good to see you today, my friend," he said as he squeezed his neck with his limber arms. "You're in good health, Charles. Looks like the Lord is showing you tremendous grace to get you out of the house and stretch your legs."

"Yes He is, Thomas. Gout is a tricky companion—you never know when it will rise and fall," Charles pulled the suitcase from Thomas's hand and placed it with the other pieces of luggage.

Charles's illness was a deceptive one indeed, as he never knew when it would flare up or lie dormant within the joints of his hands and legs. In this particular season, he felt like a new man. It had been nearly a month since any bandages or ointments were necessary, so he welcomed the opportunity to enjoy a week in the New Forest to read and write with his good companion, Thomas. Since returning to the pulpit at Metropolitan Tabernacle, he felt useful again. Yesterday's sermon at the Tabernacle had been an especially delightful one to preach, and as the Monday sun was just beginning to peek above Nightingale Lane, his heart raced with anticipation to get on the road southward from London.

"Alright—Thomas, George, Peacock, Punch—it looks like our army has assembled! Off we go." Charles carefully climbed into the carriage—his knees fragile from the previous encounter with gout—then removed his top hat and slumped into the ill-patterned, maroon and yellow seat.

Old George drove the carriage out of the front court of the Helensburgh House and turned southwest on Nightingale Lane with the hot glow of the rising sun to his back. Charles had told many stories to Thomas about the New Forest—with its charming country towns and golden sunsets—but this was the first time he had the chance to share the heavenly setting with his dear friend. As Thomas's schooling was coming to an end, Charles thought it was well suited for both of them to experience the journey, and the destination, together.

He was never more happy and exuberant when he made these excursions, yet he also was never more tempted to wrestle with thoughts of anxiety and depression—being alone and quiet was both a blessing and a curse. To fight against the Devil's whispers, Charles wised up, and often invited a student or enjoyable fellow to join. Anyone that accompanied Charles saw him at his best, both funny and charming, introspective and real.

"Did you bring your pen and paper?" asked Thomas from the opposite seat of the carriage.

"Indeed, Thomas. And you, your schoolwork?"

"Well, I was hoping to take a break from schoolwork. But I knew you would ask, so Henrietta said I should pack it." Thomas leaned towards the plush seatback and pushed his leather shoes off his feet. As rows of tall trees rushed past the window, Thomas considered how different the English landscape was from his hometown in Virginia. There was a lushness to the countryside of Great Britain that rivaled Richmond on her most fruitful day of springtime. After two years of training at the Pastors' College, Thomas had grown immensely in wisdom and confidence, and just as the trees in Great Britain seemed to stand taller and stronger than those of old Richmond, so did Thomas.

"Tell me about this forest. Where are we going?"

"The *New* Forest, Thomas. Not just any forest!" Charles pulled a cigar from his cotton vest, and lit the end.

"I thought you stopped smoking? Didn't Dr. Anderson say you should stop?"

"Well, Thomas," Charles paused to inhale a drag of sweet smoke, "I choose not to invite Dr. Anderson on these trips to the New Forest, because if I wanted someone to remind me to stop smoking, I would have asked the good doctor to come along!" His belly shook as he laughed. "And—I'd very much like to just smoke my cigar to the glory of God without any judgment."

"Whatever you say—Reverend," said Thomas with a playful grin.

The two friends sat in silence for the first few hours of the trip. As the clamors of London finally dwindled in the distance, the small town of Guildford, England, rose before them. After passing through Guildford's green-hedge fences, they drove to the foot of Martha's Chapel, and spied the brilliant stone cathedral that rose from atop a very great summit. The chapel was a hundred years old, and stood high above the valley as a king's castle. It often reminded Charles of the better King, and his better Kingdom—one that would overwhelm the moss-covered mountains and the stacked-stone cathedrals of England.

"What a pretty country," Thomas murmured as he peered through the carriage window, now open, allowing the cool morning breeze to tickle his face and dance in his hair. There wasn't much conversation as the carriage charged ahead through village after village, over hill and dale, bridge and stream. Both Charles and Thomas welcomed the silence, embracing the sweet wonders of God's imagination and creation. There are friends that require much talking—as they are insecure with silence—but there are other friends which require no words, no dialogue for enjoyment. These were the friends that Charles and Thomas had become, and as the carriage whisked them from town to town, an occasional, "Isn't that stunning?" was enough.

❊ ❊ ❊

When they finally arrived at their lunch destination in Winchester, England, their stomachs rumbled and their feet jealously waited to step onto the cool ground of the rural village. "We've arrived, sir," yelled George from the front of the carriage.

"Where are we, Charles?" asked Thomas as he returned his shoes to his feet and gazed out of the window at the wonderful town. Much different than London's Old Georgian architecture, Winchester was lively and bright. From the carriage, Charles and Thomas walked down the narrow road that intersected the middle of the town. On each side, two-story houses stood next to each other, tight and tall, painted in bright shades of white and tan, facing each other like proud brothers. Each house contained two windows and a lush planter basket beneath each one, and was welcomed by a broad wooden door, curved at the top, and painted with dazzling paint. The brisk wind of Winchester kissed Thomas's face, as they turned onto a side street and stood in front of a large stone entrance, ancient but kept, that opened to a larger courtyard with lush green grass.

"What is this?" Thomas asked, puzzled, as if he had just entered a new world.

Charles excitedly replied, "A charming place. I cannot wait for you to see. This—this is Saint Cross."

"Saint Cross?" whispered Thomas. "Who's Saint Cross?"

"Well—I don't know. Properly, this placed is called the *Hospital* of Saint Cross. But everyone that comes simply calls it Saint Cross. It's a rare old place—one that you will surely love, Thomas. So, come," Charles motioned for Thomas to follow.

As they passed under the stone archway they immediately stepped into the bright green grass. Their shoes sunk perfectly into the thick blades. To their right, just past the lawn, a looming three-story building stacked high above their heads, nearly a hundred yards in length. Nearly thirty chimneys lined the edge of the buildings, and light puffs of clean smoke chased out from the openings at the top, running towards the lovely afternoon sky. On all three stories, rows of windows lined the wall, and from the courtyard Charles and Thomas could see the brightened interior of what seemed like a hundred bedrooms. Directly in front of them, a grand cathedral with stained glass windows and tall spires cast shadows into the courtyard. As they stepped further inside the courtyard, Thomas soon realized, they were surrounded on all four sides by tall stone structures. He swore he was standing in the middle of an old castle, and couldn't stop his lips from forming into an awestruck smile. It was the greenest grass he had ever seen, the tallest cathedral he had ever viewed, and quietest calm he had ever heard.

"I have never seen anything like this. Is this a hospital?" he asked, carefully interrupting the quiet.

"It's a place for weary travelers. A place of hospitality—and rest. Some simply stop for a meal, others stay many nights," Charles said calmly as he pointed to the bedroom windows that nestled between the tall chimneys.

"Are we staying there?"

"No. We are only here for lunch," said Charles as he turned his eyes towards the cathedral.

"I've never eaten lunch in a hospital!" Thomas laughed as he continued to scan the perimeter with delight.

"But, have you eaten lunch in a cathedral?"

"No, sir. I have not," said Thomas.

"Well—there's a first time for all things, Thomas. The *dole* is exhausted at noon, but I believe we still have time." Charles began to walk towards the cathedral in front of him, unaware if Thomas was following.

"A *dole*? What's a dole?" Thomas asked with confusion, trotting forward to catch up with Charles.

"You'll see!" Charles excitedly exclaimed.

As they entered the cathedral, Thomas was immediately overwhelmed by the sheer size of its interior. Rows of wooden benches lined the center section and sat under a canopy of dark-stained cedar beams and hand-painted stained glass windows. As the noonday sun pierced through the hand-painted and stained glass windows, the magnificent scene of Christ's resurrection illuminated the entire space. Glitters of red and blue shot along the walls, poured onto the floors, and the entire cathedral was alit with the brightness of the Christ-figure's white robe. It was a truly celestial feeling that erupted in Thomas's soul.

As Thomas's eyes followed the light towards the back of the sanctuary, he noticed what seemed like a hundred men and women standing in a long line that extended from the front door to a square table in the corner. Charles pulled Thomas' arm towards the line, and as they joined the brothers and sisters who stood in silence, Thomas scratched his head in confusion.

"Charles. I have no idea what's going on. Who are these people? What are we doing here?"

"These who are standing in line—they are all wanderers. Some are very poor, without a home, without a family. Others simply pass through . . . on their way to another destination. Here at Saint Cross . . . whoever passes through . . . every single wanderer . . . gets a *spoil* of what Heaven will truly be. *That* is why we are here, brother. Because we are wanderers . . . on our way to a destination . . . taking our spoil." Charles sometimes spoke as a mystic, as he delighted in stirring imagination in others— there was nothing more boring to Charles than an unstirred imagination, so he took joy in seeing the gears of Thomas's mind turn and spin.

"Spoil? Dole?" Thomas asked, then chuckled. "You gotta tell me more, you mysterious preacher."

"Alright, Thomas," laughed Charles. "It is there"—he pointed to the table in the corner—"at the end of the line we are standing in. That is where the *dole* is given. Do you see those old brethren in their gowns with crosses?" Charles pointed towards the end of the line.

Thomas nodded.

"There are thirteen of those old priests, and they get two quarts of ale to drink every day . . . and on cold, wintry days, they get gin and hot ale!"

"Priests? Drinking two pints of ale? And—gin? Why?"

"Because, my friend! These old Saxon institutions regard *ale* as the grand necessity of life!"

"And, they make this ale?"

"Of course they do."

"Okay—I understand what ale is, but I still don't get what a *dole* is."

"Every single day, from morning until noon, these old brethren give out a portion of ale and a hunch of bread—that's a *dole*—to any hungry or poor soul. And they do it because they understand the greatest commands of Scripture are—"

"—To love the Lord your God, and to love your neighbor as yourself," said Thomas, finishing Charles's sentence.

"That's right!—and—oh, how an empty stomach feels loved when its hunger and thirst is quenched," exclaimed Charles.

"All of these people in line—are they all poor?"

"We are *all* poor, Thomas." Charles took a more serious tone, then continued. "No one feeds on Christ so fully, as the poor and hungry. The dole is exhausted about noon . . . but the mercy of God continues to the eleventh hour."

"Amen, it does," said Thomas, finally realizing the significance of the moment.

When they finally reached the wooden table, Charles and Thomas received an elk-horn cup with five silver crosses etched around the edge, and a hearty chunk of fresh-baked bread. The old brethren smiled as they poured their elk horns full of ale, then said with compassion and sincerity, "You are loved by Christ, brother."

Charles and Thomas thanked the old men, then carried their dole outside of the cathedral, where they sat on the stone steps that overlooked the green lawn.

"No one feeds on Christ like the poor and hungry," Thomas muttered as his teeth pressed into the warm bread. The delicious and salty dough swirled in his mouth and a smile of satisfaction covered his face.

"And still—" Charles finished, "the mercy of God continues forever."

As they devoured their dole on the steps of the cathedral, Charles and Thomas continued to talk about the mercy of God. They shared stories of childhood—before knowing Christ—and shared the moments of their conversion. They laughed and cried as they reminisced about their mothers, the sweet smell of her embrace, and the Lord's provision in placing women in their lives that loved and cherished them as sons. Charles told stories of his first sermons, the good and bad, as Thomas listened and gleamed. Thomas spoke of Chicago, his pastorate at Providence, and his insecurities with language and vocabulary, as Charles spoke words of encouragement and challenge.

"Brother—" Thomas spoke as he emptied his elk horn and placed it on the steps. "I've wanted to tell you this since the night I met you."

Charles waited without speaking.

"Do you want to hear how I first heard of 'The Great Charles Spurgeon'?"

"I would be delighted," Charles said gleefully, his face widened with anticipation.

"I remember the night, clearly. Even though it was twenty years ago, I remember it like it was yesterday. Me and my former master—Mr. Bennett was his name—and an old, fat preacher—"

"Careful, brother," snarked Charles as he patted his plump belly that seemed to stretch the buttons of his vest, wide.

"Well—this preacher's weight wasn't his only problem. He despised black people. And he made me drive him and Mr. Bennett all the way downtown Richmond to go to a book burning."

"A book burning? What were they burning?" Charles asked, placing his cup on the step in front of him.

"They were burnin' all kinds of stuff—books, pamphlets, newspaper clippings. In the middle of the night, all these white folk—standing around cheering—as they threw in all kinds of stuff into a big, giant fire—tall as a tree."

"Antislavery books, I would assume?"

"Yes," a wide smile crept across Thomas's face. "All *your* books, Charles."

"My books? What else were they burning?"

"Just yours, Charles."

"The whole fire was *just* for things I had written?" Charles asked with surprise. He was genuinely taken aback by the thought of such vitriol.

"The whole thing, Charles. Can you believe that?" Thomas continued to smile brightly.

"How did you come to know that it was *my* writings?"

"Because that old, fat preacher I told you about—he pushed me close to the fire, handed me a newspaper article, and told me some English preacher had written that no Christian man oughta own another man. So—right before I threw that paper into the fire—a big ol' smile crept up on my face and I thought— 'I sure would like to hear that man preach one day!'"

Charles shook his head, "That's how you first heard my name?"

Charles reeled with delight, amused by the Lord's sense of humor.

"Brother, we must get on with our journey, unless Old George has already left us," snickered Charles. "Let us not speak of the warm bread, or that Englishman would certainly sin with envy."

"That's a good idea."

❂ ❂ ❂

The carriage leapt forward as they continued their journey onward until they reached the village of Amesbury by five o'clock in the afternoon. After they passed over the Avon River, across an ancient ornamental stone bridge, Old George stopped the carriage at the edge of Abbey Park. The property, owned by the very famous Sir Edward Antrobus, sat gracefully on the shore of the river and was covered with lush trees and gorgeous shrubs. The Avon, hardly large enough to be considered a river, ran directly through Abbey Park and contained many windings, turns, and bends before it passed under the stone bridge that read, *Erected in 1791.*

Charles carried his satchel from the carriage towards the bridge, and Thomas followed suit. "Old George, why don't you leave Peacock here. But, bring Punch with you. We are going to sit here at this bridge for a while." Like a duck and her duck-lings, Charles led the men and his dog to the edge of the sturdy bridge. The ancient stones lined the edge of the road and hung elegantly above the rushing water beneath.

"Here is the plan, gentlemen. We are simply going to sit here, and listen. Sometimes—listening is the most God-honoring thing a man can do."

Thomas squinted his eyes into the setting sun as he climbed onto the edge of the bridge and dangled his feet above the water. Instantly, the beauty of the park calmed his soul, and slowed his pulse. He closed his eyes and listened to the crow of pheasants, the coo of pigeons, the cry of waterfowl, the song of countless birds, and the splash of leaping fish. It was the closest thing to the Garden of Eden he could imagine, as untouched beauty seemed to soar all around him. He did not need to open his eyes, as the song of Heaven was enough to shift his thoughts upward. There were no sounds of busy city streets, men's footsteps, congregations, or crowds. There was no bantering or dialogue, no singing or preaching—only the sounds of God's cool and refreshing creation, a healing balm to all wanderers.

Most wanderers.

As Charles climbed onto the stone edge, he wiggled himself into a squat, then dangled his feet over the edge of the bridge, hoping to bask in the glory of creation around him. He closed his eyes and drew a silent breath. The cool air stung his nos-trils and filled his lungs, then he released his breath and drew another. When Charles hung his eyes closed and the stirring of the gentlemen finally settled, he strangely felt all alone. Even though Thomas was to his left, and George to his right, and

Punch sat wagging his tail behind him—he somehow felt completely by himself. When one wrestles with depression, even a crowded room or peaceful countryside can all-at-once be compromised by depressive thoughts and hallow anxieties. Charles felt the familiar stranger rush through his mind as his vision narrowed and all of time seemed to stutter.

What if Susannah dies? he thought.

He thought of her sweet face and gentle smile, the scent of her perfume that lingered in her hair and on the back of her hand. He visualized her brown-curled hair sweeping across her pale forehead. He imagined pressing his warm lips to her cold skin as tears fell from his open eyes to hers, closed. Then, in a swift moment he saw the lid of the coffin creak closed, just before the first shovel of English soil covered the edge. *Oh, my God—what if my Susie dies?*

And, what if my hands can no longer write? What will I do during my last days?

He imagined the worst-case outcome of his gout returning, and wondered if any of his sermons, any of his teachings, would outlast his life. The last thing a man wants is to spend his whole life on things that will not matter, or last. He gripped the stone bridge beneath his hands and imagined what it would feel like to inhale his last breath. It seemed the whole earth pressed upon his body; he felt a hard lump grow in his throat. Without warning, his life was over. He saw his dead body lying in an empty hospital room, surrounded only by white-washed walls and the distant memories of a man that did not do enough, did not write enough, and did not speak enough. He imagined the newspaper headlines the morning after his death, tucked near the back pages in tiny print and misspelled fashion—

Charlie Spurgeon—the man who no one mourned.

Charles continued to grip the stone edge of the ancient bridge as he watched the rippling water beneath his dangling feet. Fish wiggled and swam forward, bugs flapped their wings and crawled forward, but Charles was unable to move, paralyzed in a stream of his own depressive thoughts. For a moment, just a second, he wondered if it were better to fall from the ancient bridge, and die.

He gritted his teeth, pressing bone to bone, and mustered the strength to open his eyes, open his ears, and open his heart. Bursting through the echoes of darkness that desperately tried to deceive his thoughts, he heard the sweetest voice of the Holy Spirit of God whisper into his heart, louder than a train, softer than a rose petal.

I am not finished with you, Charles. The sweet voice of his God instantly brought a slump to Charles's shoulders and a slowing to his pulse. *Come nestle down within My great wings which seem so close to you—they are strong as iron. Just trust Me, Charles.*

Charles inhaled deeply and savored the echo of His Father's voice within the delicious country air. Slowly, reeling from the chaos of the moment, he untied his leather satchel to reveal his notebook, Bible, and fountain pen. He coursed his hand over the leather cover of his Holy Bible, then thumbed through the pages until it laid open to the seventeenth chapter of the book of Psalms.

"'Keep me as the apple of the eye, hide me under the shadow of thy wings,'" he mumbled as he read the Scriptures, sweet to the tongue, even sweeter to the ear. As Charles read those words from the pages, a thrill of peace reached into his heart, consuming every part. He read the chapter, again and again, and drank from the wellspring much deeper than the Avon River beneath his shoes. He thought of his plight, his years of suffering, his days of depression, and prayed those words to his friend, Jesus. It had been a while since he was able to simply sit with Jesus, simply as a child of God. Too often, Charles worked himself to the point of exhaustion, then in his exhaustion forgot to sit with Jesus. He knew all too well that he was guilty of working *for*

Jesus, instead of always working *with* Jesus—and that takes a toll on a person. No matter the person.

But, there on the stone bridge, the Word of God spoke tenderly to the heart of Charles Spurgeon.

Come nestle down within My great wings.

✠ ✠ ✠

Thomas, quiet and completely unaware of what Charles had experienced, opened his eyes to the cathedral of beech trees which lined the Avon. Inside the lattice of trees, another row of dense yew trees stood, tall as steeples. Beneath them, an ankle-deep floor of brown and orange leaves that appeared softer than velvet. Above his head, a roof of silver clouds slowly moved from the east to the west, and began to drop tiny bits of rainwater into Thomas's thick black hair. As the rain continued to trickle, Thomas dared not move—there was simply too much beauty to take in.

Wild ducks flapped their wings in the sprinkled rain, then chased after each other like busy children on a playground. Swallows soared high above them, and soon after the ducks landed to eat bugs and vegetation, a hundred excited blackbirds flew from the yew trees and circled over Thomas's head like a November meteor shower.

Thomas fell into complete happiness and awe as he watched the scene unfold. *This is what Home is gonna feel like,* he thought.

"I—can't—I—don't think I ever seen anything more beautiful," whispered Thomas, adding to the silence.

"It is a *world* of beauty," Charles concurred. His voice seemed strangely weary, as if he had just been through a battle. "What does it stir within you?"

Thomas paused to carefully choose his words. "A thankful heart."

Charles nodded, still watching the water pass beneath the bridge.

"When I see all this," continued Thomas, "—I don't *just* see animals and tall trees," Thomas gestured with his hand, pointing to the trees that lined the river. "I mean—I guess a free man sees things differently than one that is tied up. When you're tied up . . . when you're in chains . . . you can only see what's right in front of you. You can only see what other people make you see. But, when you're free . . . you see *so much* more." Thomas shivered as the setting sun and the damp rain brought a chill to the afternoon air. "So, I want every person on this Earth to be free . . . so they can see things differently . . . because when you are freed by God you see *everything* differently."

Thomas nodded his head as he continued to look around, but Charles sat perfectly still, and wondered why he did not completely feel free from the shackles of darkness and depression like his friend.

"I always think of Africa," continued Thomas. "I—it's just—I can't help it. I want so badly to get there. Me and Henrietta. So we can tell everybody about Jesus." Thomas turned his head and stared at the Bible on Charles's lap. "That's what I want, brother. I want that Good News in that Bible there . . . to get all the way to Africa. So I can sit on some bridge with a new convert . . . and watch them see things with a new set of eyes."

"I want that as well, Thomas," he said firmly. "When I was a kid, there was a preacher named Mr. Knill . . . and he was one of the first people that talked to me about salvation. He was a great encouragement to me when I was a young boy wrestling to trust Jesus. Do you know what he told me one day? I'll never forget it."

"What did he say?"

"He said, 'Charles, if there were only *one* unconverted person in the world . . . and if that person lived in the wilds of Siberia . . . and if every Christian minister and every ordinary believer in the world had to make a pilgrimage to that spot before that soul were brought to Christ'"—Charles paused, placing his hand on Thomas's shoulder—"'the labor would be well worth it for that *one* soul.'"

Mr. Knill's words held their hearts as still as the ancient stone bridge beneath them. Thomas sighed and looked back at the beech and yew trees that had begun to shadow in the setting sun.

"I don't know who that one soul is—but I know that soul's gotta be in Africa."

"And, I pray it is ten *thousand* more, Thomas."

"I don't know how to make that pilgrimage, or exactly what I'm gonna do when I get there. And, Charles—I don't know how the Lord is going to fund it."

"The Lord *always* sets aside a dole for His children. He will make a way, Thomas." Charles squeezed his shoulder and smiled. "It will surely be a hard road, as there is hardship everywhere. But, with the help of the Lord—you will surely go to Africa, my friend."

Thomas sighed and lifted his head to the distant sun, setting against the horizon.

"You and Henrietta will be in Africa before you know it."

CHAPTER 20

AFRICA FOR CHRIST

Cameroon, West Africa 1879

O n the sixth day of November, Thomas and Henrietta bade farewell to London and sailed towards the west coast of Africa on the *SS Kinsembo*. After the large steamship churned through the rough ocean waters for fourteen days, Thomas's dreams of Africa were finally realized.

His final months at the Pastors' College proved to be fruitful and effective. As Thomas's love for studying increased, so did his sense of urgency in getting to Africa. Not a day passed that he didn't dream about mission work, praying over a paper map of the African continent and tracing his fingers around the edge of a country called Cameroon. "Save the lost!" he cried at night, knees to the ground. "I want You to save the lost, Jesus! Just like You saved me."

With help from Charles, Mr. Wigney, and the other professors at the college, Thomas quickly grew as a preacher and communicator of the gospel. On most Sundays, Thomas preached in churches near London, casting his vision of "Africa for Christ." As more Christians heard of his desire to see the country of Cameroon reached with the Good News, they joined him in praying for the salvation of souls. The Reverend Richardson, and his wife, soon decided to join the Johnsons in their missionary work to Cameroon, as they shared a longing for the gospel to spring up in West Africa. In 1879, there were only two Christian missionaries in the entire country, and Thomas Johnson would be the very first African-American missionary to ever step foot on Cameroon soil as an ambassador for the Good News.

❋ ❋ ❋

When the day finally came, and their boots stood upon Cameroon soil, Thomas closed his eyes and squeezed Henrietta's hand as the warm African wind blew across his face and kissed his cheeks as if to say, *Welcome*.

Victoria, Cameroon, was a beautiful little village with just under five hundred inhabitants. The dusty village sat beside the Ambas Bay, which provided stunning views of the sea. To the north, south, and east, high hills stood like medieval walls protecting the people, and were only matched by the Cameroon Mountains which stood behind the hills, soaring thirteen thousand feet above sea level. Victoria was beautifully laid out with wide streets and thatch cottages, each with a large garden of palm, lime, coconut, and plantain trees. The cottages were neat and clean, and sat cutely next to each other in long rows. Thomas was surprised with the number of converts in Victoria, so with little need to convince Henrietta and the Richardsons, they soon decided to move further inland, toward tribes that had never heard the sweet name of Jesus.

It took several weeks to get to their final destination. After they passed through terribly dangerous footpaths through ten towns and two rivers, they stumbled into a much smaller and more rugged village, Bakunda.

Their first few nights were terrifying. Thomas could hardly sleep at night—the tribal yells, beating of drums, and witchcraft rituals lasting into the early morning hours—so he found it the best time to pray and plead with God to use him and Henrietta to illuminate the hope of Jesus to the Bakunda people.

Days turned to weeks, and weeks to months. As each day passed, Thomas and Henrietta became more at home, and more comfortable with the Bakunda people. Thomas had imagined the village to be lined with human skulls on the pathways and walls, the drinking of blood and eating the hearts of enemies. But, to his surprise, they were not savage people—not cruel like other African tribes who were constantly at war—the Bakunda people were kind-hearted and gentle.

❉ ❉ ❉

"But—you are in need of Jesus Christ," said Thomas as he stood before the Bakunda king, in the center of the tiny village.

The old king, nearly ninety years of age, held a wooden bowl in his lap and occasionally sipped the thick, black liquid as he listened intently to Thomas. The king's cottage was filled with several men, his sons, Rev. Richardson, and a few other tribes-men. Since his arrival, Thomas prayed every day for him to come to salvation. A fondness for the king grew over time, and Thomas found himself conversing with the old man often.

But, as the king was very near death, Thomas's words were now more calculated, more direct. "Only Jesus can give you peace."

"Witch make me sick," the king whispered to Thomas. "Tell me not to take white man's medicine, and I take this medicine get my stomach full, but old witch still make me sick."

His weathered face bowed towards the bowl, as Thomas lifted it towards his mouth.

"All power is in the hands of God," spoke Thomas with reverence. "You must believe in Jesus, alone. And trust Him."

The king listened intently as he swallowed the foul liquid then rested his head back onto his bed. The old man was very weak, and it seemed he would soon pass from Bakunda into eternity.

"Jesus give me peace?" the king asked.

"Only Jesus can give peace."

"Give me Jesus," he said strongly as he placed his hand into Thomas's. "Give me Jesus."

Thomas told him the story of God's great love and wonderful salvation. He recited Scripture, and told him of the Heavenly City, where the great reward of Jesus would be found after death.

"Ta Ta Nambulee," said Thomas, calling the king by name, "if you believe and trust Jesus to be your King, we will meet each other in Heaven one day."

"I believe."

With that, the old king turned to his oldest son. "I go now. Whatever these men tell you—Believe. They are true men."

❊ ❊ ❊

After the death of the old king, news of his conversion spread like fire throughout the village. Very few believed in Christ immediately, but the king's oldest son, Estau, became the new king, and immediately declared that the tribe would reserve one day a week—the Sabbath—for gathering with Thomas to hear him preach from the Bible. Estau, too, trusted in Jesus, and passed a law to all the Bakunda people—

If any man or woman did work on the Sabbath they should pay a cow. If they had no cow, their house should be pulled down over their heads.

Thomas saw many conversions take place in the village, but thought often of Charles's words on the ornamental bridge. He knew that if the Bakunda king was the *only* convert Thomas and Henrietta ever saw in Africa, it was well worth the labor. He often wrote letters back and forth to Charles. He missed his friend, and desperately wanted him to share in the joys and sorrows of the Bakunda labor.

When Charles got news of the king's conversion, and the good things that were taking place in Bakunda, he was overjoyed in reporting their progress in *The Sword and the Trowel*—

Mr. and Mrs. Johnson and the Richardsons in Africa.

We have news from our friends down to the middle of May. They had been settled in their new station, Bakundu, Victoria, Cameroon, where they had commenced work under the auspices of the chief of the village, which contains about 1,000 people. On Sundays, services are held in the hut which serves as a temporary schoolroom, and by this time are probably able to preach to the people in their own language. The people appear to be very favorably inclined toward the Missionaries, and ask them many questions about the Gospel they bring.

The rainy season had commenced when the last letter was written, and Mrs. Johnson and Mrs. Richardson were suffering from the fever. They send very kind messages for all Tabernacle and other friends, and ask our prayers that they may be sustained.

Prayers were certainly needed.

The fever that crawled through the village proved to be a fierce one, and showed no mercy to those it inflicted. Thomas had suffered from its curse for a while—at one point he swore he was close to death's door—but now that Henrietta had been very sick for a few weeks, he felt helpless and worried for her life. Unable to keep food in her stomach, she had not eaten in nearly five days. The skin of her face had sunken into the bones of her cheeks and the holes of her eyes as she lay in her fever-soaked bed.

Despite all he had experienced, Thomas could not remember feeling such a level of helplessness in all of his life. Even as a motherless child, alone on the tobacco plantation, there was not the same sense of desperation that he now felt as he watched his wife's life slowly wither away. It seemed the whole world had been turned upside down.

Outside the Johnsons' cottage, the summer rain poured unceasingly. Cameroon was typically dry and hot, but the rainy season brought unusual and incessant floods. It had been raining for two weeks—without pause—and the darkened clouds and dreary rain added to the gloominess that rolled into Thomas's heart like the thick, African mud that forced its way into their cottage.

Thomas prayed for his dear wife like he had never prayed before. He begged the Great Physician to heal his beloved Henrietta. He pleaded with Him to rid her body of sickness, to take away the fever, to restore her fully.

But, the Lord was silent. The fever remained.

Each day her condition had worsened, and like the dark and agitated weather outside his door, sickness continued to press upon her body. No members of the village could offer any solace, as fevers seemed to possess a mind of their own. They either worsened, progressively moving the victim to a tragic end, or like hot breath against cool glass, they soon disappeared, leaving the tortured soul to return to the land of the living, whole and healthy. Thomas knew little as to which direction Henrietta's fever would turn.

"You really need to stop worrying," said Henrietta, her voice weak and strained.

"I'm not worried, my love," he lied, "I'm just wondering when this rain is going to stop."

"I've decided that worrying is a waste of time. If we truly believe that our gracious God is on His throne, then He and He alone is in control. To worry is to bear a burden that is not ours to carry. If anyone should know this, it's you, Thomas Lewis Johnson." Henrietta coerced a weak smile onto her face that was both loving and correcting.

Thomas turned from the window of the cottage and faced his precious wife. She knew him better than anyone in the world and their years of marriage had taught her to see through his lies. In many ways she had become a conduit of the voice of the Holy Spirit to him, constantly teaching him and pointing him to the truth during their time as missionaries in Africa. Their mission to the Bakunda people could be described as the most difficult, yet most rewarding of their lives.

On good days, Thomas was mindful of all that God had already accomplished in Cameroon. He could be found in good spirits, happy he decided to obey God's call to leave England for Africa. But in the last two weeks, his faith had seemed to whither, resonating with the prophet Jeremiah who proclaimed loudly the message of God only for it to fall on deaf ears. It had been those days that Henrietta had proven most precious to him. She held him at night and whispered to him in the dark, "God is faithful, Thomas. Regardless of the outcome of our labor and your preaching—He is faithful." She stroked his arm and placed his face in her gentle hands, as the worry of ministry faded into confidence. She possessed a faith—strong and rare—and was the sort of woman that knew Jesus well. She genuinely longed for His Word and His presence more than anything this world had to offer in sickness or in health.

Thomas sat on the edge of Henrietta's bed as he listened to the African rain beat against the thatched roof. The rain crawled through the tiny gaps of the ceiling, then ran along the small wooden joists, down the walls, and puddled in the corners. He placed the back of his strong hand gently to her forehead, and felt the hotness of the fever that raged in her blood. "Let me get a cool rag to place on your head," he urged.

"Not now," she mumbled, eyes closed, grabbing his hand. "Please, Thomas . . . read to me—read the sermon Pastor Spurgeon sent us . . . the one we received a few days ago."

"Of course, sugar. Let me get it." Rising from the bed, Thomas walked to the large dresser that lined the far wall of their bedroom. Inside the top drawer, Thomas kept his Bible and a collection of sermons that Mr. Wigley sent them from London. The manuscripts of recent sermons preached by Charles had been a lifeline and a constant source of nourishment to Thomas and Henrietta—both in their missionary work and now in Henrietta's sickness. Never a day passed where she could not be found searching the Scriptures and reading the sermons of Charles Spurgeon, her second-favorite preacher.

"I'll read the most recent one," said Thomas, leafing through the pile of papers.

"Yes," sighed Henrietta, weakly. "I love that one. It is my favorite."

Thomas returned to her bed, then began to read Charles's sermon to her slowly and deliberately, as if he were preaching the sermon himself.

Scatter your light in all un-selfishness. Be willing to make every sacrifice to spread this light which you have received.

Consecrate your entire being to the making known among the sons of men the glory of Christ.

Oh, I wish we had swift messengers to run the world over to tell the story that God has come down among us. I wish we had fluent tongues to tell in every language the story that, coming down among us, God was arrayed in flesh like our own and that He took our sins and carried our sorrows. Oh, that we had trumpet tongues to make peal through Heaven and Earth that God has come among men and cries "Come unto Me, all you that labor and are heavy laden and I will give you rest."

"Please stop," she tenderly grabbed the arm of her husband.

"Why, my love?" asked Thomas. "Have I done something wrong?"

"No, but I need to ask you something." She fastened her eyes intently to his. "Thomas, we have been those swift messengers. We left our home. We came to Africa. And—we—we have been those trumpet-tongues that have shouted through the heavens that God has come." Henrietta paused, her eyes sunken with tears.

"Yes—" Thomas stated, reassuringly.

"Do you—" she murmured. "Do you—think the Lord is pleased with us?"

Thomas lowered the sermon to the bed, leaned tenderly against his wife, and pressed his cold lips to her sweltering forehead. He gently wiped his hand across her cheeks, catching the puddles of tears that spilled from her eyes. Thomas turned his face from hers, as he could not bear to see Henrietta cry under such strain and weariness. He wanted to take it from her, to somehow trade places with her, but he knew he couldn't. He began to sob, subdued at first, then louder—louder than the African rain above his head. He felt a cold sense of guilt as he knew that he needed to be strong for his wife in this moment, still his tender heart could not muster the courage to speak any words.

As her earnest question knocked steadily on his heart, it begged Thomas to fling open a door that he desperately tried, throughout all her months of illness, to keep tightly closed. He covered this door with chains, locked them with an iron key, then boarded up the hinges to brace it for the pending storm. He dared not open it, for behind this door was the awful reality that Thomas feared more than his own death—Henrietta was dying.

Summoning the courage to speak, Thomas wiped away the tears of his own, then smiled deeply at his beautiful lover and friend.

"My dear—I happen to know that the Lord is very pleased with you," he whispered, stroking her hair and face. "You are, in fact—one of His favorites. He told me as much just the other day. And—He also told me that you should not ask such questions, because He has had His eye on you since you were a little girl—and you have brought Him more joy than He could ever express."

Henrietta smiled back at Thomas and relaxed. Peace enveloped her.

"What do you think Heaven will be like?" she asked, barely above a whisper.

"It will be more wonderful than you've ever imagined," said Thomas, tears once again welling in his eyes. "Your momma will be there. I know she can't wait to see you. And, Ezekiel—" Thomas stopped, choking on his friend's name. "Ezekiel—he'll be there too. I know he loved you like a daughter. You give him a hug for me and tell him that I'll be there soon. Tell him that I can't wait to tell him all the stories of our time here in Africa."

Thomas stood from the bed and walked to the door next to Henrietta's bed. With tears falling from his face to the dirt floor, he gently turned the doorknob and pushed open the door. The hinges creaked as it swung wide, revealing the storm outside and the dirt path that led into the village. A coolness blew into their bedroom and gently kissed Henrietta's warm body. From her bed and through the now-open door, she saw the blurry city in the distance.

"And, my dear Henrietta," he said returning to her bed, "when you walk into the gates of Heaven—best thing of all—is that your sweet Jesus will be there to greet you. He will run to you and wrap you in His arms—and say, 'Well done, my good and faithful servant.'"

She looked past him, through the opened door, as if she saw someone in the distance that was calling to her.

"I don't want to leave you, Thomas," her voice weak and strained.

"Darlin', please rest." He leaned in to hold her, wrapping his arms under her back, his cheek pressed to hers. Her body was light and frail in his arms, her breathing slow and small. In that moment he knew he was holding her for the last time on Earth, and to let her go would be to let go of the most precious gift the Lord had ever given him. He gently stroked her hair, kissed her forehead, then whispered, "Go to Him, Henrietta."

With those words, an otherworldly expression of peace softened Henrietta's face. She inhaled sharply, then slowly released her final breath. The doors of Heaven had flung wide where Henrietta Thompson was welcomed and embraced by Jesus.

CHAPTER 21

IN CURSIVE LETTERS

Cameroon, West Africa 1879

Thomas sat alone in the corner of the thatch cottage, elbows on his desk, eyes towards the blank and pale-green wall. The pain of Henrietta's passing was as hot as the day it happened, nearly three weeks ago. With her absence, Thomas decided he must leave Africa and return to either America or England, neither of which the Lord had made clear. He knew the Lord had not abandoned him, but his face shifted heavily with loneliness, and he often spent entire days sitting at his desk, unable to think or move, or breathe.

When someone loses a spouse, it is as if a piece of their heart is literally stolen away. The heart still beats. It still pulses blood to and from its corridors. But, it is not whole. It never can be again. Thomas's heart was missing a significant portion, and although he did his best to dream of Henrietta dancing and singing with Jesus in Heaven, he missed the sweet savor of her presence on Earth.

A knock came to the door, startling Thomas from his numbness. The knock rang loudly through the cottage, breaking the monotony of the silence.

"Hello, Thomas," Mr. Richardson said as Thomas slowly opened the door.

"Come in, my friend," spoke Thomas. He lumbered back towards his desk. His head hung from his slouched shoulders and he slid his feet across the ground, barely lifting them. "Please sit down."

"Oh—no, but thank you, Thomas. I'm here just to give you a letter that came to us in this morning's mail. It comes from London. Charles and Susannah heard of Henrietta's passing— and I—I wanted to deliver it to you, as soon as I saw it arrive."

Mr. Richardson handed Thomas the letter. Thomas took the letter and traced his hand along the crisp edges and over the stack of colorful stamps that cluttered the corner. He smiled with fondness, as he missed his friend, Charles. As he read the front of the envelope, he noticed it was addressed from the Rev. and Mrs. Charles Haddon Spurgeon, but not written in Charles's handwriting.

He sighed, and his head slouched even lower as he knew Charles's sickness must have surely returned. That would be the only explanation as to why his good friend wouldn't address the letter personally and in his own handwriting—large with cursive swoops and bright purple ink. Thomas was filled with another sense of sadness—a different one than that of Henrietta's departure—as he thought of his dear friend Charles, sure that his hands were too swollen and bandaged to even write a letter.

"Thank you, Mr. Richardson." At once, he left Thomas alone. He slid the metal blade of a paper opener under the seal of the envelope and pulled out a tiny letter written in Susannah's neat print. His lips moved ever-so-slightly as he read silently—

News has come to me from Africa of the passing of our dear Mrs. Johnson. She was a source of great joy and encouragement to me, as she sang so sweetly to Charles and I on our night together before you left for your missionary work. She is now singing a new song and has full realization of the blessedness of being "forever with the Lord." I have heard that she was stricken with a fatal fever, and has laid down her life in the land of her fathers, without having much time to tell 'the sweet story of old' to those whose sake she bravely dared danger and death. We weep, not for her; For Jesus has come and taken her to Himself, and her bliss is perfect; but for the desolate heart, of you, her husband. Please know that you have our deepest sympathy and constant prayers. Please also know that Charles will be writing of you and your ministry in his upcoming article of The Sword and the Trowel. *I pray that your testimony and the testimony of your dear wife will be a source of encouragement to many.*

Yours Truly,

Susannah and Charles Spurgeon

Thomas folded the letter and returned it to the envelope. He stood and pushed his chair, sliding it under the desk, then began slowly placing his few possessions into a leather suitcase.

There was nothing left for him in Africa.

CHAPTER 22

The Fog of 1880

London, England 1880

I n the year 1880, a deep fog settled on London. Years of over-expanded industry, as well as air pollution from the factories that lined the bank of the Thames River, had caused the air to darken and stifle with smoke. Nearly every portion of London was greyed, and on most days the sun never had the chance to shine and warm the city below. Weeks could pass without any-one seeing the glorious rays of the sun, and the lack of fresh air gave a fierce strength to cholera, causing it to spread like angry weeds across the landscape. Hospitals soon filled to capacity with coughing patients, desperate for help. When men traveled the city streets from home to work, they wrapped their face in silken clothes, hoping to keep the toxic fog from entering their lungs. Still, no matter how hard they tried, their lungs sucked in the fog. Their stomachs soured, and their eyes blotched with red splinters.

The Helensburgh House, too, was filled with fog. Old George did his best to keep the windows tight and the doors shut, but like a tired thief in the winter, the damp fog found its way into the warm house, then settled—unwelcomed—in every room. Charles coughed from deep within his gut, causing his ribs and back muscles to throb with pain. He stumbled to the sink in the corner of the kitchen where he coughed and spit up bits of black tar into the drain. Onto his face he splashed the water from the spout, warm and clear, and washed the fog from his eyes and mouth.

Susannah's lungs must have been stronger—most likely due to her abstaining of smoking several cigars each day—and unlike Charles, the fog was only a nuisance to her as it blocked the pretty sun from warming her bedroom.

The only place in the city that was fortunate enough to have clean air was the Upper Norwood neighborhood that stood high above the city on Beulah Hill, just south of London. There, one could see the breadth of the city as it stretched and crawled in every direction. The crisp mountain air was a delicious contrast from the London fog, and soon the Spurgeons realized it was necessary to leave the Helensburgh House on Nightingale Lane, and head toward higher ground and cleaner air.

Leaving the Helensburgh House was much harder than Charles expected. As a man who was unaccustomed to treasuring earthly things, he was surprised by the strong sadness that came as he placed books into cardboard boxes, and tied cotton sheets around furniture. So many profoundly beautiful and impossibly sorrowful things had taken place on 99 Nightingale Lane, and in many ways it was much more than a house to Charles—much more.

A house requires only a few things: a sturdy foundation, walls with tiny holes to frame windows and doors, a roof to keep the rain from flooding the floors, and a few articles of furniture to rest a weary body at the end of a day. But, a *home* is altogether different and more wonderful. It requires much attention, costs more than money can afford, and often takes decades to build. Homes are not built by hammer or nail, brick or cement, stick or mud, but by the mingling of sorrow and joy, tension and thrill. A house can be erected in a matter of months, but the amount of nurturing required to build a home cannot be measured by the rising and setting of the sun.

Once the contents of their home were packed into parcels and placed onto carriages, Charles sat within the empty walls of his study and reminisced the countless conversations, the tireless nights of study, and the many fire-lit evenings spent covered in bandage and ointment. He reached in his coat pocket to pull out a scrap of paper, then wrote a simple poem and tacked it under the windowsill before walking away.

> *Farewell, fair room, I leave thee to a friend:*
> *Peace dwell with him and all his kin!*
> *May angels evermore the house defend!*
> *Their Lord hath often been within.*

Charles took one final glance at the vacant bookshelves, the spotless fireplace, and the barren porch that fostered so many wonderful conversations, then closed the door to the study and made his way downstairs to the carriage where Susannah waited with Punch and Old Dick.

"Do we *really* need to take Old Dick with us, Susie?" Charles smirked as he climbed into the carriage.

"You love this old cat," she smiled.

"Ah—wifey." Charles placed his hand on her knee and turned his face towards the front door of the Helensburgh House. The lilies were just beginning to bloom their yellow buds, as plump bumble bees spun and circled the front porch and stone pathway hungry for pollen. "This was a good home, was it not?"

"Truly—a gift from the Lord." Susannah gently laid her head onto his shoulders as Old George steered the carriage out of the driveway and into the cobblestone road that lead from Clapham Common toward Upper Norwood. "May it continue to be a home for the next pilgrims."

"Yes, Lord. May it be so," Charles agreed.

Their next house, named Westwood, was purchased with the profits from the sale of the Helensburgh House. Although it spanned nine gorgeous acres in the hills and contained an expansive house, stables, garden, and pond, the Spurgeons' new home was not purchased with debt or excessive spending. Still, those that desired to speak ill of the Spurgeons found Westwood an easy way to cast a negative spin on the Charles's stewardship and character.

"Ah! The Reverend Charles Spurgeon has established his kingdom at Westwood," wrote an American visitor who published a grossly exaggerated account in the newspaper. "It's park, and meadows, and lakes, and streams, and statuary, and stables rival those of the Queen at Windsor Castle!" But, Charles refused to let the negative press affect him, as he thought it was the better decision for his own health and his wife's.

At first, the property did seem too grand for Charles, but as the Westwood house quickly morphed into the Spurgeon's home, it became a place of refuge and solace not just for his family, but for every person that visited. Westwood was perhaps more utilized than the Helensburgh House, as students and guests constantly appeared and enjoyed the lush property. From the entrance at Upper Norwood Road, a shady carriage-path stretched to the large house. In the center of the house, a large circular tower covered in thick vines, rose to the sky. From its balcony, the tops of tall buildings and the spires of Windsor Castle could be seen poking through the London fog in the distance, just past Beulah Hill. The front door was located at the bottom of the tower, and the stone steps emptied to a grass-bordered path that led around the house, through a rose garden, down a pathway shaded by limp-hanging trees, over a tiny wooden bridge, along the edge of a lake, then spilled out into a wide-open stretch of lizard-green grass. The expansive property reminded Charles of the Essex hills, as well as the picturesque English landscape in the New Forest.

The beauty of Westwood was soothing for Susannah, and the higher altitude allowed her to sleep restfully at night. In daytime, Susannah tended to the lovely fernery that sat just beyond the rose garden. There, she trimmed the ferns, pulled weeds from the fertile soil, and poured fresh well-water onto their wide leaves. When the proper time came, she cut a slender portion from the "mother fern," then carefully replanted that smaller portion into a new pot. She loved watching the new baby fern take root and develop into a full-grown fern. Then, appropriately, when that full-grown fern shot new offshoots that were ready for replanting, she trimmed again and replanted. It reminded her of discipleship—the growing, nurturing, cutting off, and planting that happens when lives are replicated.

To the left of the fernery, in the middle of the expansive area that overlooked the lake, stood a large and lonely oak tree. Charles immediately loved the old oak tree with its stretched branches and wide leaves. It stood as tall as the Westwood house, and perfectly provided a place of conversation and view of the city below. Charles appropriately named the tree, the *Questioning Oak,* as he found that most guests that visited Westwood enjoyed sitting under the tree and asking "The Governor" questions. He embraced the opportunity, allowing anyone to ask him any question they wanted. No questions were off limits. On most nights of the week, his guests included students from the Pastors' College, preachers from America, political and social figures, as well as old friends. Some asked theological or political questions, others asked personal and intimate questions about his health and mental well-being. Whether hard or easy—every single question was answered without a moment's hesitation from their vulnerable and honest pastor underneath the Questioning Oak.

"When did you first know you wanted to preach the gospel?" asked the Earl of Shaftesbury on one of Charles's first nights under the tree. To christen the oak, Charles had invited the Earl, Mr. Fullerton, and Mr. Harrald for lively conversation and "brother time." Charles, still recovering from the latest episode of gout, sat under the oak tree, wrapped in a blankets and oversized bandages.

"Ah! I think, even as a child—I knew I would tell others of Christ. Not long after my eyes were opened—the eyes of *faith*—I remember wanting to tell everyone I could." Charles smiled as he recollected memories of his grandfather, and Stambourne, with a fondness. "My grandfather was the finest preacher in Essex. One spring, when I was just a boy, I learned that a member of his church frequented the local tavern. I could not reconcile how a church member was able to *frequent* a tavern, so I marched over—flung open the door of that pub—and confronted that man face-to-face."

The Earl leaned forward in his chair with anticipation as Charles continued to tell the story with a charisma and charm that only Charles Spurgeon could muster. "What did you say?" the Earl asked.

"I pointed my scrawny finger in his face and asked, 'What doest thou *here*, Elijah? Sitting with the ungodly? And you—a member of a church? Breaking your pastor's heart? I'm ashamed of you! I wouldn't break my pastor's heart, I'm sure!'" The Earl laughed hysterically. His round belly and rosy cheeks shook as he imagined a young Charles shouting at an old man in a pub.

"And—what happened next?" he inquired, curious as ever.

"I yanked his tobacco pipe from his mouth, pushed aside his beer, and ran out the door!" Charles spouted through a blast of laughter, slapping his knees with his swollen hands. "I wouldn't suggest that sort of evangelism these days. But—for whatever reason, the Lord used it in that old man's life."

"Fascinating. How do you mean?"

"His name was Thomas Roads, and a few years later I heard of his conversion. He wrote me a letter and told me that after he left the tavern, he hurried away to a quiet spot and cast himself before the Lord. His conversion proved real and lasting." The men nodded, affirming the beauty of conversion. "See—it only proves that God can use anyone—even an ignorant, over-zealous boy—to move a heart towards repentance and faith in Christ. If he can use me, he can use anyone."

"Charles, what has it been like—" asked Mr. Fullerton, "—to see so many conversions in London? I mean—the Tabernacle—it started with only a few hundred people . . . and now there are nearly fourteen thousand that attend services on the Sabbath."

"It can only be accredited to a work of the Spirit, brother. God may have used us to some degree, but it has been Him—all Him." Joseph's square face nodded. He sighed as he buttoned the top button of his dark-blue vest, bracing as the night coldened further.

"The only part I play is to remain faithful. Just like a *lamplighter* within the city streets," Charles continued, looking over the fogged-city past Joseph's shoulders.

"What do you mean—*lamplighter*?" William chewed his lip with curiosity as he listened.

"Joseph—every lamp in that city below us must be lit *individually*. Although they each burn by gas, a human hand must strike a match and light each one that stands along every single intersection in London. Those men are the lamplighters." Charles stood from his chair to peer over the Upper Norwood hills that sloped toward the London skyline. "One Thursday in the late autumn, I was coming home from an engagement. And do you know of the steep road that ascends to the top of Herne Hill Ridge on the way to my first house on New Kent Road?" he asked.

"Yes."

"Just before my carriage ascended that steep hill—while I was on the level part of the road—I asked the driver to stop so I could stretch my legs for a moment. The night was cool, and it was so good to stand for a moment, gazing upward at the stars and the hill that stood before me. Then, I saw a single gaslight turn on, just up the road. And beyond that light . . . a few moments later . . . another light just up the hill. A few minutes later . . . beyond that light . . . another . . . higher up the hill. Suddenly with my eyes, I could see a line of gaslights, gradually ascending all the way from the foot of the hill to its top. And, do you know what thought ran through my mind?" he asked rhetorically. "I never saw the lamplighter. I do not know his name, or how old he is, or where he is from. But—I saw the lights that he had kindled, and these remained long after he was gone. How earnestly—*earnestly*—do I wish that my life be spent in lighting one soul after another with the sacred flame of eternal life. I may be unseen while at my work, and I will certainly vanish into eternity when my work is finished—but," Charles raised his hand and extended his forefinger, pointing at each man in the circle, "but—the lights will have been lit. *That* is what matters most, Joseph. That is why we preach . . . why we serve . . . why we tell everyone we can about Christ. We are *lamplighters*."

Many wonderful conversations took place under the Questioning Oak during the first few months at Westwood, but in the final months of 1880, gout worsened, his lungs filled with fluid, depression was aggravated, and Charles's aloneness was amplified. Susannah's sickness also took a turn for the worse, so all the houseguests were quickly refused and lively conversation with family and friends were stowed in the London fog beneath Westwood.

The orphanage and almshouses continued to run effortlessly from a financial and operational standpoint, as the sales of Charles's books provided all the funding needed. But, the children desperately missed Charles, their only father figure.

Every time he wandered into the large home to pass out candy and squeeze the children in his bulky arms, they knew they were loved, deeply.

The publishing house continued to flourish, but they missed their leader and their pastor. His sermons continued to be printed, and in that year, twenty-five thousand copies were printed every week in twenty-two languages. They never missed a printing release, but the staff members didn't have the same sense of belonging and passion as when Charles had his hand at the helm.

The Metropolitan Tabernacle—the largest Congregationalist church in the world—remained fruitful, but the people desperately missed their preacher. No one can replace the unique role of a preacher to his flock, and when the church doesn't have one, she wanders. Charles knew the reality of all this, and it only worsened his sadness and remorse that he had been removed from the front of the battle, a prisoner to his sickness and grief.

One Saturday, as Charles desperately tried to muster up energy to preach on the following Sabbath, he wept as he could not even hold his pen in his inflamed hands. His thumb bent towards his wrist, while every finger locked as iron beams. They seemed to weld together, forming a heavy and unmovable extremity. As he wept, his body slid from his desk chair, then fell to the wood floor of the Westwood study, where he landed in the fetal position, feet tucked, teeth clenched, bandaged hands tucked into his trembling chest.

Susannah, hearing the commotion from the adjacent study, rose from her bed and inched toward Charles.

"Husband—are you alright? Charles!" she yelled as she approached his round body that seemed to cling to the wood beams of the floor.

"Wifey, what shall I do?" he cried. His cheeks pressed to the floor. "How will I preach again?"

Susannah delicately nestled herself next to his sobbing body, where she, too, wept.

His tendency to wander into depression seemed to overwhelm him, sometimes shackling him to his bed for days at a time.

You're worthless, Charles, whispered the darkness as Charles laid in his bed, staring at the oak beams that held the ceiling of the Westwood study.

"Perhaps you are right, old friend," muttered Charles. "Perhaps I am."

You'll be forgotten, Charles, the voice rang through his heart like the St. Petersburg cathedral bell in the midnight hours.

"Probably will be."

You ought to die.

"Sometimes I want to."

You're mine.

"Am I?" Charles whispered, then closed his eyes to sleep.

"Charles—you must get out of bed. Stretch your legs. You've been in bed for two days," said Old George, with stern compassion as he opened the curtains of the Westwood study, exposing the afternoon sun. But, Charles did not speak. Coiling into the fetal position, he pressed his tangled beard into the pillow, then drifted to sleep.

"Tirshatha—" whispered Susannah into his ear. "It's been three days. You must rise from your bed, dear—you must." She held a cup of warm mint tea to his parched lips, and waited for him drink. After he finished the cup, Charles turned his face from his bride, lobbied his eyelids closed, and whispered, "I cannot find the strength today, wifey."

"It is Thursday," said Joseph. His freshly shaven skin only accentuated the worry on his face. "Governor—it has been four days. We are all fearful for your life. You *must* rise. Eat. Stretch your legs."

"Joseph," Charles mumbled, staring into the blankness of the study. "I have tried. But, I cannot. I am very distrustful of my mental powers. I feel so entirely broken down and crushed. My incessant pain is wearing me down."

"What can I do to help you? Tell me," Joseph asked mournfully.

"What is the end of this perpetually recurring affliction, Joseph?" he cried.

"I do not know, Charles." Joseph's face fell onto his pastor's shoulder as he cried to God, begging for healing. Charles moaned with pain, as both of his legs had swollen to horrific levels. The skin cracked and opened, oozing fluid through the layers of thick bandage that covered them. Immense pain jolted through his body. Incredible sorrow drowned his heart. Still, as Joseph prayed, Charles could be heard affirming the requests for healing. "Yes," he mumbled. "Please."

"Take a pen, Joseph," said Charles after the prayer was finished. "Write a letter to my brother, James."

Joseph rose from the bed, wiped his tear-soaked hands on his brown trousers, then retrieved a pen and paper from the desk. "What shall it say?"

"Dear Brother," Charles whispered as Joseph wrote in simple letters. "I am attacked . . . with such violent neuralgia in my head . . . that I cannot keep up. And must beg you . . . to preach for me tonight. My legs are heavy with the gout feeling. Blue pill and black draft have had a fair trial, but it is a huge foot and full of fire. I cannot be sure of a swift deliverance."

Joseph wrote every word as Charles prescribed, then held his pen, waiting for Charles to finish.

"Your loving brother, Charles Haddon Spurgeon."

On the fifth day of affliction, Charles was awakened at six o'clock by a familiar and comfortable voice. The English sun had barely begun to poke through the white cotton curtains of the Westwood study, slowly emblazoning the rows of Puritan books and old commentaries on the mahogany shelves with pure-white light. Punch lazily raised an eye, wagged his tail, then returned to sleep as he soon realized the intruder was an old friend.

"Charles. Wake up," said the voice.

Charles—famished and weak—peeled open his eyes to see a blurry figure sitting on a stool next to his bed. The incoming sun made it difficult for Charles to make out the figure's face, but he felt a consoling hand rest on his forearm, then another hand firm upon his shoulder. As Charles's eyes began to adjust, he blinked his eyes, raised his head, and looked into the eyes of his kindred, brother.

"Thomas?" he moaned.

"It's me," answered Thomas. The terrible sight of his dear friend in such anguish caused a flood of emotion to well within him. Tears spouted and ran along his dark skin, then trickled into his beard, along the corners of his mouth.

"Is it you, Thomas? You have come back to England?"

"Where else would I go, Charles?"

"Henrietta." Charles shuffled forward. "Oh—your dear Henrietta. I'm so sorry, Thomas."

Thomas was silent.

"Help me sit," said Charles as Thomas pulled his fragile body to a sitting position, and rested his bandaged hands on his bandaged knees. "Water."

Thomas held a cup of water from the old Westwood well to his lips, and Charles drank deeply until it was emptied. "Another, please."

"Old George told me about your oak tree."

"Ah—my oak tree."

"He said you just let people ask you questions under that tree. The Questioning Oak? Is that what you call it?"

"Aye."

"What you say about getting out of that bed and showing it to me?" Thomas smiled deeply and pushed the tears from his cheeks and eyes.

"I am not able to find the strength, Thomas. My legs are full of fire. My knees knock with pain."

"Well—I guess you need to lean on me. Because, one thing is for sure this morning. You and me are going down to that old tree. Even if I have to carry you, old man."

"Susannah's wheelchair," said Charles, smiling only with his eyes. As Thomas retrieved the wheelchair from the hallway, Charles—with his hands—pushed his legs to the edge of the bed. Like suspended cannons, they hung, motionless, to the wood floor.

"Let's go." Thomas braced his strong back and helped Charles slide from the bed onto the wheelchair. Charles cleared his throat and brushed his hands through his messy, silvered hair. "Why are you here, Thomas? You should not have come."

Thomas, ignoring Charles's argument, pushed the wheelchair out of the study door and onto the grass-edged pathway that led from the Westwood house to the Questioning Oak. The birds cheered the morning air overhead, and Charles lifted his head toward the morning sun. His face was instantly warmed by its heat and beauty. Once they made it to the oak tree, Thomas locked the wheelchair in place, and took his seat next to Charles.

"I'm—I was so—sad," Charles said, slowly, "—to hear the news."

"Henrietta is—was—the best woman I knew. I miss her every day."

"Why would God take her?" asked Charles as an innocent boy, which caught Thomas off guard. "Do you ask that, Thomas? I have not lost a spouse. I imagine it hard to believe He is still good."

"He's still very good." Thomas nodded his head, exaggeratedly, with firm belief.

The two men sat in silence for a few minutes, breathing in the fresh morning air and the rare opportunity to simply be together.

"Why are you here, Thomas? I'm in a shameful place."

"That's exactly why I'm here," he paused to gather his thoughts. "I guess—God wanted me here this morning so I could sit under your big *questioning* tree, and let you ask the questions for once."

Charles had never conceived the idea of being the one asking questions. For years, he had been the answer-giver, the sage who poured out all the answers—sometimes as if he had learned them all by rote. But, for the first time in a long time, Charles felt like he was being seen, for when Thomas saw him, he saw the *real* Charles—full of pain, sorrow, suffering, and grief.

"The gout is painful, Thomas. But—it is not the only thing shackling me to the bed. Do you know what else does?" asked Charles.

"Tell me."

"These old depressive thoughts. The whispers of the Devil in the darkness. Sadness—uncontrollable sadness."

Thomas earnestly listened.

"Tell me, Thomas. Why would *I* give ear to the Devil? I have seen God do so many wonderful things. Why would *this* man of God war against depressive thoughts and sadness?"

"Because you are *just* a man, Charles."

"Yes, I am—" Charles said before raising his tired and scratchy voice. "But—why after all these years . . . after knowing Christ . . . as a true Friend . . . Why would I *still* be enslaved to feeling so low . . . lower than the bottomless pit of hell? Why would I have Christ and still seem to spiral down it?"

Thomas leaned towards Charles and fixed his dark, steady eyes into his disillusioned face. "Because, the Devil *hates* you, my friend. The very last thing he wants . . . is for you to find all your happiness and freedom in Christ *while* you suffer!" he spoke with conviction, raising his voice. "Don't you see? When you have gout, and depression, and bandaged hands, and big swollen joints—Satan doesn't want a man to rejoice in Jesus when he's suffering. What he really wants . . . is for you to curse God."

"Seems the Devil has been throwing fiery arrows at me for a long time. I'm tired from the fight, Thomas. I fear I have no faith."

"Let me tell you something," said Thomas, eyes widening with passion. "The Devil loses one of his fiery darts when he can't whisper—'God forsakes you, and your friends forget you.' You take *that* weapon out of his hands, and he loses. That old weapon is made out of lies."

"How do I do that?" asked Charles sullenly, staring at the dense fog that lay beyond.

"You remember the story about the boys in the fiery furnace," Thomas said.

"Shadrach, Meshach, and Abednego." Charles nodded.

"You know who tied those boys up and put them in that furnace in the first place?"

"The king. They refused to worship a false god," answered Charles rotely.

"Nah—you know better than that, Reverend. No king has that much power. Who tied those boys up?"

Charles waited silently, watching the morning sun slowly crest above the fog. He knew the answer to his question as it hung beneath the oak tree, still he waited to hear it with the fresh ears of faith from a friend he trusted to speak truth.

"God tied them up." Thomas interrupted the silence. "*He* chose to put them in that furnace. And, it's never a mean thing to be chosen by God. Just like Shadrach, Meshach, and Abednego, you were chosen for the furnace. 'Cause, in the furnace . . . when the coals burn the hottest . . . that's when all your human strength is melted. All your human pride is burned up. When the furnace of affliction burns hot—" he paused, thinking. "God says—'Don't you worry. I chose this for you. You're Mine. Ain't nothing gonna crush you.'"

Charles lifted his head to the canopy of oak leaves above his head. The bright sun seemed to smile and wink as the oak leaves danced with the morning wind. All around him, the brightness of morning awakened his senses and pushed the fog from his cold and weary heart.

"So, I say this," continued Thomas as he leaned back in his chair with a kingly confidence. "If the furnace gets heated seven times hotter, you ain't gonna dread it no more. Because the Son of God is walking right there next to you. Right there in the glowing coals."

"In the realms of sorrow I am blessed," Charles mumbled, preaching to his own soul.

Thomas took a deep breath, then steadied his eyes once again on Charles's sunken and purpled eyes. "The best blessing God could give any of us is health," he swallowed and nodded his head. "—*Except* for sickness."

Charles listened, fixated on the Spirit of God that was speaking through his friend under the oak tree.

"A sick wife . . . a freshly dug grave . . . a lonely and terrified slave . . . poverty . . . gout, depression, and fear . . . they all teach us lessons we can't learn nowhere else. Trials drive us to Jesus. Sickness has been more useful to the saints of God than health ever has. The furnace is a blessing, Charles. Embrace it."

With that, mysteriously and suddenly, the fog lifted from Charles's heart. His eyes opened wide, as a newfound revelation echoed in the chambers of his imagination.

> *Trials make the promise sweet,*
> *Trials give new life to prayer,*
> *Trials bring me to His feet,*
> *Lay me low, and keep me there.*

Charles sat still in his wheelchair, and traced the masterfully written story that had been woven into his life. It seemed time stood still as he thought of his salvation as a young man, the Lord's kindness in giving him a flock, his lovely Susannah, his two sons, his good friends. He thought of the nights of misery and the changing of bandages, but now clearly, he saw God's faithfulness in allowing his words to be scattered all over the world, despite his own strength.

Then—Charles's thoughts wandered back to his grandfather's garden, just past the parsonage, tucked inside the hedges of yew.

"God does what we can't. So, we wait." He remembered his grandfather said as he pushed the apple seedling into the sparkling wine bottle and released it into the air.

He knew the apple seedling died decades ago, but was also keenly aware that the faith that was originally placed into his heart all those years ago—although tested and tried—could never be quelled. The Good and Faithful Gardner was doing what no one else could: water, nourish, and sustain his faith.

Darkness whispered nothing to Charles. Instead, it hastily sped into the distant hills, fearful of the light's invading presence. The hot morning sun continued to merrily run into every corner of the Westwood yard—up and down the gravel pathway, into the rose garden, past the fernery, across the tiny wood bridge, past the lake, and into the branches of the Questioning Oak—where it fully warmed Charles's fragile body.

"Will you write something down for me, so I shall not forget this?" asked Charles.

Thomas fished into his back pocket to retrieve a leather-bound booklet, half-full of sermon notes and scribbled prayers. "You say it. I'll write it."

"God often sends us trials that our graces may be discovered." Charles spoke with precision. "God often takes away our comforts and our privileges in order to make us better Christians. He trains His soldiers, not in tents of easy and luxury, but by turning them out and using them to forced marches and hard service. He makes them forge through streams, and swim through rivers, and climb mountains, and walk many a long mile with heavy knapsacks of sorrow on their back."

Thomas continued to write every word, desperate to catalogue each sentence perfectly.

"Thorns and thistles shall bring forth to you, but there is a Land coming . . . where everlasting springs abide . . . and never-withering seedlings bloom into plump, delicious fruit."

CHAPTER 23

JUBILEE

London, England 1884

When a great fog finally lifts, the entire city celebrates. Children throw open their windows, climb with all their strength, then jump from the sill to the bed of grass below. They shout and smile, dance and sing, as their grey-soaked landscapes suddenly burst with color again. Mothers break open the windows of the kitchen, boil pots of celebratory meat and potatoes, then gently pile them on fine sets of china for the entire family to gorge. Fathers, with a renewed sense of joy, leave their silken scarves behind, traveling to work with mouths open to taste the fresh air, swallowing it like cups of melted chocolate. The day of infamy is forever scribed into their calendars, and like the statue of a prized warrior within the courtyard of the city square, their day of jubilee is forever recognized.

After the fog dissipated on that warm morning beneath the Questioning Oak, Charles Spurgeon was never the same. As the years continued to climb forward, so did Charles's ability to embrace suffering. He no longer resisted, but saw suffering as a comfortable companion that only nudged him towards His sweet Savior. As the crushing of a flower causes it to yield its aroma, so Charles—having endured in the long-continued illness of Susannah and his own constant pains—was able to sympathize most tenderly with all sufferers.

When Charles was well enough to visit the orphanage, he sat for hours, talking, listening, and playing with the children. A single-mindedness took over his previously anxious heart, a deep sense of empathy for anyone who was lonely, especially orphaned children, compelled him to exhaust every moment he had with them.

Charles made it a point to personally meet with every new member of the Tabernacle, and when he did, he pressed into their needs and sinful desires, then counseled them with the hope of Christ. He knew what it felt like to be a man full of need and sinful desire, and felt a profound joy in leading others towards hope.

When his gout lessened and he was able to preach, Charles preached as he had never before. He gained from illness a wealth of knowledge and sympathy which he could not have gained elsewhere. Undergirding all of his experience in suffering was his conviction that his ill health was God's gift, and he used that gift every time he opened his mouth, inscribed pages for a book, or preached a sermon from the pulpit of the Tabernacle.

While he sat at night to read *The Pilgrim's Progress* to Susannah, he stroked her hair and kissed her cheeks, empathizing with the unsmooth road of suffering she had endured for so long. He thanked the Lord for her faithfulness, her sweetness, and her consistency in always pointing his eyes towards Jesus.

Perhaps Charles's most prevailing sensitivity to others was found in his ability to resonate with anyone who was in bondage—bound by either physical or spiritual chains. He detested darkness with all his heart, and when he stumbled across news of women and children enslaved by evil men, or foreign tribes bound and bruised by oppressors, or men and women enchained to depression or addiction of any kind, his heart sank, as he knew all too well the darkness that came with being enslaved.

⊠ ⊠ ⊠

Thomas had taught Charles many things throughout the years. After he returned to America for mission work in 1881, they remained faithful friends by pen and paper, often instructing each other as good brothers do.

Charles—How I miss you and pray for you often. I do hope you remember—a free man lives like a free man. I am praying that you continue to resist the Devil's attempt to put you back into those old chains of depression and sadness.

Chicago is cold. Give my love to Susannah. And rub Punch's belly for me.

—Your friend, Thomas.

Charles savored and kept each letter in a neat stack in the bottom drawer of his study desk. When the old darkness tried to knock on the door of his heart, Charles would read the Scriptures and occasionally peek into that desk drawer to read truths from a fellow freed man. As he thought of Thomas, Charles would inevitably pull out a thin sheet of white paper, and craft a return letter to his friend.

Thomas—The night is still. Work is done. And the Lord Himself draws near. Possibly there may be pain to be endured, the head may be aching, and the heart may be throbbing. But, if Jesus comes to visit us, our bed of languishing becomes a throne of glory.

I pray He is visiting you often, my friend. —CHS

The year 1884 marked one of Charles's and Thomas's most important years, as both men celebrated milestone jubilees. Their jubilees did not call for the blowing of trumpets or the fanfare of parades, only the uplifting of holy hands to acknowledge God's sweet grace to use mortal men for eternal causes. To celebrate both of these landmarks, Thomas made the trip from America to London, and was able to spend many months with Charles and Susannah at Westwood.

During the summer months, Mr. Harrald, Mr. Fullerton, and Mr. Wigney organized the jubilee that celebrated Charles's fiftieth birthday. Most people in the city of London were surprised to find he was only fifty years old since, for three decades, he had been a prominent and influential figure in London.

"At first he was a curiosity," penned *The Gazette*, announcing his year of jubilee. "Then, a notoriety. But, he has long since been recognized as one of the first celebrities of his day. His position is absolutely unique."

By the age of fifty, Charles had pastored and preached to countless men and women in numerous countries around the globe. On June 18, Charles sat behind a desk in the pastor's vestry of the Tabernacle from twelve to five o'clock, to receive all the members of the congregation, one by one. As they filed through, they hugged their beloved pastor, thanking him for his years of pastorship and endurance. Some church members brought gifts, but most only blessed him with kind words of affirmation and gratitude.

Once the procession was completed, every seat in the sanctuary of the Tabernacle filled with enthusiastic church members. They buzzed with joy as they awaited their pastor's address. The line of people outside the Tabernacle overwhelmed the amount of seats available, so the elders decided to do multiple meetings on two nights so that everyone was able to attend the jubilee. Thankfully, Susannah was able to make the journey from Westwood for both evenings, and as Charles made his way to the pulpit to give his address, he spotted Susannah, neatly dressed in a pale green dress on the second row, sitting squarely next to Thomas.

"I do not think anybody imagines that I ought to speak at any great length tonight," he addressed the congregation, smiling outrageously. "After the kind words which many of you have spoken to me, I feel very much like weeping now. But, let me say this for my speech: the blessing which I have had here, must be entirely attributed to the grace of God, and to the working of God's Holy Spirit among us. I hope I have never preached without an entire dependence on the Holy Ghost. I defy the Devil himself ever get that truth out of you if God the Holy Spirit once puts it in you. I thank you, dear friends, for all your love and kindness towards me. I cannot see any reason in myself why you should love me. I confess that I would not go across the street to hear myself preach!" He laughed, instantly conjuring laughter from the congregation as well.

"But I dare not say more about that matter because my dear wife is here." The crowd erupted in laughter again, as they squirmed in their seat and scanned the room to see Susannah's response. "It is the only point upon which we decidedly differ. I differ in total from her estimate of me, and from your estimate of me too." Susannah shook her head and cast a gentle and loving grin.

"And, yet," he said with a more serious tone, "I do not wish you to alter your love for me." As Charles continued his address, he set his eyes on the thousands of individual faces that cluttered the room. In those faces he saw men he had discipled, couples he had married, children whose parents he had buried, deacons, elders, and precious co-laborers in the gospel. He could not remember feeling more godly pride.

As Charles finished his sincere speech and offered a final prayer of blessing over his congregation, he was followed by a closing address from Pastor D. L. Moody, who had traveled from America to attend the celebration.

Pastor Moody stood confidently behind the pulpit. His round face and neatly trimmed, silver beard offered a trustworthiness to his sound speech. After a few moments of recounting his own story of conversion and his first encounter at the Tabernacle many years ago, he paused to look directly at Charles, who sat on the second row, next to Susannah and Thomas.

"God bless you," Rev. Moody proclaimed as he pointed his finger directly at Charles. "I have read your sermons for twenty-five years. You are never going to die. Your words will live forever, Charles Spurgeon. We may never meet together again in the flesh, but—by the blessing of God—I will meet you up yonder."

A river of peace seemed to overflow the banks of Charles's and Susannah's hearts as they sat in the packed sanctuary of the church they had served faithfully for so many years. Charles lifted Susannah's hand to his lips and gracefully kissed the back of her palm.

"This jubilee of my life is a true jubilee of joy. Not only to me, Susie. But, to you as well," he whispered in her ear.

❋ ❋ ❋

A few months later, Thomas attended a jubilee of a different kind, the 50th Anniversary Meeting of the Abolition of Slavery in the colonies. Invited by the secretary of the Anti-Slavery Society of England, Thomas was given the honor to sit on the platform with dignitaries from around the United Kingdom, his chair perfectly situated between the Prince of Wales and the Archbishop of Canterbury. He thought of the irony of a former slave with no status now reclining in the plush cashmere chairs of royalty.

As the Prince of Wales stood and motioned for the audience to take their seats, the Great Hall of Guildhall stalled to a silence. The hall was neatly trimmed with gold-embossed wood and was amply lit by nearly a hundred filament lightbulbs that hung from black iron chandeliers. Every face, from the back of the room to the platform, was engulfed by the modern, bright light.

"Ladies and gentlemen," he said from behind the podium, "This is a great and important anniversary." The Prince's long-flowing and ornate coat hung over his shoulders, and was decorated with golden cords and bright silver metals of armor. His bald head, shining from the glowing filament bulbs, gave him a regal appearance. "Today we celebrate the jubilee of the emancipation of slavery throughout our colonies." The crowd burst into enthusiastic cheers as the he finished his sentence. "It is also a day which has been looked forward to with pleasure and satisfaction by this excellent Society, which has worked so hard in this great cause of humanity, as there are many human beings still enslaved all over the Earth."

Thomas glanced towards Charles, who sat on the corner seat of the front row of the Great Hall, accompanied by Old George and Joseph. Charles slouched in his seat, adjusting his neck as the pain from sitting on a wooden bench already began to stir in his lower back. Thomas was proud that Charles made the journey to attend such an important day in history, and offered a gentle nod to Charles as the Prince continued.

"Fifty years ago, throughout all the colonies, the churches and chapels had been thrown open, as slaves eagerly awaited the news of their freedom. They then sprang to their feet as the proclamation passed throughout the colonies. On every island, that glad song of freedom rang as chains were broken and human beings freed, as they should."

The crowd stood and cheered.

"A decade later, slavery was abolished in India," the crowd shuffled to their seats as he continued. "All it required was the passing of an Act, destroying its legal status. Then, in 1848—the abolition of slavery in France. And, 1861—Russia. In the United States of America, in 1865, the fetters of four million slaves in the Southern States were melted in the hot fires of the most terrible Civil War of modern times. And, in Egypt, and the Gold Coast of Western Africa in 1874. Passing to South America, Brazil, and Spain, the abolition of slavery continued.

"A great work in the world has been accomplished in these fifty years, and still there is more to do. The chief end of this jubilee is not merely to celebrate what has been done, but to also rekindle the fires of English enthusiasm. To carry on the act until the light of freedom radiates from every corner of the Earth."

The Prince of Wales spoke with fierce passion and convincing firmness as he knew the plight of slavery in the world had not been fully conquered. He turned to back to Thomas, respectfully tipped his head, then addressed the crowd again.

"Now, I would like to introduce you to the Reverend Thomas Johnson from the United States of America. Reverend Johnson is in the fight against slavery of all types around the world. Twenty-eight years a slave in the Southern States of America, Thomas knows the bitterness and evil of human slavery more than most in this Great Hall. As a display of our absolute intolerance for human slavery, we will now sit in silence as Reverend Johnson places his old relics into the Society's conservatory, where they will forever remind each of us of the despicable nature of slavery."

Thomas nervously stood from his seat, and buttoned all four buttons of his long, black coat. From behind his chair, he pulled a wide, wooden box, and slid it all the way to the edge of the platform. One by one, Thomas lifted twenty chains and neck harnesses that were used on Mr. Bennett's slave plantation in Richmond, Virginia, then draped each chain over his shoulders, as the crowd helplessly watched. The clanking of the hard metal pierced the ear of every patron in the Great Hall, and it echoed up and down the aisles, bouncing to the ceiling, then back again to the platform. As Thomas added the last chain onto his shoulders, he began to weep. Memories of the whipping post, Ezekiel, and Quentin Ellis flooded his mind.

Charles, without thinking, hurried to his feet. He gripped his wooden cane, and although his legs shook under the weight of his body, he continued to stand, fixated on his friend who stood at the front of the platform covered with iron chains. Thomas had never described details of his chains to Charles, and as he had now seen them for the first time, Charles was overwhelmed with reverence.

Slowly and quietly, other members of the audience—Old George, Joseph, and a thousand others—rose to their feet. Some hung their head, unable to look at the terrible sight, but others forced themselves to look, so the terrible image of slavery could be forever ingrained in their thoughts, and their hearts never grow stale to the vile institution.

Thomas, full of grace and poise, stood tall as he carried the chains from the platform, down the short row of steps, into the center aisle of the silent crowd. The weight of the chains did not buckle Thomas's strong back, and their hold on him had shattered years ago. Arriving at the back of the Great Hall, he placed each chain on a long, wooden table that was covered in a bright linen tablecloth. The contrast of the black iron against the white cloth was illuminated by the bright lightbulbs that hung overhead. There was no greyness on the table, nor was there greyness in the hearts of those who stood in the Great Hall, for when you see the terrible relics of slavery and hear the clanking of iron harnesses that once held image-bearers of God, you are forever enlightened.

Thomas turned his back to the chains he would never bear again, then walked towards the platform, where he took his seat with dignitaries of the kingdom, and gentlemen of rank, wealth, and stature.

⌗ ⌗ ⌗

When the ceremony and a brief procession was finished, Thomas and Charles embraced, as this was the last time they would see each other for some time.

"When does your ship depart, Thomas?" Charles held Thomas firmly by his elbow.

"I set sail for America at five o'clock."

"Go forth, beloved brother."

"Pray for me as I continue to preach of freedom in Christ!" he smiled.

"May I speak a prayer of blessing over you, Thomas?"

"Please." Thomas closed his eyes, held out his empty hands, and heard the prayer of a fellow saint and kindred brother.

"May you have your heart right with Him. And He will visit you often. Every day, may you walk with God—as Enoch did— and so turn days into Sabbaths, meals into sacraments, homes into temples—and Earth into Heaven. So be it with us! Amen."

CHAPTER 24

FALLING ASLEEP

1892

Susannah placed a silver letter opener in the corner of the paper envelope and slowly slid it forward until it revealed the contents. With careful hands, she slid open the letter and held it between her fingers.

The air was pleasant, as one of her caretakers had flung all of the windows open, inviting the tasty English air to flap the curtains and chase through her brightened bedroom. Her hair was neatly brushed and she sat comfortably in her armchair. It was the first time she had escaped her bed in several weeks. She deeply missed the companionship of her husband, and chuckled as she switched on the filament lightbulb of the lamp next to her chair.

Charles hated these bulbs! She laughed to herself, as no one was there to join her.

It had been some time since she had seen Charles. His sickness had taken a toll for the worse, so he and Old George found lodging in Mentone, in the sunny south of France. He had frequented the quaint town many times in the past year, as the temperature was perfect and the scenery gorgeous. It seemed to be a proper place for a mortally wounded man to spend his final days reading, writing, and studying.

❈ ❈ ❈

With Old George at the helm, Charles loved the short drive around the Boulevard Victoria, along the breaking water of the Mediterranean Sea. One great help to him was the bright sunshine in which he was able to spend so much of his time. He almost lived in the open air, usually going for a drive in the morning, and in the afternoon having a ride in a bath chair, along the Promenade St. Louis.

When he worked on his writing, Charles enjoyed the plush gardens of the tiny house where he stayed. A walk up the hillside led to the numerous quiet nooks where the Pastor and his sec- retary spent many a delightful day. He was nearly finished with a commentary on the book of Psalms, one that required decades of writing, editing, and nurturing. Most of its beginning pages were written in the New Forest, atop the ancient stone bridge above the Avon River, but as he toiled to finish the commentary, he found Mentone to be a place of inspiration, where he could dictate the final pages to a secretary if his hands were unable.

The Treasury of David, he thought. *That's what we shall call it.*

Some of Charles's best writings took place during the years he was most sick. Volumes of sermons had been crafted, nearly three thousand. By 1892, his works made up the most of any English author in history. Whether in pain or pleasure, his mind tirelessly worked to craft texts that all seemed to point to the glory that is found when a man or woman suffers, and glories, in God.

� � �

As Susannah continued to hold the letter, she thought of Charles's last sermon at the Metropolitan Tabernacle, just a few months prior. Sometimes pastors know when they are preaching their last sermon. They plan for it, brace for it, then enter the spiritual arena for the last time to deliver a sermon they have meticulously poured over—their *last*.

But, Charles had told her of his promise long ago—beneath the canopy of trees in gardens of the Crystal Palace—to preach every sermon as if it were his last. From that day, and every sermon since, Charles preached as if Gabriel's trumpet might sound in the seconds following his last amen.

Susannah sighed with a fondness as she recalled his final sermon on June 7, 1891. Charles sat in the front pew of the Tabernacle and waited for the service to begin as thousands streamed in to fill the sanctuary. Charles always loved the minutes before the service began, as the room bustled with the movement and chatter of soon-to-be worshippers. Normally, Charles used this time to walk among the people, shaking hands, hugging children, and meeting visitors, but on that Sunday, it simply was not possible. His gout was severe, and before he left for Mentone for a few days of rest, Charles was determined to preach the text from the thirtieth chapter of First Samuel.

� � ✵

"Are you ready, Governor?" asked James, jarring Charles from thought. "It is time for the service to begin."

"I am," said Charles, offering a jovial smile.

As he approached the pulpit, a surge of excitement and adrenaline coursed through him. He felt it every time he stood to preach. Try as he may, he could never articulate that feeling to anyone, not even Susannah.

"It's like breathing, Susie—when the Holy Spirit takes over your preaching, it just flows forward!" he tried to explain with no avail. "When a preacher is truly anointed with the power of the Holy Ghost, the flesh is no more in control of his words than he is the oxygen that sustains his body."

As the adrenaline began to subside, Charles entered the pulpit with sobriety. Perched high above the crowd, it had offered an incredible view of his flock, which had been his pulpit throne for thirty years. There, he had proclaimed the gospel to at least twenty million souls, while the printed versions of those sermons had reached a far greater number than anyone would know.

He took notice of the wooden railing that lined the outer edges of the pulpit, extending to his left and his right. Within the top, there were two palm-sized and lightened places on the ornate wood. They were smooth and worn from the years of oil and sweat from his fiery grip, and the dark stain had faded some time ago. He smiled, traced them with his swollen fingers, and thought, *If only the wooden floors in my study were that worn and smooth from my knees bent in prayer—how might the Lord have used me in this life?*

As he began to preach, the Word of God flowed powerfully from his lips. He preached as he always had—for the lost soul to come home, the sick to find healing, and the parched to drink from the living water of Christ.

"This morning—I want to utter God-given words of comfort to those who are faint and weary in the Lord's army." The congregation leaned forward in their seats with every eye fixed on Charles. Their hungry souls longed for more than bread and choice wine, so Charles continued to preach the Bible, a dole for their hunger.

"I shall begin by saying, first—that faint ones occur even in the army of our King. Among David's army heroes, there were hands that hung down, and feeble knees that needed to be confirmed. There are such in Christ's army at most seasons. We have among us soldiers whose faith is real, and whose love is burning. And yet, others whose strength is weakened. They are so depressed in spirit, that they are obliged to stop behind, with the baggage."

Charles reached the place in his sermon that was more personal than he dared to admit. Earlier in the week, he sat at his desk and wrote these words as a weary man. He had fought the Lord's battles for forty years, and although his love for Christ was strong, and his faith as firm as the ground on which he stood, his body was clearly failing.

"Sometimes the body fails," he continued, "God's loyal-hearted ones are placed on the sick list. Sometimes they must keep in the trenches for a while.

"What I have to say is this: If you know Christ, you will find Him so meek and lowly of heart that you will find *rest* for your souls. He is the most magnanimous of captains. There never was His like among the choicest of princes. He is always to be found in the thickest part of the battle. When the wind blows cold, He always takes the bleak side of the hill. The heaviest end of the cross lies on His shoulders. If He bids us carry a burden, He carries it also. If there is anything that is gracious, generous, kind, and tender, lavish and superabundant in love—you *always* find it in Him."

For the congregation, the time it took for their pastor to complete his sermon passed as in an instant. Most people who heard the great prince of preachers would leave the presence of the Tabernacle, wishing earnestly that Charles had preached a moment longer, for the taste of milk and honey never grows old to those who feast at the table of the Lord. That day's sermon proved the same.

"These forty years and more have I served Him, blessed be His name! I would be glad to continue yet another forty years in the same dear service if so it pleased Him. His service is life . . . peace . . . joy. Oh, that you would enter on it at once. God help you to enlist under the banner of Jesus even this day. Amen."

Susannah saw the look on Charles's face as he closed his Bible, and the entire congregation stood, erupting in applause. The people of Metropolitan Tabernacle had never clapped at the end of a sermon, but on this day, they applauded—not for Charles or his ability, but as an act of worship to the Lord. Susannah beamed with humility as Charles exited the platform, walked to his seat next to her, and joined the congregation in applauding.

She clapped too, in worship and gratitude to the Great Savior that always fills weary bodies with the river of life.

❊ ❊ ❊

Oh, what a day that was, she thought as she carefully unfolded the paper letter in her bedroom. As she pulled each corner wide, the familiar purple ink of her soulmate's pen covered the white paper. She smiled, and her stomach fluttered as if butterflies were swarming. She slowly read each word, carefully deciphering the shaky and now-messy handwriting.

Wifey,

I am very low in spirit, but I am reminded that our God is yet alive. I have enjoyed the rest very much, but young married couples remind me of our early days, and the cloud which covers us now. Still—He who sent both sun and shade is our ever-tender Father, and knows best. If it be good for us, He can restore all that He has withdrawn, and more. And if not, He designs yet our greater good.

I believe you should make your way to Mentone. My days are numbered, and only our Father knows how many. In a few days, I should see you. And, it will be a fairer sight than any my eyes have rested on during my absence. — CHS.

Susannah inhaled a deep and sober breath, as she placed the letter in the envelope and wiped her tears on the sleeve of her dress. The season had come, the hour was near, and Susannah knew it was time to travel to Mentone for her last days with Charles.

After her things were packed in bulky parcels of luggage, Susannah wrote a few handwritten letters to old friends to inform them of Charles's impending death. She closed their envelopes and sealed them tightly, then handed them to an official of the Royal Mail service before they scattered to their recipients.

Joined by James, his wife, and Joseph Harrald—Susannah was lifted into a carriage to begin their thousand-mile journey to the southern region of France. The trip was long and tiring, but when they finally arrived in Mentone, the reunion was sweet.

❇ ❇ ❇

A few weeks later, a few of Charles's other close friends made the pilgrimage to Mentone, after receiving the sad news in Susannah's letter. For days on end, Charles's closest friends sat beside his bed to pray, read Scripture, and tell stories.

"Read me a Puritan hymn," Charles insisted. Faithfully, a friend would read every verse and chorus of as many hymns as he wanted to hear.

"Tell me a story," he asked his brother James, who quickly offered a story of their childhood, their dear grandfather, and games of hide-and-seek played in Mr. Tagley's horsing block.

Finally, on an unsuspecting day in January, Charles called for his friends to circle around his bed as he knew it was his final day as a mortal man. They stood in silence, holding hands, whispering only prayers of adoration and gratitude for all the work God had accomplished.

As Susannah looked at each dear friend in the circle, one after another, she thought of that Great Day around the throne room of God, when she would see every single saint that had gone before, and her husband's unmarred body dancing on the golden streets.

A great deal can be said about the character of a man, not by the measure of his influence, or the earthen things his hands once crafted, but by the glimmer of confidence in the eyes of the few friends that surround his death bed—their hands clasped, eyes clear, and hearts assured of his triumphant entrance into the courts of the Heavenly City where Jesus most surely will say, "Well done! Come dance with Me."

Charles, mostly bound to his bed, had lost several teeth and most of the use of his fingers, hands, and arms. His face was shriveled and small, and his round belly had dissolved into the pure-white bed sheets that tucked beneath his body. His breathing was short, and the blue blanket atop his legs and chest barely moved as he struggled to inhale the sweet oxygen of Mentone, and exhale it into the sober-reverence of the room. The white walls were barren and unfanciful, but the small balcony doors opened to the smiling hills and rolling sea in the distance.

His eyes slowly turned to his brother James, his wife, and Joseph Harrald. He savored each glance, grateful for the moments lived with each person. As he inhaled again, his eyes met Old George's, the man who had selflessly cared for him for so many years. As he passed Old George, near the end of the circle, he looked into the eyes of the man who taught him what it meant to find freedom in Christ. He lifted his left hand, and Thomas held it without wavering.

Then Charles turned his eyes to his right. He squeezed the hand of Susannah and felt the warm rush of the pilgrim's hand that he had loved most dearly. Her face, confident and caring, reminded him that the greatest earthen treasure God had given him was the girl he fell in love with in a cold London kitchen so many years before. He looked into the eyes of his bride and whispered, "I love you, Susie."

"Charles—I love you," she said sweetly, kneeling close to his face.

"I—" he whispered into the quiet and still room, his mouth half-open, barely able to speak. "I have been cast into the waters to swim . . . But for God's upholding hand . . . they would have proved waters to drown in."

"You were no dry-land sailor," Susannah smiled. "Charles—it's time to go Home."

She nodded and knelt closer to Charles's ear. She lifted one hand to the heavens and held the other tightly to Charles's bandaged hands who were now steady and unmoved.

Slowly, and only at a whisper, Susannah sang a song of hope, of freedom, of home.

> *My Lord, He calls me.*
> *He calls me by the thunder.*
> *The trumpet sounds within my soul.*
> *I ain't got long to stay here.*

She took a deep breath, then continued—

> *Steal away, Steal away.*
> *Steal away to Jesus;*
> *Steal away, Steal away home;*
> *I ain't got long to stay here.*
> *So steal away, Steal away to Jesus.*

Charles drew his final breath and closed his eyes to the sound of angels singing and trumpets calling from a distant shore.

The End.

ACKNOWLEDGMENTS

Matt and Aaron would like to thank our wives and families for your endless support and sacrifice during the writing of this book; the elders and staff of the Austin Stone for believing in us and building a church that glorifies God and exalts Jesus; Devin Maddox, Hunter Powell, and Lindsay Lundin for so much wisdom and insight during the editing process; Dr. Christian George and the Spurgeon Library at Midwestern Seminary, who helped us immeasurably in the research phase of the project; Brice Johnson and Dietrich Schmidt for doing more things than we can list in seeing this project to completion; John Onwuchekwa, Léonce Crump, and Propaganda for offering invaluable insight into the nuances of writing from the voice of Thomas Johnson. Robert Patterson and Gary Schwarz for providing beautiful, open spaces for us to dream and write; and Matt Kirk, Randy Leifeste, and the amazing people of the Castell General Store in Castell, Texas, for keeping us fed during the long weekends of writing. Most important, we would like to thank our Lord and Savior, Jesus Christ, the creator of beauty and every story worth telling.

About the Authors

Matt Carter serves as the Pastor of Preaching and Vision at The Austin Stone Community Church in Austin, Texas, which has grown from a core team of fifteen to more than eight thousand attending each Sunday since he planted it in 2002. Matt has coauthored multiple books including a commentary on the Gospel of John in The Christ-Centered Exposition Commentary series and two group studies, *Creation Unraveled* and *Creation Restored*, which traced the gospel message through the book of Genesis. He holds an MDiv from Southwestern Seminary and a Doctorate in Expositional Preaching from Southeastern Seminary. He and his wife, Jennifer, have been married for over twenty years, and they have three children, John Daniel, Annie, and Samuel.

Aaron Ivey is the Pastor of Worship at The Austin Stone Community Church in Austin, Texas, where he pastors a team of nearly three hundred worship leaders, artists, storytellers, and musicians. Aaron has written and produced ten worship albums, and has written hundreds of congregational worship songs. His songwriting includes works represented in Worship Together, Jesus Culture, Capital Music Group, Doxology & Theology, and Austin Stone Worship. Passionate about mentoring and developing young leaders and world changers, Aaron spends much of his time communicating on topics of leadership, theology, art, and culture. He and his wife, Jamie, have been married for fifteen years, and have four children, Cayden, Amos, Deacon, and Story.

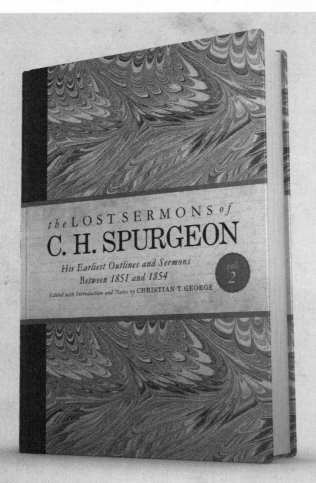

These volumes feature never-before published sermons from Charles Spurgeon's earliest years of ministry. See how one of history's greatest preachers began in ministry, complete with biography, full color charts and graphs, and facsimiles of each of the original sermons.

Celebrating the
"Prince of Preachers"

AVAILABLE 11.1.17

The
Spurgeon
Study Bible

CHRISTIAN
STANDARD
BIBLE®

FAITHFUL AND TRUE

General editor:
Alistair Begg